REBELS

Rebels is an exciting and innovative series looking at contemporary rebel groups and their place in global politics. Written by leading experts, the books serve as definitive introductions to the individual organizations, whilst seeking to place them within a broader geographical and political framework. They examine the origins, ideology and future direction of each group, whilst posting such questions as 'When does a "rebel" political movement become a "terrorist" organization?' and 'What are the social-economic drivers behind political violence?' Provocative and original, the series is essential reading for anyone interested in how rebel groups operate today.

ALREADY PUBLISHED

Alex Khasnabish, *Zapatistas: Rebellion from the Grassroots to the Global*
Garry Leech, *The FARC: The Longest Insurgency*
Christina Hellmich, *Al-Qaeda: From Global Network to Local Franchise*

ABOUT THE AUTHOR

Dr Paul White works as an independent consultant in Jakarta, Indonesia. He has taught Middle East Politics courses at Deakin University in Melbourne; at Macquarie University in Sydney; and at the University of Sydney's Centre for Peace and Conflict Studies. He is the author of *Primitive Rebels or Revolutionary Modernizers? The Kurdish National Movement in Turkey* (Zed Books, 2000). He was a member of the editorial board of the *Journal of Arabic, Islamic and Middle Eastern Studies* and serves on the board of directors of the Kurdish Institute, Washington DC.

THE PKK

Coming Down from the Mountains

PAUL WHITE

For Andrew Vincent: a close friend, colleague and adviser whom I sadly miss. His unstinting assistance to my research, critical insight and positive personal reinforcement were essential to my formation as a scholar.

The PKK: Coming Down from the Mountains
was first published in 2015 by Zed Books Ltd,
Unit 2.8 The Foundry, 17 Oval Way, London SE11 5RR, UK

www.zedbooks.co.uk

Designed and typeset in Garamond by illuminati, Grosmont
Index by John Barker
Cover designed by www.alice-marwick.co.uk
Printed and bound by CPI Group (UK) Ltd, Croydon, CR0 4YY

A catalogue record for this book is available from the British Library

ISBN 978–1–78360–038–0 hb
ISBN 978–1–78360–037–3 pb
ISBN 978–1–78360–039–7 pdf
ISBN 978–1–78360–040–3 epub
ISBN 978–1–78360– 041–0 mobi

Contents

Glossary of organizations, cities and towns

Organizations

KURDISH OR TURKISH NAME	ENGLISH NAME
Adalet ve Kalkınma Partisi	Justice and Development Party
Anayasa Mahkemesi	Constitutional Court
Ankara Yüksek Öğrenim Derneği	Ankara Higher Education Union
Apocular	'Apoists'; followers of Apo
Artêşa Rizgariya Gelê Kurdistan	People's Liberation Army of Kurdistan
Barış ve Demokrasi Partisi	Peace and Democracy Party
Demokratik Özgür Kadın Hareketi	Free Democratic Women's Movement
Demokratık Toplum Kongresi	Democratic Society Congress
Demokratik Toplum Partisi	Democratic Society Party
Derin devlet	Deep state
Devrimci Doğu Kültür Ocakları	Eastern Revolutionary Cultural Centres
Doğu Çalışma Grubu	East Working Group

Eniya Rizgariya Netewa Kurdistan	National Liberation Front of Kurdistan
Fazilet Partisi	Virtue Party
Genelkurmay	Military General Staff
Hâkimler ve Savcılar Yüksek Kurulu	Supreme Board of Judges and Prosecutors
Halkın Emek Partisi	People's Labour Party
Halkın Kurtuluşu	People's Liberation
Hêzên Parastina Gel	People's Defence Forces
Hêzên Rizgariye Kurdistan	Kurdistan Liberation Force
Jandarma police (Jandarma Havacilik Komutanligi)	Jandarma (Jandarma Havacilik Komutanligi): paramilitary police attached to the Ministry of Interior
Jandarma İstihbarat ve Terörle Mücadele	Intelligence and Fight against Terrorism Gendarmerie
Koma Ciwakên Kürdistan	Kurdistan Communities Union
Koma Jinên Bilind	High Women's Council
Koma Komalên Kurdistan	Council of Associations of Kurdistan
Komünizm İle Mücadele Dernekleri	Associations for Struggling with Communism
Kongra Netewiya Kurdistan	National Congress of Kurdistan
Kongra-Gel	Kurdistan People's Congress
Kongreya Azadî û Demokrasiya Kurdistanê	Kurdistan Freedom and Democracy Congress
Kordînasyona Civata Demokratîk a Kurdistan	Coordination of Democratic Communities in Kurdistan
Milli Güvenlik Kurulu	National Security Council
Milli İstihbarat Teşkilatı	National Intelligence Agency
Milliyetçi Hareket Partisi	Nationalist Action Party
Özel Harp Dairesi	Special Warfare Department
Partiya Carseravi Demokratik Kurdistan	Kurdistan Democratic Solution Party

Partiya Jiyana Azad a Kurdistanê	Kurdistan Free Life Party
Partiya Karkerên Kurdistan	Kurdistan Workers' Party
Partiya Yekîtî a Demokratik	Democratic Union Party
Refah Partisi	Welfare Party
Tevgera Jinen Azadiya Kurdistan	Kurdistan Women's Freedom Movement
Teyrêbazên Azadiya Kurdistan	Kurdistan Freedom Falcons
Türk İntikam Tugayı	Turkish Revenge Brigade
Türk Silahlı Kuvvetleri	Turkish Armed Forces
Türkiye Halk Kurtuluș Partisi–Cephe	Popular Liberation Party–Front of Turkey
Türkiye İșçi Partisi	Workers' Party of Turkey
Ulusal Kurtuluş Ordusu	National Liberation Army
Yekîtiya Demokratîk a Gelê Kurd	People's Democratic Union
Yekîtiya Jinen Azad	YJA STAR – the Free Women Units
Yekîtiya Jinen Azadiya Kurdistan	Association of Free Women of Kurdistan

Cities and towns

KURDISH NAME	TURKISH NAME
Amed	Diyarbakır
Çelê	Çukurca
Cizîr	Cizre
Colemêrg	Hakkâri
Dêrsim	Tunceli
Êlih	Batman
Gewer	Yüksekova
Mêrdînê	Mardin
Şemzînan	Şemdinli
Şirnex	Şırnak
Wan	Van

Glossary of key figures

NAME	ROLE
Başbuğ, İlker	General, Chief of the Turkish General Staff
Bayık, Cemil	PKK joint acting leader with Besê Hozat
Bookchin, Murray	Deviser of 'democratic confederalism'
Buçak, Mehmet Celal	In 1979 Buçak and other large landlords were the first persons targeted for assassination by the group headed by Abdullah Öcalan.
Cansız, Sakine	PKK co-founder, assassinated on 10 January 2013 in Paris, together with two comrades.
Catlı, Abdullah	Mafia boss and putschist
Demirtaş, Selahattin	BDP chairman
Dicle, Hatip	Former independent candidate for the Diyarbakır province. Elected with a big vote, but his election was annulled; replaced by the sixth-placed candidate, a member of the government party.
Doğan, Fidan	PKK activist, assassinated on 10 January 2013 in Paris, together with two comrades.
Emek, Fikret	Retired Özel Harp Dairesi operative, implicated in Ergenkon putsch

Erbakan, Necmettin	Refah Partisi leader
Erdoğan, Recep Tayyip	Prime Minister of Turkey 2003–14; President of Turkey 2014–
Eruygur, Şener	Four-star general implicated in Ergenkon putsch
Gül, Abdullah	Formerly Refah Partisi deputy chairman, then President of Turkey in the Erdoğan government
Gülen, Fethullah	Hizmet leader
Güney, Ömer	Man accused of murdering Sakine Cansız and her comrades
Hozat, Besê	PKK joint acting leader with Cemil Bayık
Huseyin, Fehman	'Doctor Bahoz': responsible for training guerrilla fighters
Kalkan, Duran	Real name Selahattin Abbas; a senior PKK commander
Kaplan, Leyla	The youngest PKK suicide bomber, at 17 years, in 1996.
Karasu, Mustafa	PKK deputy commander
Karayılan, Murat	A senior PKK leader
Karer, Haki	PKK cadre, whose assassination convinced the *Apocular* to establish a political party.
Kınacı Zeynep (Zilan)	PKK female suicide bomber on 30 June 1996.
Kutan, Recai	Fazilet Partisi chairman
Öcalan, Abdullah	PKK founder and leader
Öcalan, Osman	Abdullah Öcalan's brother. Formed the Partiya Welatparezen Demokraten Kurdistan with Kani Yilmaz.
Örnek, Özden	Four-star general implicated in Ergenkon putsch
Özal, Turgut	Prime Minister of Turkey 1983–89; President of Turkey 1989–93
Pir, Kemal	PKK co-founder

Sakık, Şemdin	'Parmaksiz Zeki'; former PKK member and commander
Söylemez, Leyla	PKK activist, assassinated on 10 January 2013 in Paris, together with two comrades.
Taş, Nizamettin	Former senior PKK leader. Formed the Partiya Welatparezen Demokraten Kurdistan with Kani Yilmaz and Osman Öcalan.
Tekin, Muzaffer	Retired Özel Harp Dairesi operative, implicated in Ergenkon putsch
Tolon, Hurşit	Four-star general implicated in Ergenkon putsch
Tuğluk, Aysel	Demokratık Toplum Kongresi chairwoman
Türk, Ahmet	Democratic Society Congress president
Yilmaz, Kani	Real name Faysal Dunlayıcı. Former commander of the PKK guerrilla training camp in Lebanon, then PKK political organizer in Europe. He split from the PKK after the *Serok*'s arrest, forming the Partiya Welatparezen Demokraten Kurdistan with Osman Öcalan. The PKK is accused of assassinating him on 11 February 2006.
Zana, Leyla	In 1991 she became the first Kurdish woman to win a seat in the Turkish parliament. She was imprisoned for ten years. She was re-elected to parliament in the June 2011 elections and is a member of the Barış ve Demokrasi Partisi. She received the Rafto Prize in 1994 and the Sakharov Prize in 1995.

Chronology of significant events

1974 Kurdish members of a radical leftist Turkish group meet and decide to form a distinctly Kurdish organization. Abdullah Öcalan is elected leader of the group.

1978 The Partiya Karkerên Kurdistan (PKK – Kurdistan Workers' Party) is established.

1978 27 November: The PKK holds its founding congress.

1979 30 July: Mehmet Celal Buçak and other large landlords are targeted for assassination by the group headed by Abdullah Öcalan.

1980 August: Abdullah Öcalan and a few other PKK members deploy to the Beka'a Valley in Lebanon, for political and military education.

12 September: A military coup is staged in Turkey.

1982 20–25 August: The PKK's Second Congress is held and resolves to return to Kurdistan, undertake diplomatic activities, establish military and political organizations, and retain Abdullah Öcalan as leader. The Hêzên Rizgariye Kurdistan (HRK – Kurdistan Liberation Force) is formed at the Congress.

1984 15 August: Simultaneous armed raids by PKK forces staged on Jandarma police stations, killing several soldiers. These were the first attacks against direct state representatives.

1985	21 March: Eniya Rizgariya Netewa Kurdistan (ERNK – National Liberation Front of Kurdistan) formed.
1986	25–30 October: PKK Third Congress. Artêşa Rizgariya Gelê Kurdistan (ARGK – People's Liberation Army of Kurdistan) replaces HRK.
1990	26 and 31 December: PKK Fourth Party Congress.
1991	Prime Minister (later President) Turgut Özal makes overtures to the Kurds. The overtures continue until 1993.
1992	Congress of PKK women held. Abdullah Öcalan rules that the congress's decisions are null and void.
1993	17 March: Abdullah Öcalan announces a unilateral ceasefire.
	24 May: Ceasefire ends with the killing of 33 unarmed Turkish soldiers.
1994	8 March: International Kurdish Women's Conference is held on International Women's Day.
1995	24 January: PKK Fifth Party Congress.
	8 March: On International Women's Day the first official Congress of PKK Women is held. The Congress elects an Executive, which subsequently founds the Tevgera Jinen Azadiya Kurdistan (TJAK – Kurdistan Women's Freedom Movement), which later changes its name to the Yekîtiya Jinen Azadiya Kurdistan (YJAK – Association of Free Women of Kurdistan), and then to Yekîtiya Jinen Azad (YJA STAR – the Free Women Units).
	10 December: PKK announces a unilateral ceasefire with Turkey.
1996	16 August: Ceasefire ends.
1998	January: PKK holds its Sixth Party Congress in Kurdistan.
	24–26 May: The Kongra Netewiya Kurdistan (KNK – Kurdistan National Congress) is formed.
	1 September: PKK declares a new unilateral ceasefire.
	9 October: Abdullah Öcalan expelled from Syria.
1999	15 February: Abdullah Öcalan captured in Kenya.
	19 January and 16 February: PKK Sixth Party Congress.
	The PKK Presidential Council ends the ceasefire.

August: PKK restores the ceasefire, following Abdullah Öcalan's intervention via a message to the Congress conveyed by his lawyers.

2000 January: PKK Seventh Extraordinary Party Congress adopts policy of moving from armed struggle to 'democratic transformation' with a democratic republic.

The ARGK is renamed the Hêzên Parastina Gel (HPG – People's Defence Forces).

2002 April: PKK briefly changes its name to the Kongreya Azadî û Demokrasiya Kurdistanê (KADEK – Kurdistan Freedom and Democracy Congress) at its Eighth Party Congress.

2003 KADEK renames itself Kongra-Gel (KGK – Kurdistan People's Congress).

2004 1 June: Ceasefire finally formally ended by Kongra-Gel.

2005 28 March–4 April: PKK Ninth Congress. KGK returns to the name PKK at the Congress.

17 May: Koma Ciwakên Kürdistan (KCK – Kurdistan Communities Union) is founded, as the sovereign authority body of the PKK movement, overseeing all the movement's activities in all parts of Kurdistan. It is run by an administrative council with Kurds representing all parts of Kurdistan.

19 August: New ceasefire announced by the PKK, scheduled to last until 20 September, and then extended until 3 October.

2006 Fighting between the PKK and the Turkish military intensifies, before the PKK declares a new unilateral ceasefire on 1 October.

2007 Dialogue between the PKK and the Turkish state in Oslo.

April: PKK declares a further unilateral ceasefire.

June and October: Turkish attacks on PKK bases in Iraqi Kurdistan and clashes in south-east Turkey end the ceasefire.

2008 August: PKK Tenth Party Congress.

2009 25–31 August: New PKK unilateral ceasefire lasts only one week.

11 May: 'Kurdish Opening' announced by President Abdullah Gül.

11 December: The Kurdish DTP is banned.

2010 May: The Kurdistan National Congress claims that more than 1,500 politicians, human-rights advocates, writers, artisans and leaders of civil-society organizations have been arrested since April 2009.

13 August: New PKK unilateral ceasefire.

2011 28 February: PKK ends ceasefire.

2012 18 October: Ankara acknowledges the existence of peace talks between the MİT and Öcalan.

2013 10 January: Three PKK members – Sakine Cansız, Fidan Doğan and Leyla Söylemez – are shot dead in Paris.

21 March: Abdullah Öcalan declares end of the conflict between the Turkish government and the PKK on Newroz (Kurdish New Year).

I offer the Turkish society a simple solution. We demand a democratic nation. We are not opposed to the unitary state and republic. We accept the republic, its unitary structure and laicism [secularism]. However, we believe that it must be redefined as a democratic state respecting peoples, cultures and rights. On this basis, the Kurds must be free to organize in a way that they can live their culture and language and can develop economically and ecologically. (Öcalan, 2009: 38–9)

Negotiation and struggle are both important processes in determining the future of peoples' movements. It is not those who are feared but rather those who have the confidence of their people that can lead those processes. (Öcalan, *Guardian*, 2014)

Introduction

'I, myself, am declaring in the witnessing of millions of people that a new era is beginning, arms are silencing, politics are gaining momentum' (Dalay, 28 September 2013). With these simple words from his prison cell on 21 March 2013, the Kurdish nationalist guerrilla leader Abdullah Öcalan put an end to armed hostilities between his PKK guerrillas and the Turkish army, which have taken in excess of 45,000 lives (overwhelmingly PKK militants) since 1984 (*Hürriyet*, 16 September 2008).

Turkey captured the PKK leader in February 1999. It is now well known that Abdullah Öcalan was apprehended as a result of cooperation between Greece and the CIA. A leading officer in Greece's Intelligence Service (the EYP), Colonel Savvas Kalenterides, admits that Athens collaborated with the CIA to deliver the Kurdish leader to Turkey (Smith, 19 February 1999). Abdullah Öcalan himself alleges: 'I was handed to Turkey at the end of a plot carried out by an international force' (Öcalan, 17 February 2011). He has labelled his abduction an international conspiracy backed by an alliance of secret services, comprising a 'complex mix of betrayal, violence and deception' (Öcalan,

13 February 2010; Öcalan, 2009: 27–8). Since then, much has changed – and much has remained very much the same.

The present book is in many ways a sequel to and an updating of *Primitive Rebels or Revolutionary Modernizers?* (Zed Books, 2000), a Turkish-language edition of which appeared recently in Turkey entitled *İlkel İsyancılar Mı, Devrimci Modernleştirmeciler Mi?* (2012, Vate Publishing House, Istanbul, 2012).

The earlier book examines the transformation of peasants from 'social rebels' into modern Kurdish nationalists, and the changing nature of political leadership in Kurdish society in what may be described as the 'modern' period. It shows that the Kurdish national movement emerged in the late nineteenth century as a product of traditional Kurdish society. Affected by Ottoman and Kemalist economic and political changes, the movement evolved towards a less parochial, 'purer' nationalism, led centrally by urban Kurds formed in the Turkish left. It also demonstrates that ethnic differentiation was a central cause of the failure of several armed uprisings in the name of Kurdish nationalism. This differentiation is a problem that Kurdish nationalists in Turkey are still coming to terms with.

That book goes on to argue that, in many significant respects, the present-day Kurdish national movement, in Turkey the Partiya Karkerên Kurdistan (PKK – Kurdistan Workers' Party), represents a qualitatively different sort of leadership from that of its historical predecessors. Initially a group of 'primitive rebels', with both millenarian tendencies and some 'modern' political features, the PKK eventually emerged as a modern revolutionary nationalist organization, with a burgeoning diplomatic presence, which contemplated bringing a complete end to its armed activities before this political evolution was curtailed by its founder's capture. Öcalan's apprehension in February 1999 raised the distinct possibility of a political 'de-evolution' on the part of the

PKK, back towards practices of social banditry. In other words, were Turkey's Kurdish nationalist leaders 'primitive rebels' or revolutionary modernizers?

This new book reveals the PKK's initially contradictory evolution since 1999, its apparently enthusiastic return to a non-violent, democratic road, and the even more astounding evolution of the Turkish state from denouncing Öcalan as a mass murderer to dealing with him on the PKK's proposed 'democratic confederalism', which the PKK maintains will eventually develop into full-blown self-managed autonomy.

Given that the PKK previously advocated nothing less than full independence for a united Greater Kurdish state, engaging in bloody feuds with Kurdish nationalist groups favouring a perspective of mere autonomy, this alone is a remarkable change for the PKK. The fact that this new outlook represents a decisive step away from Marxism–Leninism in the vague direction of semi-anarchist ideas is arguably even more astounding.

The first two chapters of the book set the scene, laying out the origins and aims of the PKK – its foundation, organization and membership and the role of ideology in the organization. The notorious 'under-underdevelopment' of Turkey's Kurdish region is discussed, and its violent consequences explained.

Chapters 3 and 4 discuss key events of the modern Kurdish national movement in Turkey, showing the impact of the ideologies developed by Abdullah Öcalan and propagated by the PKK. The ideas and perspectives of Öcalan (known affectionately as 'Apo' by his followers) have impacted deeply on political life throughout Turkey as a whole. Indeed, Apo's ideology (*Apoizm*) has changed Kurds and Turks in Turkey forever. The influence of the Kurdish *Apocular* diaspora is also elaborated in these chapters.

Chapter 5 examines the peace process between Ankara and the PKK that began in late 2012. An analysis of Turkish responses to the process – by the AKP government, the far right, the military and the conservative Gülen sect – and the reality or otherwise of the process is offered. The contradictory, perilous, nature of this process is shown.

Chapter 6 considers the PKK's ideological evolution from Marxist–Leninist guerrilla status to 'democratic confederalism', via the radical municipalism of Murray Bookchin. It is shown that this enabled it to exchange its traditional stance of struggling for nothing less than a united independent Kurdistan to a new perspective of 'democratic confederation', leading to self-managed Kurdish autonomy within the borders of the Turkish state. An investigation of the PKK's fascinating feminist transformation rounds off this chapter's examination of the PKK's ideological evolution.

The final chapter, 'Coming Down from the Mountains', sums up the PKK's transition from 'terrorists' to legitimate (or almost legitimate) rebels. It explores future directions for Turkey's Kurds and Turks. The future of the PKK in a democratic Turkey is critically examined and final conclusions drawn on PKK ideology and organization.

ONE

'The time of revolution has started'

'Events, however great or sudden', as John William Draper once reflected, 'are consequences of preparations long ago made' (Draper, 1875, vol. 2: 152). The emergence and evolution of the Partiya Karkerên Kurdistan provides sound verification of this astute observation. It was the product of nationalist and proto-nationalist uprisings and events hundreds of years earlier, which had divided Kurdistan into enclaves subservient to domination by a number of foreign states, as Figure 1 illustrates.

The Kurdish and Turkish left in Turkey almost universally regard Turkish Kurdistan as feudal. PKK *Serok* (Leader) Abdullah Öcalan is no exception, still maintaining:

> the Kurds have not only struggled against repression by the dominant powers and for the recognition of their existence but also for the liberation of their society from the grip of feudalism. (Öcalan, 2011: 19)

As several scholars have observed, the actual picture in Turkish Kurdistan is more complex. In fact, all ancient Anatolian society stagnated under a dominant 'Asiatic' mode of production.

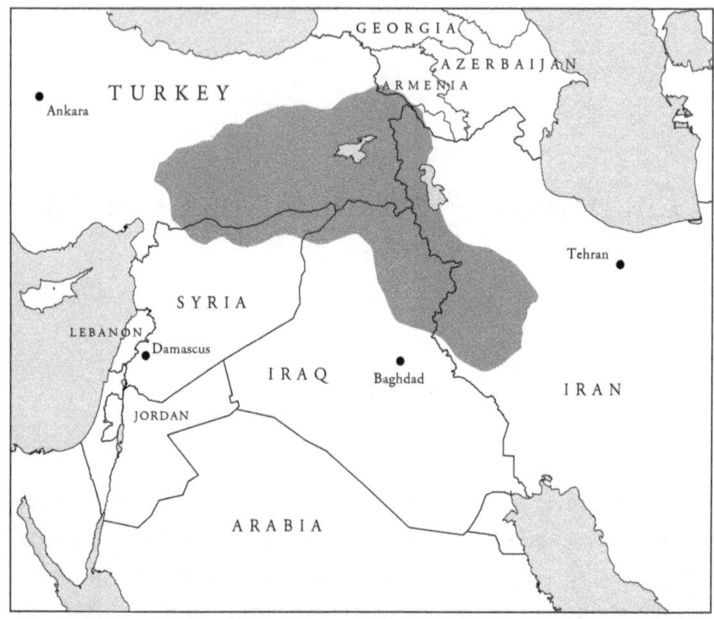

FIGURE 1 Map of Kurdistan

Interaction with Europe increasingly evoked feudal forms there from the seventeenth century onwards. But Mustafa Kemal's Turkish nationalist takeover in 1923 ushered in an openly modernizing regime – albeit Turkey remained a weak, underdeveloped economy, subordinate to the economies of those great powers that had successfully industrialized centuries earlier. Nevertheless, Turkey was integrated into the world economy during the 1920s and experienced real growth, including industrialization from the 1950s onwards.

Yet Turkish Kurdistan stumbled backwards in comparison, relatively speaking. Peasants have remained mostly landless. Kurdish economic development problems were not resolved by the economic modernization of the 1980s onwards, and political 'democratization' was not achieved for the Kurds. The Kurds were effectively excluded from citizenship.

As Majeed R. Jafar (1976) masterfully explains, the Kurdish region in modern Turkey is not merely underdeveloped, like Turkey as a whole, but is an exceptionally underdeveloped sector within the latter – or, as he puts it, Turkish Kurdistan suffers from 'under-underdevelopment'. Zülküf Aydin (1986) shows that the region's peasants remained mostly landless sharecroppers. He verifies the general verdict of severe economic underdevelopment for the region. Aydin, along with Ronnie Margulies, Ergin Yıldızoğlu (1987) and Kemal H. Karpat (1973), explain how the mechanization of agriculture, beginning in the 1950s, forced vast numbers to migrate either to western Turkey or even abroad. The landless rural Kurds who remained were caught in a horrendous poverty trap, as not even a modest degree of stunted industrial development in Turkish Kurdistan soaked up the jobless and underemployed.

The continuing war in Turkish Kurdistan has massively impacted upon all who live there. Kurdish sociologists estimate that about 3,500 Kurdish villages have been destroyed, rendering some 4 million people homeless. Severe unemployment prevails even in Amed (Diyarbakır), the largest city. In Turkey as a whole the mean annual income is US$7,000, whereas in the four poorest neighbourhoods in Amed it is a mere US$500 (Tatort Kurdistan, 2013: 70; Cagaptay and Jeffrey, 2014: 10).

İsmail Beşikçi's *Doğu Anadolu'nun Düzeni: Sosyo-ekonomik ve Etnik Temeller* (1969) documents the serious effects of agricultural mechanization on the Kurdish region's economy. Seyfi Cengiz's work (1990; n.d.) establishes that, despite grave economic underdevelopment in the region, a Kurdish working class not only exists but periodically organizes strikes and other forms of economic and political struggle, both inside and outside the trade unions. Basing himself on Turkish government statistics, Cengiz proves his case, showing that industrial activity by Kurdish workers in the region is intimately connected to similar action by workers throughout the Turkish state. This is potentially significant for understanding the objective factors impelling Kurds into political action, for Kurdish industry and economy today are linked with Turkish industry and economy, not that of Kurdistan as a whole. Cengiz's research thus reveals potential counter-pressures to Kurdish nationalism in Turkey.

Precursors of the PKK

Taking its prehistory into account, a schematic chronological typology of the Kurdish national movement in Turkey from its earliest murmurings up to the present day would be as follows:

- 1514–1879: the period from division to the Sheikh Ubaydallah rebellion.
- 1879–1908: the period from the defeat of Ubaydallah to the (Turkish nationalist) Young Turk rebellion.
- 1908–1925: the period from the Young Turk rebellion to the Sheikh Said rebellion.
- 1925–1938: the period from Sheikh Said's rebellion to Dêrsim (Tunceli).
- 1938–1965: the period from the Dêrsim rebellion to the dawn of the modern national movement.
- 1965–the present: the period of the modern national movement.

All of these risings unquestionably took place on the historic territory of Kurdistan, although – as discussed in the present writer's earlier book on the Kurds (White, 2000) – the Kızılbaş and Zaza peoples also claim most of them. Naturally, modern Kurdish nationalists reject these claims, also asserting that the Kızılbaş and Zaza are Kurds. It is quite clear that the modern

Kurdish national movement considers this asserted rebellious patrimony essential for its legitimacy.

These rebellions were all evoked by a heady mix of territorial particularism (the desire to rule their own lands themselves) and economic motives. Sheikh Said's 1925 rebellion was also animated by Islamic concerns. The modern Kurdish national movement is the product of the interaction of territorial particularist and economic motives, with leftist political radicalization, in the wake of Turkish political development and the explosion of radicalism in Western countries during the 1960s. It is Kurdish leftist political radicalization, especially, which differentiates the modern Kurdish national movement from its historical antecedents.

Emergence of the modern Kurdish national movement

In May 1960, Turkey's armed forces – which since the establishment of the Turkish Republic in 1923 have considered themselves the Republic's guardian – staged a military coup. The military hierarchy asserted that the military has both the right and the responsibility to intervene in affairs of state when absolutely necessary in order to guarantee the system's continuance. It was not a left-wing coup, but the military brought in a new, and surprisingly democratic, constitution. The prime minister and two of his ministers were executed and hundreds of right-wingers were imprisoned in 1961. The result of all these events was an unprecedented leftist resurgence.

From 1968, a rising tide of strikes began, supplemented by left–right political violence, culminating in a series of political murders in early 1970. Hundreds of thousands of workers and students repeatedly clashed with police on the streets. On 12 March 1971 another military coup took place.

For a brief moment during this period, the need of the 1960 junta to repress the right allowed the left a breathing space. A staggering range of leftist publications emerged – from radical populist and social democratic in inclination, such as *Yön*, *Ant* and *Türk Solu*, through to ostensible Marxist, 'Marxist–Leninist' and Maoist. All of these groups looked towards a leftist reworking of the tradition of military intervention in national politics. In this scheme, the elite, technocrats (including, in some versions, the students) and officers would lead Turkey 'independently' on behalf of the workers and rural poor – 'for the people, despite the people'. 'Students would agitate, officers would strike, and a national junta would take power' (Samim, April/May 1981: 65–72).

This strategy soon proved to be a failure. The radicalism sweeping across Western countries in the 1960s then swept over Turkey as well – despite the reality that in this country right-wing radicalism had a much stronger popular base than in Europe at the time. Left-wing radicalism in Turkey now took the shape of a different leftist approach, the urban guerrilla strategy of Che Guevara (Landau, 1974: 31).

Turkish Kurdistan was not immune to these developments. Indeed, many Kurdish intellectuals were deeply affected by the political cauldron of 1960s' Turkish politics. Confused political and organizational links soon developed between the movements in Turkey proper and these intellectuals (Bozarslan, 1992: 97–8). Crucially, this confused intellectual leftist renaissance occurred at a time when Turkey's

> Kurdish population ... was both more mobile and more susceptible to influence from regions to the West. Migratory movements, which were intensified by industrialization, ultra-rapid means of communication and the massive presence of Kurdish students in major Turkish towns, together with a more heterogeneous political environment were crucial in transforming East–West relations in Turkey. (Bozarslan, 1992: 98)

A number of bilingual (Turkish/Kurdish) nationalist journals emerged, only to be swiftly suspended (Kutschera, 1979: 4–5). Then in 1965 the Democratic Party of Turkish Kurdistan (PDKT in Turkish) was formed (Vanly, 1986: 64). The new party name referred to the Iraqi Kurdish Democratic Party of Iraq (KDP), founded and led by the famous Barzani clan, although in the beginning it was controlled by Ibrahim Ahmad, who had nothing to do with the Barzanis. At the time, the KDP was waging a highly successful guerrilla war against the Ba'athist authorities in Baghdad (Bozarslan, 1992: 98–9; Kutschera, 1979; More, 1984: 68, 70, 193–4; Ghareeb, 1981: 7–8; Kendal, 1982: 91–2).

The PDKT was never an effective organized force. Nevertheless the social and political issues that ripped it apart in the late 1960s were significant for the emergence of a fully modern national movement of the Kurds. At their core, these disputes involved the role of both traditional leaders and intellectuals in the Kurdish national movement and the relationship of the national movement itself towards the international working-class movement (Bozarslan, 1992: 98–9). The PDKT was clearly unable to adapt to the rapid radicalization occurring among Kurdish workers and intellectuals during the late 1960s. The organization was soon branded 'bourgeois nationalist' by most of the radicalized Kurdish organizations that subsequently emerged.

The catalyst of racist provocation

Kurdish resentment was growing, spurred on not just by centuries of perceived ill treatment, but also now by immediate outrages. In April 1967, a provocative article appeared in the extreme right-wing Turkish magazine *Ötüken*, journal of the far-right Milliyetçi Hareket Partisi (MHP – Nationalist Action Party). The article stated that the Kurds were a backward people, devoid of history and culture, who wanted to cut Turkey into pieces. The author suggested that the Kurds get out of Turkey, since Turkey was only for the Turks, adding that Kurds 'do not have the faces of human beings' (cited in Vanly, n.d.: 41–3).

Demanding that Ankara punish the author and ban the magazine (Section 12 of the Turkish Constitution proclaimed the equality of all citizens), a furious Kurdish protest movement erupted. The government did nothing, even when a follow-up article appeared in the June issue of *Ötüken*, entitled 'The Howlings of the Red Kurds', which declared:

> the Kurds may represent a majority as high as 100 per cent of the population of the eastern provinces; yet their dreams to establish a Kurdish state on the soil of Turkey will always remain a dream comparable to that of the Armenians in a Greater Armenia...
>
> But the day when you will rise up to cut Turkey into pieces, you will see to what a hell we shall send you... (cited in Vanly, n.d.: 42)

The Kurds were well aware that the Armenians were massacred by the Ottoman Turks (with assistance from some Kurds). Now a Turkish writer was implying that the same thing might happen to the Kurds.

These articles provoked a swift and widespread response by Kurds. A public statement signed by nineteen student committees was sent to the president and the prime minister (Vanly, n.d.: 42). Protest demonstrations organized by Kurdish students on 3 August 1967 attracted 10,000 people in Silvan and over 25,000 in Amed. Large demonstrations were also held in most of the other towns of Turkish Kurdistan (Heinrich, 1989: 8; Ghareeb, 1981; Vanly, n.d.: 42). The demonstrations protested not only against the articles and the government's inaction in the face of them, but also against Ankara's 'policy of national oppression and of planned underdevelopment' of Turkish Kurdistan. This was the first time in the three decades since the disaster at Dêrsim that the Kurds had vented their anger politically and publicly (Ghareeb, 1981; Vanly, n.d.: 42).

Retribution from the Kurds' Turkish adversaries was swift. Shortly after the demonstrations, unknown assailants – suspected by some to have been Turkish secret police – killed PDKT founder Faik Buçak. The other leaders of the PDKT were briefly arrested in early 1969 (Kutschera, 1979: 340). Specially trained commandos were despatched to the Kurdish region. According to some accounts, these 'clearing operations' were carried out with great force and to the accompaniment of frequent racial insults hurled at ordinary Kurds (Bozarslan, 1992, 5; Kutschera, 1979: 341–2). Chris Kutschera (1979: 342) relates an incident that occurred on 8 April 1970, involving 2,000 commandos and military police and six helicopters, against the town of Silvan. All the men of the town, 'exactly 3,144', were made to line up. They were beaten, while being addressed thus: 'Dogs of Kurds! Spies of Barzani! Tell us where you have hidden your arms!'

Matters were now well past the point where simple intimidation could prevent the open manifestation of Kurdish disaffection. Over the next two years mass nationalist demonstrations were repeatedly held throughout Turkish Kurdistan (Besikçi, 1969: 131–2). Frustrated by the failure of the previous 'left Kemalist' strategy of the Turkish left – especially with the orientation to the 'patriotic' section of the army – many young Kurdish radicals looked for a new organized alternative. The result was the foundation in 1969 of the Devrimci Doğu Kültür Ocakları (DDKO – the Eastern Revolutionary Cultural Centres) (Heinrich, 1989: 13–14). The DDKOs were the first legal Kurdish organization in Turkey. Despite their diplomatic substitution of the term 'East' for the name of their motherland Kurdistan, the DDKOs were symbols of radicalism. Propagandizing against cultural oppression and economic backwardness, the DDKO's monthly bulletins pointed to American imperialism as the central cause and accused local large landholders and capitalists of facilitating this exploitation through their collaboration with the United States (van Bruinessen, 1997).

DDKO militants were Kurdish students of varying ideologies, who broke free of the political control of the Türk İşçi Partisi (TİP), the main communist party at the time in Turkey (More, 1984: 69). Strongly supporting the preservation of Kurdish culture and language, the DDKO built a network of support in Kurdish towns and major Turkish towns. The DDKO represented a radical break for the Kurdish national movement. Convinced that attempts to conciliate Kemalist nationalism must be abandoned, DDKO members looked at events in Vietnam and elsewhere in the developing world, and foresaw that Turkey also faced major upheavals. They viewed the Kurdish problem as centrally a colonial problem, in which, as Hamit Bozarslan explains, in their view 'a "policeman of global imperialism" dominated an oppressed nation with the aid of local collaborators'. This was simultaneously both a 'class' and a 'national' problem. Only 'progressive forces' could resolve the situation 'by liberating Kurdistan – not necessarily as an independent state – from this double yoke' (Bozarslan, 1992: 100–101).

The DDKOs were destroyed when all their leaders were arrested in October 1970 (More, 1984: 69; Bozarslan, 1992: 101; McDowall, 1996: 409). It was some measure of the growing support for the widespread Kurdish radicalization which had developed that the military claimed it was acting to foil a Kurdish uprising (Kutschera, 1979: 343; Ghareeb, 1981: 9; Vanly, n.d.: 65). Specifically, it was alleged that the DDKO aimed at the partial or complete removal of constitutional public rights on grounds of race and to conduct propaganda to destroy national feeling. This charge was based on a rather contentious theory of racism – so-called 'minority racism' (Bayır, 2010: 310–11). This occurred

> when those who are numerically a minority constantly demand that they belong to a different race other than the majority race people and give weight to their racial particularities and by changing their race ask for special demands other than the general rights provided for members of the nation, although in the main laws there is no differentiation or no laws which create difference. (cited in Bayır, 2010: 311)

DDKO leaders such as Musa Anter, Tarik Ziya Ekinci, Sait Elci, Necmettin Büyükkaya and the young scholar İsmail Beşikçi faced the courts in Istanbul and Amed. Beşikçi produced a 150-page legal vindication, defending the Kurds' existence, history and unique identity. The DDKO leaders received jail sentences of up to ten years. Some of these – notably Musa Anter, Sait Elci and İsmail Beşikçi – went on to play active roles in the Kurdish national movement following their eventual release from prison (McDowall, 1996: 409–10; van Bruinessen, 1997). Musa Anter was assassinated by an undercover Turkish security agency (JİTEM) in September 1992 (Romano, 2006: 135).

TWO

PKK origins and ideological formation

It was in this political hothouse that, by 1974, Abdullah Öcalan was to be found working in the Ankara Higher Education Union (AYÖD – Ankara Yüksek Öğrenim Derneği). AYÖD based itself, at least partially, on the tradition of an earlier organization, the Guevarist Türkiye Halk Kurtuluş Partisi–Cephe (THKP–C, or Popular Liberation Party–Front of Turkey). AYÖD provided Öcalan with the foundations of an ideological, political and strategic outlook. Öcalan and several other Kurds in AYÖD were not satisfied, however, and they began to develop a separate, distinct 'political-ideological' grouping (Institut de Criminologie, 1995; Ismet, 1992: 10–11; Ersever, 1993. See also More, 1984: 188; Heinrich, 1989: 42–3; Ismet, 1992: 9; McDowall, 1996: 418–19; Gunter, 1990: 25).

One day in 1974 in the Ankara suburb of Tuzlucayir, between seven and eleven of these militant Kurdish nationalists met and drew up rudimentary plans for the formation of a distinct Kurdish leftist organization, which would have no ties with Turkish leftist groups, all of which had ignored the Kurds' specific needs. Öcalan reportedly asserted at this meeting that the conditions existed for the establishment of a 'Kurdish national liberation movement'. Öcalan was elected the leader of this group in the process of formation, which became known simply as the *Apocular*, or 'followers of Apo', until the provisional name of Ulusal Kurtuluş Ordusu (UKO, National Liberation Army) was adopted by the group, indicating its intention to eventually undertake 'armed struggle' (Heinrich, 1989: 43; Ersever, n.d.; Ismet, 1992: 10–12).

The PKK later described its initial development as a series of stages (*Serxwebûn*, October 1991: 4–13). The initial stage, between 1973 and 1977, was as an 'ideological group'. During this period, says the PKK today, a 'revolutionary youth group' was established, which was involved mostly in theoretical work – ideological struggle and propaganda. By 1974 this group was already distributing leaflets, in an attempt to draw Kurdish youth and intellectuals towards it. The core, founding members, of the tiny *Apocular* propaganda group abandoned any studies or full-time work they were involved in, to become full-time 'professional revolutionaries' (PKK, 1991; Gunes, 2012: 99; Ersever, n.d.). As the grouping grew, it maintained its initial struggle – discrediting political rivals (both Turkish and Kurdish leftists), which the group dismissed as 'revisionist and reformist'. These included several Kurdish groups – including Türkiye Kurdistan Demokratik Parti, Kürdistan Ulusal Kurtuluşcuları, Kürdistan İşçi Partisi, Devrimci Halkın Birliği and Halkın Kurtuluşu. The PKK stands accused of physically attacking members of these organizations. On the Turkish left the PKK clashed with the Türkiye İşçi Partisi and the TKP–ML/TİKKO, among others. In November 1978 the organization's first congress agreed upon a 'self-criticism' of the previous policy of armed confrontation with rival groups, saying that these had been a mistake. Nevertheless occasional armed confrontations continued to occur between the PKK and other organizations for some years, before ceasing altogether.

The movement's next phase was between 1978 and 1980. This stage saw the party organized and its politics refined, to allow the organization to become a political force. The group's ideology and programme were taken to villages as well as to workers. During this three-year period, the initial ideological formation evolved into a political party, the Partiya Karkerên Kurdistan, which was officially launched on 27 November 1978 in the village of Fis, near Lice, in Diyarbakır province (Heinrich, 1989: 42; Imset, 1992: 12–20; *Serxwebûn*, October 1991: 5). The party issued a founding declaration, asserting that 'The time of revolution has started…' It added:

> For some centuries, the people of Kurdistan have directed a war of liberation against foreign domination and its local collaborators. In order to raise the struggle to the level of a war of national liberation for which the situation is mature, and so as to combine the fight with the class struggle, the Kurdistan Workers' Party has been founded. It is the new organization of the proletariat of Kurdistan. (More, 1984: 187–8)

By all accounts, the PKK's founders were all from humble origins. There were no intellectuals in the very early (pre-PKK) organization, except perhaps Haki Karer, who died early on. The intellectuals were only attracted gradually from the cities of eastern and south-eastern Anatolia.

The story of the PKK's engagement in political and military struggle up until the present day is told in later chapters. The remainder of the present chapter outlines the PKK's organizational evolution, dealing with the party's reformation in the early 2000s, as well as considering the role played by *Apocular* ideology.

From disorientation to refounding

The initial period after Abdullah Öcalan's capture was one of great disorientation for the PKK. An estimated total of 1,500 militants left the party between 2003 and 2005. Yet, as Casier and Jongerden aptly point out, it would be foolhardy to gauge the PKK's strength 'in terms of the number of its armed members' (Casier and Jongerden, 2012: 10 n1). They add that the PKK is primarily a political organization, noting Hamit Bozarslan's assessment that PKK violence 'was rational/instrumental, in the sense that it sought to change the political and juridical status [of the Kurds]' (Bozarslan 2004: 23, cited in Casier and Jongerden, 2012).

Stuck in his prison cell, Abdullah Öcalan nevertheless managed to hold the situation together, calling for a 'Preparatory Rebuilding Committee' to oversee the PKK's refounding in 2004. The PKK Ninth Party Congress from 28 March to 4 April 2005 'marks the PKK's rebirth' (Casier and Jongerden, 2012: 10 n1).

The PKK's Seventh Extraordinary Party Congress in January 2000 had already officially adopted the policy of striving for a democratic republic. Stressing that the party now sought to move from armed struggle to 'democratic transformation', the same Congress also resolved to replace the Artêşa Rizgariya Gelê Kurdistan (ARGK – People's Liberation Army of Kurdistan) and its political front the ERNK (Eniya Rizgariya Netewa Kurdistan – National Liberation Front of Kurdistan) with the Hêzên Parastina Gel (HPG – People's Defence Forces) and the Yekîtiya Demokratîk a Gelê Kurd (YDK – People's Democratic Union) respectively. The YDK worked within the European Kurdish diaspora, until it was superseded by the Kordînasyona Civata Demokratîk a Kurdistan (KCD – Coordination of Democratic Communities in Kurdistan). Then, in April 2002, attempting to build credibility for its peaceful orientation, the PKK briefly changed its name to the Kongreya Azadî û Demokrasiya Kurdistanê (KADEK – Kurdistan Freedom and Democracy Congress). In late 2003, KADEK renamed itself again, now becoming

Kongra-Gel (KGK – Kurdistan People's Congress). Each name change represented a further attempt to change its image and broaden its appeal, as if to say that the 'new' organization was qualitatively different from the original PKK. In 2005 the KGK returned to the original name: Partiya Karkerên Kurdistan (PKK, 2005), apparently deciding that historical continuity with its heritage was most important.

The party's initial guerrilla force, formed in 1984, was the Hêzên Rizgariye Kurdistan (HRK – Kurdistan Liberation Force). The PKK's 'armed struggle' began officially on 15 August 1984, with attacks by HRK guerrillas in the Eruh and Şemzînan (Şemdinli) regions. Announcing its existence, the HRK declared on 15 August 1984:

> Patriotic People of Kurdistan! It is time to raise the struggle against colonialism, which aimed to destroy our nation for hundreds of years, it is time to ask for the oppression, torture and cruelty, and the blood we have shed for hundreds of years and have become barbaric more than ever in the last four years. This is the duty of all members of Kurdistan who want an honourable life. (Bozarslan, 2002: 861)

In an effort to remind the world that the PKK per se was merely a political party with a separate armed wing, the party's Third Congress on 25–30 October 1986 changed the name of its fighting force from the HRK to the ARGK. In 2000 the Seventh Extraordinary Congress of the PKK again rebadged the force: the ARGK became the Hêzên Parastina Gel (HPG – People's Defence Forces). The name change was intended to indicate the new, purely defensive, nature of this armed wing, in line with the PKK's declared aim of seeking a peaceful settlement to the conflict.

The PKK has a fundamentally political front, the ERNK, formed in March 1985 (Heinrich, 1989: 43–4). As well as being the leading element in a broader political front, the ERNK until recently had its own reserve guerrilla militia in Turkish Kurdistan, which could be mobilized when necessary (Imset, 1992: 130–33).

The first guerrilla training camp was established in 1982 in Lebanon's Beka'a Valley – which was at the time under Syrian control. In achieving this, the PKK was assisted by the Popular Democratic Front for the Liberation of Palestine (PDFLP), a radical armed faction of the PLO, which had its own camp on a plateau adjacent to the PKK's camp (White, personal observation, Beka'a, July 1992). In late 1994 and 1995 the ARGK's strength was variously estimated at between 10,000 and 30,000 active guerrilla fighters (Korn, 1995, 34; Panico, 1995; Kutschera, 1994: 14; US Department of State, 1994; Immigration and Refugee Board of Canada, 1996), supported by a part-time (ERNK) militia of 75,000. The organization then operated out of Syria, Iran and Iraq (Bell, 1995; *Middle East Times*, 25 June–1 July 1995; Panico, 1995; US Department of State, 1994). PKK 'staging areas' in Turkey's Munzur, Gabar, Tendurek, Cudi, Ağri and Dêrsim (Tunceli) regions were also reported by some sources (Panico, 1995; Immigration and Refugee Board of Canada, November 1996–April 1998).

Following massive pressure from Turkey, Syria largely ejected the PKK in the early 1990s, compelling it to recentre its operations in Iraqi Kurdistan, where the organization established a number of small camps along the border with Turkey, including in Sinaht, Haftanin, Kanimasi and Zap. A few camps equipped with field hospitals, electricity generators and arsenals were also established in Iraqi Kurdistan (Jenkins, 2007). The headquarters of the PKK is still to be found in the Qandil Mountains, around 100 kilometres from the Turkish border.

ARGK/HPG fighters were uniformed and organized in units, platoons and regiments. The units were further subdivided into Military Units, Local Units and People's Defence Units. Formally under the authority of the *Serok* and the PKK Central Committee, a Military Council directly supervised them, via a network of subordinate bodies:

> Field Commands, Provincial Military Councils, Regional Command Offices and Local Stations. These military forces operate out of three forms of bases, which are identified as (1) Supportive base (2) Main Base and (3) Operations Base. (US Department of State, 1994)

The PKK of today is a far cry from the founding band of ragged guerrillas. What can perhaps best now be termed 'the PKK movement' (PKK founder Kemal Pir, cited by Jongerden and Akkaya, 2014) consists of a network of organizations across putative Greater Kurdistan. Apart from the PKK itself, there are also affiliated parties in Iraqi, Iranian and Syrian Kurdistan. The PKK's affiliate in Iran is the Partiya Jiyana Azad a Kurdistanê (PJAK – Kurdistan Free Life Party), in Iraqi Kurdistan the Partiya Çareseriya Demokratik a Kurdistanê (PCDK – Kurdistan Democratic Solution Party), and in Syria the Partîya Yekîtî a Demokratik (PYD – Democratic Union Party).

The Koma Ciwakên Kürdistan (KCK – Kurdistan Communities Union) is the sovereign authority body of the PKK movement, overseeing the movement's activities in all parts of Kurdistan. The KCK is an umbrella or executive organization for the entire PKK movement, consisting of the pro-PKK parties and other organizational units throughout putative Kurdistan, including the PYD, the PJAK and the PCDK, as well as the HPG. Several civil society organizations are also KCK members. Abdullah Öcalan is the honourable president of the KCK (Çandar, 2012: 82).

The PKK's organization and membership

According to Öcalan, the PKK has 'a very natural structure; it hasn't got many formalities' (interview by White, 2000: 212). It is also true, of course, that the PKK has an impressive transnational organizational configuration, at the peak of which is the *Serok*, or Leader. Initially the party had the structure of a typical Communist Party: a leader, supported by a Central Committee, and a party Congress that was the organization's highest formal authority. As we shall see below, the party has evolved considerably since 1978.

Abdullah Öcalan remains accepted by the organization as its leader, despite his life sentence (Brandon, 2007; White, 2000: 189–90). In some ways, this is purely symbolic, since subordinate leaders run the day-to-day operations of the PKK. And yet that was always the case, prior to Öcalan's capture – hence the lack of 'formalities'. As a 'charismatic' leader, Öcalan's role is to 'inspire' the organization and to provide its strategic direction – while intervening, as necessary, in prosaic organizational matters (White, 2000: 210). Öcalan was also confirmed as president by the PKK Sixth Party Congress, in March 1999. Certainly, the *Serok*'s successful declaration that the PKK ceasefire that began on 1 September 1998 was to resume, along with the current peace process, speaks volumes for the continuing effectiveness of his leadership from prison. His ability to lead under such difficult circumstances has not gone without challenge within the organization, however.

After Öcalan's capture, the Turkish press speculated about a 'leadership struggle' it claimed was being waged among Cemil Bayık, Osman Öcalan and Mustafa Karasu (*Hürriyet*, 14 March 1999). Meanwhile the Turkish daily *Milliyet* reported that Cemil Bayık had been appointed the PKK's 'high authority', while

Abdullah Öcalan remained the organization's formal leader (*Milliyet*, 3 March 1999).

The PKK Central Committee swiftly appointed a new Ruling Council, consisting notably of Cemil Bayık (the most senior military wing commander), Osman Öcalan (Abdullah Öcalan's brother and a senior military wing commander) and Murat Karayılan (another senior military wing commander) (Med TV, 18 February 1999).

Interestingly, the first issue of the PKK's publication *Serxwebûn* after Öcalan's capture confirmed the new leadership structure. In addition to the usual pictures of Abdullah Öcalan on the front page, this issue also carried photos of the next six most senior leaders: Cemil Bayık, Osman Öcalan, Nizamettin Taş, Murat Karayılan, Sakine Cansız and Mustafa Karasu. All were small and of uniform size, but that of Bayık was prominent. Most of those pictured on the front page had articles in the issue'; again, Bayık's was prominent (*Serxwebûn*, February 1999: 1, 8, 9, 10, 11, 24).

As the PKK's new 'high authority', Cemil Bayık was subject only to Abdullah Öcalan's veto (*Milliyet*, 3 March 1999). Bayık has served in the PKK leadership as a military commander, a Central Committee member and on the Presidential Council. His personal history gives every indication that he is a thoughtful man, capable of independent thinking and with a demonstrated ability to strive for his own perspectives within the organization, when circumstances permit this. Successful in his studies, he secured a state scholarship to the Malatya Teacher Training College, after which he pursued university study in Ankara.

Bayık successfully asserted his own authority in Abdullah Öcalan's absence, initially reversing the PKK's drive towards peace with Ankara, and putting it once again on a war footing.

Given that his authority in the organization derives substantially from his historical closeness to Öcalan, however, Bayık can only lead by continually deferring to him. Shortly after his arrest, Öcalan (through his lawyers) relayed successive letters over some weeks directing the organization to adhere to the 'ceasefire announced on September 1, 1998'. These communications were initially successfully ignored by Bayık (*Reuters*, Istanbul, 28 March 1999), who apparently argued that Öcalan's declarations were the product of torture (PKK Central Committee, 15 March 1999). Yet, merely by continuing to issue statements via his lawyers, Öcalan was very soon able to rein in Bayık and return the PKK to his perspective (White, 2000: 191).

Öcalan is well aware of the dangers that Bayık potentially poses. Perhaps significantly, he used his courtroom testimony during his trial to criticize Bayık, alleging that he prefers to stay behind the front lines, and reportedly accusing him of killing seventeen wounded PKK fighters in 1992, to avoid his own capture (Jamestown Foundation, 2008). Hidir Sarikaya, a former PKK member, further alleged in 2007 that Bayık had executed around 300 PKK members for 'disloyalty' since the 1980s (*Cumhuriyet*, 2007), although there exists no independent proof. There have been no allegations that he has executed PKK members in recent years.

Cemil Bayik in some ways represents the 'old' PKK – especially his ignoring of the ceasefire after Abdullah Öcalan was captured. Ironically, it is Bayık's legacy as a PKK 'hawk' that makes him valuable in Öcalan's strategy. With Öcalan in prison, the *Serok* cannot warn Turkey too strongly of the consequences were it to walk away from the peace process. Öcalan seems genuinely to want a lasting peace, but he also perceives the need to keep pressuring Ankara to keep its word This is where Bayık comes in handy.

Bayık's interaction with reporters on October 2013 – when he warned of the danger of civil war (Candar, 2013c) – illustrates this. Claiming that Turkey is supporting armed gangs in Syrian Kurdistan (West Kurdistan), Bayık warned:

> If the Turkish government continues with its war against the people of west Kurdistan by arming bandit groups, then the Kurdish people have the right to carry their war to Turkey. (Candar, 24 October 2013)

Furthermore, Bayık remains a PKK leader with an alternative perspective, should the current peace process definitively fail. He takes the lead in the organization's relations with Iran (*Tempo*, 18 October 2007, cited in Jamestown Foundation, 2008). Nevertheless, he was supplanted by Murat Karayılan as acting leader between 1999 and 2013 (Shekhani, 2013; *Akşam*, 2012; *Independent*, 2007; *Middle East Newsline*, 2008). Since mid-2013, however, Cemil Bayık and Besê Hozat have been the first joint acting leaders, supplanting Karayılan. The four most senior leaders of the PKK are: Cemil Bayık, Besê Hozat, followed by Murat Karayılan and the current military commander, Dr Fehman Huseyin (Kurdpress News Agency, 2013; Shekhani, 2013; *Tempo*, 2007; Arsu, 2013).

Besê Hozat, for her part, strongly advocates the PKK's feminist positions, as may be expected. A co-founder of the PKK, she is serious-minded and an eloquent speaker. Given that she is an Alevi from Dêrsim, Hozat's appointment will please 'Alevi Kurds' close to the Turkish opposition party the CHP (Gediman, 2013; Çandar, 2013b). Alevi PKK members are known to have had reservations about the peace process, which requires them to make up with Ankara – which supports Sunni opposition forces in Syria against that country's Alawite regime. Alevism is distinct from Alawism, but the two religions are distantly related. Alevi PKK members have been unhappy about making peace with Ankara while Turkey is opposing Assad (Uslu, 2013) and arming Syrian opposition fighters.

Fehman Huseyin ('Doctor Bahoz' – a Syrian-born Kurd from Western Kurdistan) is in charge of training guerrilla fighters. Accustomed to the exigencies of guerrilla warfare, where commanders must of necessity make independent decisions if they are to survive, Huseyin is also known to act on his own initiative and has broad appeal among Syrian Kurds (Pollock and Cagaptay, 2013). His inclusion in the central leadership team, as a capable military leader, is also a warning to Turkey to be wary of abandoning the peace process.

In contrast to Cemil Bayik and Doctor Bahoz, Murat Karayılan possesses a personality similar to that of Abdullah Öcalan. When interviewed by the author in mid-1992, Öcalan communicated a very quiet, withdrawn personality – an embodiment of the PKK/Öcalan ideal of the 'Kurdish personality' (White, 2000: 137–9). Like the *Serok*, Karayılan weighs his words very carefully, pausing when necessary, and closing his eyes as he searches for the right words. He projects a conciliatory outlook, stressing the desire for non-violence and peaceful resolution. This reflects Öcalan's current preferred perspective of seeking democratic reform. Karayılan has been appointed leader of the PKK's HPG guerrilla force. This positions him as a potential counterweight to the 'hawk' Cemil Bayık, should the need arise.

The new party leadership was reportedly required by Abdullah Öcalan in a letter to the PKK leadership (*Taka*, 2013). Turkish journalist Emrullah Uslu suggests that Karayılan secured his post as HPG leader 'for the sake of the peace process' (Uslu, 2013). Uslu reports that an Iranian general had approached the previous PKK leadership group, urging it not to enter into a new ceasefire with Ankara. The general presumably offered some inducements to the PKK. However, Karayılan rebuffed him. Uslu speculates that by removing Karayılan and appointing the 'pro-Iranian' Bayık as leader, 'the PKK has demonstrated a desire to work with Iran' (Uslu, 2013). This is certainly plausible, as it fits the PKK leader's perceived desire to strengthen his hand against Ankara, to compel it to honour its commitment to the peace process.

Founded by a grouping of Kurds who had been active in the Turkish left, the *Apocular* advanced from being a tiny propaganda group in 1974 to a fledgling political party, the PKK, in late 1978. The party met formidable obstacles – not only when it took up armed struggle in 1984 after a protracted period of preparation, but also internally, with an estimated 1,500 militants leaving between 2003 and 2005, due to serious disorientation following their leader's arrest. The *Serok* nevertheless contained the problem by summoning a 'Preparatory Rebuilding Committee' to oversee the PKK's refounding in 2004. The PKK Ninth Party Congress the following year resolved to move from armed struggle to 'democratic transformation'. The contemporary 'PKK movement' now comprises a complex of organizations. In mid-2013 Cemil Bayık and Besê Hozat became the PKK's first joint acting leaders upon Abdullah Öcalan's request.

THREE

Early years of struggle

The PKK's initial name of Ulusal Kurtuluş Ordusu (UKO – National Liberation Army) declared its perspective of armed struggle. The organization's founding ideology was a mix of Kurdish nationalism and radical Marxism–Leninism, leading it to designate Turkish Kurdistan as an 'internal colony'. Just as the countries of Asia and Africa were once characterized by Marxist–Leninists of all stripes as being subjected to 'imperialist domination', the *Apocular* asserted that the Turkish state – while itself being subjected by the West – had acted in a similar manner towards Turkey's Kurdistan, with a fascistic feudal class exploiting it (Silverman, 2013).

These ideas emerged and gradually gained support between 1973 and 1977. During this period, *Apocular* cadres took the ideas to Kurdish intellectuals, workers and villagers – to any Kurds who would give them a hearing. The outcome of this patient process was the formation of the PKK in 1978.

Towards armed struggle

This emerging new movement faced an ideological climate in which the state and Turkish nationalists denied the very existence of the Kurdish people generally – and readily resorted to violence in an effort to stifle the movement. PKK co-founder Sakine Cansız argues that this 'denialism' (of the Kurdish reality) was a very tangible obstacle, preventing the *Apocular* from 'expressing and representing' their ideas. The killing of group member Aydın Gül in 1977 – widely believed to have been done by the Halkın Kurtuluşu leftists (Gunes, 2012: 79), although this cannot be proved – was a seminal event for the new movement, reports Cansız, who states that it was through Gül's murder that

> the use of violence was brought to the agenda. Resorting to violence was as a matter of fact a necessity against this obstacle, and we grounded our movement on ideological and political struggle and revolutionary violence. Necessary defense was actually a way of struggle that our movement [was] based on since the very beginning. (*ANF News*, 27 November 2013)

The *Apocular* advocated the destruction of all such 'colonialism', by violently ejecting the various state forces 'occupying' the different sectors of Kurdistan as a whole. In Turkish Kurdistan this led to armed confrontation with the Turkish state, beginning in 1984. The PKK was not the only Kurdish radical organization with such an analysis at the time. But it became the 'the most radical, most strictly organized and most violent' of these dozen or so Kurdish parties (van Bruinessen, 1995: 2–3; Jongerden and Akkaya, 2011: 123–5). This makes it imperative to outline the nature of the PKK's early physical struggles.

The 18 May 1977 killing of a PKK cadre, Haki Karer, in a Antep coffee shop convinced the *Apocular* that they needed to move towards the establishment of a party. Cansız reports:

'This incident brought along the need to give a more serious fight. With the determinant [*sic*] approach of the leader, an organization was brought into existence in Kurdistan' (*ANF News*, 27 November 2013).

Organized training of a guerrilla force began early the following year in Lebanon's Beka'a Valley. The 1980 military coup disrupted the PKK's operations in Turkey, but by 1982 a force of 300 fighters had been established, based in Southern Kurdistan (Kurdish Iraq), from where they crossed into Turkish Kurdistan, beginning in 1984. The party's Second Congress, held 20–25 August 1982, set the PKK's military strategy, comprising three phases: defence, balance and offence. Reminiscent of Mao's strategy of protracted war, this envisaged an armed struggle proceeding in stages from asymmetrical guerrilla attacks up to conventional war, aiming to eject Turkey from Turkish Kurdistan (McDowall, 1996: 420; Jongerden and Akkaya, 2011: 130, 136, 139 n6).

Armed struggle unfolds

The initial targets for these guerrillas were widely disliked repressive landlords and tribal chiefs (Eccarius-Kelly, 2011: 110–11), whom the PKK accused of collaboration with Turkish colonialism. The first such target, in 1979, was Mehmet Celal Buçak, a big landlord who owned over twenty villages and was a prominent member of the Justice Party. This attempted assassination failed. However, a number of subsequent efforts, against similar targets, were successful (Jongerden and Akkaya, 2011: 139 n6).

In 1984 PKK armed units began reconnaissance operations in Turkish Kurdistan. On 15 August 1984 simultaneous armed raids by PKK forces were staged on Jandarma police stations in the Eruh and Şemdinli (Şemzînan) regions of Colemêrg (Hakkâri)

(Jongerden, 2008: 128). Several soldiers were killed or wounded in this twin operation. Guerrillas distributed propaganda and hung banners on coffee houses. These were the first direct attacks on state representatives. The guerrilla war had now been officially launched (Jongerden and Akkaya, 2011: 131).

In a harsh move to stem the rising tide of attacks, the Turkish state deforested swathes of Turkish Kurdistan and destroyed over 3,000 Kurdish villages, creating an estimated 2 million Kurdish refugees – many thousands of whom fled to Iraqi Kurdistan (van Bruinessen, 1995: 11). From 1985 the state also employed 'village guards' (*korucular*, rangers) – pro-government militias armed by the government to fight the PKK in certain Kurdish villages (Gunes, 2012: 104; van Bruinessen, 1995: 11). These included notorious criminal bands, such as that of Tahir Adıyaman. Some big landowners (*ağhalar*) pocketed their men's *korucu* wages, enriching themselves in the process. David McDowall reports:

> Those tribes refusing a government invitation to join the village guards risked retribution. Some were expelled from their villages, which were then razed. In the case of one chief, the security forces persuaded him to reconsider his position by executing his brother in front of his villagers. (McDowall, 1996: 423)

The PKK killed many *korucular*, in some cases attacking their families as well (McDowall, 1996: 423–4; van Bruinessen, 1995: 4).

Many guerrillas were killed and thousands imprisoned and brutalized. Martial law had been in place across Turkey until 1983. This was made permanent in ten Kurdish provinces with the 1987 declaration of the *Olağanüstü Hal Bölge Valiliği* (OHAL – Governorship of the Region under Emergency Rule). Entire communities were exiled (Silverman, 2013; Gunes, 2012: 104).

In the face of the state's response, the PKK now turned to strengthening its military capabilities, resolving at its Third

Congress in October 1986 to transform the HRK into the ARGK guerrilla army (Gunes, 2012: 104). Significantly, especially when compared to the PKK's later development, the Congress decided that military development was the central objective of the movement in that period, with even 'ideological-political', cultural and 'external relations' being subordinated to it. The Congress envisaged that these other aspects would 'emerge from the people's war'. As if to underline the dominance of the Kalashnikov and the RPG over other forms of struggle in that period, the Congress also resolved to introduce a PKK 'compulsory conscription law' (Gunes, 2012: 104–5), according to which each Kurdish family was expected by the PKK to provide one guerrilla fighter.

By the end of the 1980s the ARGK guerrilla forces not only increased appreciably numerically but also succeeded in building connections to local populations (Levitt, 1991: 24). Local PKK militias (*milis*) were established and ARGK attacks on military targets intensified, especially during 1987, when multiple deaths of military personnel in single operations occurred (Gunes, 2012: 105–6). ARGK units in the mid- to late 1980s managed to remain in villages – and from 1987 in some towns – for several hours, while making continuous propaganda (Rathmell and Gunter, 2014; Gunes, 2012: 106).

Clashes between the ARGK and Turkish security forces only intensified in the 1990s. Battles now lasted for days on end and the area of PKK activities widened. Cross-border attacks by Turkish forces into PKK bases in Iraqi Kurdistan began in late 1991, but were unable to stem the tide of ARGK attacks and the PKK's growing popularity (Gunes, 2012: 106–7). 'The people of Kurdistan … is now presented for the first time with the opportunity to assume power' declared the PKK (*Kurdistan Report*, 1991: 1). Convinced of this possibility, Cemil Bayık stated in late 1998: 'President Apo has explained on various occasions that it is quite possible that the Kurds will be able to claim a peace for themselves by the year 2000, and we are convinced that this can be achieved' (*Kurdistan Report*, 1998). In reality the situation was, militarily speaking, approaching stalemate (Silverman, 2013). Neither side could destroy the other. Turkish security forces possessed overwhelming military force, but could not bring this to bear effectively in the harsh mountainous terrain and given the PKK's growing popular support among Kurds (Levitt, 1991: 24; Gunes, 2012: 107). The PKK in this period imagined that it could secure victory by military means, but this was merely a fantasy.

The period in Turkish Kurdistan surveyed in this chapter so far, from 1973 to 2004, witnessed the unfolding of a guerrilla struggle. Beginning with tiny forces, the movement that became the PKK managed eventually to attract mass support, in both the villages and the towns of Turkish Kurdistan (Levitt, 1991: 24).

As the guerrilla war expanded and deepened across Turkey, the state responded with devastating force. One consequence of this was a massive new Kurdish migration westwards, to the cities of western Turkey. But PKK operations spread to these as well, increasing the state's pressure on the Kurds, pushing growing numbers out of Turkey altogether. Some, as we have seen, fled to Iraqi Kurdistan. A larger number uprooted their families and sought refuge in Western Europe – especially in Germany. This provided the PKK with the opportunity to spread its increasingly formidable supporters' network (Bozarslan, 1997: 358).

The PKK in Europe

The PKK has never been content to limit its activities to the four corners of Kurdistan. It has long been committed to organizing support for its goals among Kurds globally. Alynna J. Lyon and Emek M. Uçarer observed in 1998 that 'current technological innovations provide a conduit for diffusion of contentious politics from state to state' (Lyon and Uçarer, 1998). They pointed out further that 'the rapid growth of communications and transportation provides the mechanism in which Kurdish dissension is sent.' They note that these technological tools are effortlessly relocated from one country to another.

This explains how the PKK has also established itself firmly in the Kurdish diaspora. Hamit Bozarslan (1997: 358) estimates that the PKK has a 'massive presence' in all sectors of the Kurdish diaspora, but particularly in Germany – the West European country with the most Turkish Kurds (*Reuters*, Ankara, 25 November 1998). The PKK reportedly divided Germany into eight 'regions', around thirty 'sub-regions' and numerous 'lodges' or boroughs, all under the umbrella of YEK-KOM, the Federation of Kurdish Associations in Germany (Lyon and Uçarer, 1998).

The PKK continues to accumulate prodigious amounts of money from Kurds in Europe. It also maintains full-colour printing presses that produce large quantities of political and cultural books, magazines, newspapers, pamphlets and posters in various languages, which – together with cassettes and DVDs – are distributed as far afield as Australia. Sophisticated PKK websites are based in Europe. The PKK also maintains facilities in Europe for the ideological and cultural training of Kurdish youth.

It is estimated that in excess of 1,300,000 Kurds live in Western Europe (*Today's Zaman*, 9 August 2012; *CNN*, 11 January 2013; *Ethnologue*, 2015a; *Wereldjournalisten.nl*, 23 May 2007; Institut Kurde de Paris, 2015; Northern Ireland Neighbourhood Information Service, 2011; Scotland Census, 2013; *Ethnologue* 2015b; *Jyllands Posten*, 8 May 2006; *Christian Science Monitor*, 12 January 1998; *Ethnologue*, 2015c; *Ethnologue*, 2015d; Statistics Finland, 2015; *Ethnologue*, 2015e; *Dublin People*, 11 February 2013; *Cyprus Mail*, 22 May 2010; *Rudaw*, 28 November 2011; *Times of Malta*, 25 October 2014). Diaspora Kurds live principally in Germany (800,000 Kurds; *Today's Zaman*, 9 August 2012) and France (150,000 Kurds; CNN, 11 January 2013). Pro-PKK Kurds in Germany and France especially have long ago 'successfully organized themselves along political lines in Europe' (Eccarius-Kelly, 2002: 91, 92).

The PKK's ability to mobilize large numbers of its supporters in Germany has a solid history. In April 1990, the PKK organized 10,000 Kurds to demonstrate in Cologne against Turkey's military attacks on Kurds. Some 8,000 gathered on 9 December 1991 in Bremen to celebrate the PKK's thirteenth birthday. A 120-person hunger strike was begun simultaneously in Hamburg and Kiel, also in the early 1990s, at the same time as a 700-person hunger strike in Brussels (Lyon and Uçarer, 1998).

On 25 August 1992, protesting the then recent killings by the Turkish army in the south-west of Turkey, 2,000 demonstrated in front of the Turkish consulate in Hamburg (Lyon and Uçarer, 1998). In the same period, the PKK organized human blockades of German highways as a form of protest, including on the Franco-German border. In one such protest, pro-PKK demonstrators crossed the border on foot without valid visas. The border guards were forced to permit the massive crowd to cross and proceed to their cultural festival in Frankfurt – which was attended by 45,000 Kurds.

On 24 June 1993, pro-PKK Kurds (some of whom were heavily armed) stormed the Turkish consulates in Munich, Marseille and Bern, taking embassy personnel hostage. More or less simultaneously, many Turkish banks and travel agencies were attacked in major German cities, causing heavy damage. Perhaps realizing that it had gone too far, the PKK's front organization in Europe claimed that these actions had all occurred 'spontaneously'. Nevertheless, strong suspicions arose that these actions had been orchestrated by the PKK from outside Germany (Lyon and Uçarer, 1998).

The French and German governments banned the PKK and its front organizations after these incidents, in November 1993. In retaliation, supporters and members of the banned organization staged new demonstrations, including the occupation of a pro-PKK cultural centre that had been closed under the ban. Protesters threatened to immolate themselves if they were forcibly removed (Lyon and Uçarer, 1998).

The US Department of State (1995) reports that the PKK clashed 'frequently' with police in some Western European countries during 1994, in a strategic targeting of 'Western interests in Europe'. On 22 March 1994 the PKK blocked highways in Germany between Karlsruhe and Stuttgart (Lyon and Uçarer, 1998). It organized demonstrations in several German cities, some of which ended in violent conflicts with the police (US Department of State, 1995). When German police killed a Kurdish youth in Hanover, the PKK organized sit-ins at the German embassy in Athens. It did the same at Denmark's German consulate, in October 1994, when British immigration authorities detained Kani Yılmaz, the senior PKK leader in Europe. At this time the PKK also opened offices of the ERNK in Italy and Greece (US Department of State, 1995).

Despite the ban on the PKK, the party laid on busloads of Kurds to show that nothing would prevent them from organizing in Germany. Some 200,000 PKK supporters rallied in Bonn on 17 June 1995, brandishing ERNK flags and Öcalan posters and chanting *Bijî PKK!* (Long live the PKK!). Throughout the mid-1990s pro-PKK demonstrators frequently grappled with police in Germany as they attempted to disperse these illegal assemblies. On 16 March 1996, some 2,000 PKK members and sympathizers gathered in Dortmund when their demonstration permit was refused, and attacked the police. These PKK mobilizations were frequently multi-country affairs. For instance, busloads of PKK supporters from Belgium attempting to link up with the Dortmund protesters on 16 March 1996 were stopped at the German border. So some 1,500 of them crossed the border on foot (Lyon and Uçarer, 1998: 45–6).

In an interview with Med TV on 24 March 1996, Öcalan warned Europe – especially Germany – of serious disturbances if Turkey's government did not respond positively to the PKK ceasefire in Turkey. Öcalan threatened to make an assault on Turkish holiday resorts, which are very much favoured by German tourists. Claiming that 'Germany has launched a war against the PKK', he added ominously: 'Should Germany decide to stick to this policy, we can return the damage. Each and every Kurd can become a suicide bomber' (Lyon and Uçarer, 1998).

Vera Eccarius-Kelly notes that the PKK's demands – Kurdish-language education, independently managed Kurdish radio and television stations, and the legalization of Kurdish political parties – all parallel requirements for Turkey's membership of the European Union. She submits that this provides PKK leaders with potential leverage in future negotiations by Turkey over accession and encourages Kurdish leaders to reach out to Kurds pursuing university degrees in Western Europe (Eccarius-Kelly, 2002: 114). Despite granting in principle permission for Kurdish-language teaching, Turkey's Higher Education Council permitted only two universities (in Mêrdînê and Amed) to create Kurdish Language and Literature departments – with only postgraduate students granted access. A third university's application was rejected by authorities as an attempt to 'support terrorism'. Students at all other levels (including school) were denied admittance to Kurdish-language programmes across Turkey. Generally speaking, 'The use of the Kurdish language is still seen as a sign of support for "separatist activities"' (Eccarius-Kelly, 2002: 168).

Young educated Kurds from as far afield as Australia have long been invited to Europe by pro-PKK organizations to participate in its key European undertakings – especially its media projects. Med TV, a PKK-dominated television station (Barkey and Fuller, 1998: 33) based in London and Brussels, formerly broadcast eighteen hours daily. The broadcaster began transmission in 1995; within six months it was apparently attracting an audience of 50 million, in thirty-four countries – including Turkey – according to one usually conservative source (Gunter, 1997: 54). Apart from cultural programmes in Kurdish languages, the station also showed ARGK guerrillas in the field, sometimes even engaged in battle. On 22 March 1999 Britain's Independent Television Commission closed the station (Med TV press releases, 1 April and 23 April 1999). Med TV was succeeded by Medya TV, which began transmitting from Belgium via a satellite uplink from France, until its licence was in turn revoked by French authorities on 13 February 2004. A few weeks later Roj TV began transmission from Denmark. The PKK was once again showing it could not be silenced.

From time to time there have even been PKK guerrilla training camps in European countries. Reported camps have been dismantled (*Expatica*, 2004; *NIS News Bulletin*, 2004) at Liempde and near Eindhoven in the Netherlands and in Belgium (United Nations OHCHR, 2004: 276–7).

The PKK has a sophisticated leadership structure in some European countries (Bongar et al., 2006: 97). The formidable power of the PKK's political and communications network was dramatically verified by its campaign for the liberty and physical safety of Abdullah Öcalan, in late 1998 and early 1999. Ordered to leave Syria by President al-Assad, the PKK leader was variously reported to be in Russia, Lebanon, North Korea, Greece and Kenya. When he was arrested in Rome on 13 November 1998, the PKK's illegal networks in Germany staged demonstrations attracting over 2,000 Kurds in several German towns (*AFP*, 17 November 1998).

Meanwhile, the PKK Central Committee beseeched Kurdish 'patriotic people':

> Our nation's every true eye, ear and heart must be upon Rome and by the side of our national leadership. All who have the means to do so must make their way to Rome, and stand up for our leadership. For every honourable Kurd there is but one task, at home and abroad, in the situation in which we find ourselves: That is to march, to demonstrate, to join on hungerstrike [*sic*] and to undertake whatsoever democratic action may be necessary to stand up for our leadership. No acts other than those of a democratic nature must be resorted to. (PKK Central Committee, 1998)

The Kurds indeed stood up for their leader. When Öcalan formally requested political asylum in Italy on 15 November, a couple of thousand Kurds had already congregated outside the military hospital near Rome where Öcalan was being held. Demonstrators arrived from Germany, Romania, Denmark, Russia, Armenia, the Netherlands, Sweden, Finland, Australia, North America, Syria, Lebanon, Switzerland, France, Austria and other lands (*Reuters*, Rome, 15 November 1998; *Reuters*, Beirut, 16 November 1998).

'An eye for an eye! A tooth for a tooth! We are with you until death, Öcalan', chanted the Kurdish demonstrators in Rome (*Reuters*, 17 November 1998). An estimated 10,000 marched through the city demanding asylum for Öcalan on 18 November (*ABC News*, 1998). On the *Voice of America* Amberin Zaman reported that Öcalan was being lionized in the Italian media as a 'freedom fighter' (Zaman, *Voice of America*, 16 November 1998).

Demonstrations and hunger strikes took place in many other countries, as well as in Amed and Istanbul. Pro-PKK websites provided contact points in Rome for Kurds arriving there. The appeals of the PKK Central Committee to the Kurdish diaspora were carried around the globe via the Internet. The diaspora's strong response proved the tremendous mobilizing power of the PKK's political and communications network. From an initial fighting force of a hundred guerrilla fighters, the PKK had transformed itself into a movement with mass appeal to Kurds in both Turkey and the Kurdish global diaspora.

From its original ideological melange of Kurdish nationalism and radical Marxism–Leninism, the *Apocular* slowly became more sophisticated in its guiding ideas and organizational structure. The PKK soon became the most radical, the most violent and the best organized of all Kurdish parties in the Turkish state. Turkish repression convinced it to deepen its military preparations. A guerrilla training camp was established in Lebanon in 1978. Guerrilla attacks began in 1984, meeting fierce opposition from Turkey's army. Nevertheless the PKK Third Party Congress in 1986 resolved that military development remained the party's central objective. This approach brought the PKK a great deal of support in the villages and towns of Turkish Kurdistan, especially from the 1990s onwards. However, the cost to the Kurdish population was so heavy that many fled to Western Europe. Yet this provided the PKK with the opportunity to construct a formidable supporters' network across the continent.

FOUR

From ceasefire to all-out war

Peace continued to elude the Kurdish–Turkish conflict. In fact, for a long time the conflict grew visibly bloodier with the passage of time. The 1980s and 1990s were the peak of the PKK's armed struggle against the Turkish state. Numerous authors, and of course the Turkish state itself, have consistently alleged that the PKK during those two decades was guilty of perpetrating widespread atrocities against civilians, including liquidating entire villages (White, 1997: 227). As the present author has shown, several of these acts were actually perpetrated by Turkish Special Forces (White, 1997: 249 n5). One well-known case is that of the massacre of 12 July 1993, in which at least twenty-six villagers (including fourteen children) were murdered at Giyadîn (Diyadin) village in Van province. Both the pro-PKK newspaper *Özgür Gündem* and the local PKK commander denied the organzation's involvement, blaming the massacre on the crack Turkish army *Özel Timler* (Special Teams) (*Özgür Gündem*, 1993). Witnesses confirmed to the *Turkish Daily News* that the Turkish state, in the form of *Özel Timler*, was behind both this massacre and an earlier one, which had also been attributed to the PKK. Independent investigators, including Deniz Baykal, leader of the Kemalist Cumhuriyet Halk Partisi, also confirmed that state forces were responsible for the killings (*Turkish Daily News*, 1993; Kutschera, 1994: 14). The Turkish state's portrayal of the PKK as wantonly violent terrorists was facilitated by the rigid censorship of events in Kurdistan and the obliging attitude of most of the Turkish press.

Nevertheless, Abdullah Öcalan conceded in 1989 that civilians – including women and children – had been killed by the PKK (*İkibine Doğru*, 1989: 23; Öcalan, 1999: 114). Those classified as civilians by the *Serok* did not include the *Korucular* employed by the Turkish state as a bulwark against the PKK, on the grounds that the *Korucular* were no longer civilians but a traitorous portion of the security forces.

A deadly pattern has marked the Kurdish–Turkish conflict in Turkey: wholesale bloodletting is followed by fruitless attempts at peacemaking – which are followed by even worse bloodletting. The PKK's unilateral ceasefire declaration on 1 September 1998 did not result in a viable peace process and violent attacks continued from both sides. Ankara excused itself with the traditional mantra that it was only 'fighting terrorists'. The PKK retorted that the state was uninterested in peace and that the guerrillas needed to defend themselves against the security forces. Öcalan's capture unleashed a particularly ferocious disruption of the proclaimed ceasefire, when PKK forces wreaked furious havoc on the state. The *Serok* managed to restore the ceasefire on the PKK side, but still no viable peace process emerged. Ankara did introduce some very timid reforms in this period, to appease its Kurdish population. Most notably, in 2003 limited use of the Kurdish language was permitted in state television broadcasts. This was not designed as a government confidence-building measure to prepare the way for a lasting peace process, however.

The prime function of such limited reforms at that time was to attempt to wean Kurds off supporting the PKK.

The unilateral ceasefire ends

Speaking subsequently of the period from late 2004 to May 2011, Abdullah Öcalan stated that the Turkish state's illegal paramilitary organization Jandarma İstihbarat ve Terörle Mücadele (JİTEM – Intelligence and Fight against Terrorism Gendarmerie) 'attempted two or three coups' against the Turkish government. A meeting between George W. Bush and Recep Tayyip Erdoğan on 5 November 2007 saw the United States openly switch its support from the army and begin 'to support the AKP', according to Öcalan. The *Serok* concurred with the verdict (Uslu, 8 September 2008) of the former JİTEM founder, retired Brigader General Veli Küçük, that the generals were 'sold out' at the Bush–Erdoğan summit (Öcalan, 2013).

On 1 June 2004 the PKK/Kongra-Gel finally formally ended the ceasefire that had been in existence since August 1999. The Kurdish party claimed that the state was continuing to attack it. Armed clashes between Kongra-Gel and Turkish security forces recommenced in late 2004, proceeding on an escalating scale into 2005. Already in May 2004 the PKK had warned that its unilateral ceasefire would end soon, due to what it alleged were 'annihilation operations' against its forces (Cutler and Burch, 2011). On 2 July 2005, six people were killed and fifteen injured by a bomb planted by 'Kurdish guerrillas', on a train travelling between Elâzığ and Tatvan in Bingöl province. Attacks attributed to Kurdish nationalists multiplied throughout July (Cutler and Burch, 2011).

The full truth regarding these incidents may never be known. Nevertheless, evidence suggests that Kongra-Gel might not have been responsible for those attacks that it did not claim. At least some of the incidents were the work of the shadowy Teyrêbazên Azadiya Kurdistan (TAK – Kurdistan Freedom Falcons). First appearing in 2004, the TAK maintained a website (www.teyrebaz.com) between 2 April 2006 and 6 February 2012. The TAK is alleged to be either (i) a splinter group of former PKK/Kongra-Gel members disgruntled with the organization's perspective of seeking a peaceful settlement, or (ii) a front for the PKK/Kongra-Gel. PKK leaders deny there is any connection with their group (National Consortium for the Study of Terrorism, 2013). Lending some credibility to the first assessment, one analysis claims that TAK sought to attract recruits who believed that the PKK/Kongra-Gel was 'too soft' (Bekdil/Jamestown Foundation, 2008). Academic Francesco F. Milan (2012) describes TAK as a 'hard-line offshoot' of the PKK/Kongra-Gel.

A press release dated 5 August 2006 published on TAK's website stated that the group was dissatisfied with the struggle of Kongra-Gel and its armed wing, the Hêzên Parastina Gel, for 'taking political balances into consideration… We are calling on the HPG to become more active in their struggle.' The same statement noted that TAK militants had for a period fought within the ranks of the PKK, but they had concluded that the latter's approach of trying to seek peace with the state caused the PKK to become weak. Therefore, the statement continued, the TAK 'separated from the organization and established the TAK'. Nevertheless, in justifying its attacks, the TAK repeatedly referred to 'Chairman APO our historical leader', concluding: *Yaşasın Başkan APO*! (Long Live President APO!) (TAK website, 5 August 2006).

It is impossible to state with certainty what the real nature of TAK is, due to the extremely shadowy nature of the group. However, in the past *Kontrgerilla* have been deployed by illegal Turkish armed units, to perpetrate atrocities that are falsely attributed to the PKK, in order to both discredit the organization and prevent a peace settlement between the PKK and Ankara. In other words, it is quite feasible that TAK comprises (at least in part) former PKK fighters, yet acts solely under the direction of Turkey's 'deep state'. It is known that sections of the Turkish state have no wish to see a peace settlement successfully concluded.

TAK has perpetrated a series of bombings: a supermarket; a tourist resort near Antalya (Cutler and Burch, 2011); the coastal resort town of Çeşme; a bus station in Istanbul; a district office of the Justice and Development Party in Istanbul; and in Kızılay (Cutler and Burch, 2011; National Consortium for the Study of Terrorism, 2013).

The TAK website contained details of numerous TAK operations, including the burning of Turkish forests in no fewer than fifteen regions. These acts were said to be revenge for 'fascist Turkey's' depredations against the Kurdish population in Dêrsim, Bingöl, Şirnex, Colemêrg, Amed and Elazığ. Two attacks were claimed in Istanbul's Sultanahmet district, as were many other acts of sabotage in the city (TAK website, 2 April 2006 to 6 February 2012).

TAK vowed that its 'attacks would continue and become more violent', targeting the 'military bureaucracy, economy and tourism' as its 'top priority targets, while the state of terror does not stop'. TAK also promised to attack the 'traitors and compradors … military officers, civil bureaucrats, fascists, traitors' who make Kurdish people's lives 'a living hell'. The website contained detailed illustrated technical guides for the preparation of radio-controlled time bombs (TAK website, 2 April 2006 to 6 February 2012).

TAK's terrorism heightened anti-PKK feelings among ordinary Turks – and ultra-nationalist Turkish forces sought to capitalize on this. For example, a bombing in Amed on 12 September 2006 killed ten civilians. The Türk İntikam Tugayı (TİT – Turkish Revenge Brigade), a violent Turkish ultra-nationalist organization with strong military connections (*Zaman*, 2007), claimed responsibility for the attack, threatening to kill ten Kurds for every Turk killed in the conflict (*Voice of America News*, 2009). A TAK bombing in Mersin on 30 August 2006 was condemned by the PKK. The latter declared yet another ceasefire on 1 October 2006. Nevertheless minor clashes continued in the south-east as Turkish security forces continued operations (MAR Project, 2010).

On 22 May 2007 the Turkish capital Ankara was the target of a suicide bombing, which killed eight and wounded over a hundred. The Turkish authorities attributed the attack to the PKK. However, the organization hotly denied this (Goktas, 2007; *People's Daily Online*, 23 May 2007). Whoever was responsible, the incident was a perfect opportunity for the Turkish military to announce an imminent attack upon PKK strongholds in Kurdish northern Iraq. On 2 June the United States withdrew all its troops from Iraqi Kurdistan. An estimated 100,000 Turkish troops were mobilized on the border between Turkey and Iraq.

On 5 June 2007 shelling and air strikes by the Turkish army were reported, targeting PKK bases in Iraqi Kurdistan (*Oakland Tribune*, 7 June 2007; Torchia, 8 June 2007). Two days later, several thousand Turkish troops apparently crossed into Iraq in a 'hot pursuit' raid against the PKK there. Turkey's foreign minister denied that his troops had entered Iraq. Nevertheless two senior Turkish security officials admitted that the armed incursion had indeed taken place, acknowledging that the troops ventured almost 2 miles inside Iraq. This attack marked a decisive ratcheting up of the AKP government's conflict with the Kurdish nationalists, given that the last major Turkish incursion into northern Iraq had been as far back as 1997, when almost 50,000 troops were sent to the region (*BBC News*, 9 June 2015; *Oakland Tribune*, 7 June 2007). The new incursion was preceded by the declaration of a three-month period of martial law in Kurdish areas near the Iraq border and a ban on civilian flights to the area (Torchia, 2007).

The Patriotic Union of Kurdistan (PUK), an Iraqi Kurdish party, reported that Turkish artillery shells hit the Sidikan area in Irbil province during this operation, affecting nine villages. It also confirmed that the Iranian military shelled the adjacent area in Iranian Kurdistan at about the same time. 'Huge damage was inflicted on the area', the PUK stated, adding that residents had 'left their houses, fearing for their lives'. Lt Ahmed Karim of the Iraqi border guards force told the *Associated Press* that seven Turkish shells landed on a forest near Sakta village in the Batous area (Torchia, 8 June 2007). The justification for this sortie was a PKK grenade attack that killed seven soldiers and wounded six at an army base in Dêrsim on 4 June 2007 (*BBC News*, 4 June 2007).

In late September and early October 2007, similar attacks upon the Turkish military paved the way for severe measures against the *Apocular* by the Turkish state. On 27 September, two Turkish Jandarma policemen were killed in Bitlis province by a bomb allegedly planted by 'Kurdish separatists' (Cutler and Burch, 2011). Then on 7 October a force of forty to fifty PKK fighters ambushed an eighteen-man Turkish commando unit in the Gabar mountains, killing fifteen and injuring three, making it the deadliest PKK attack since the 1990s (MAR Project, 2010).

The Turkish parliament passed a law sanctioning renewed Turkish military action inside Iraqi territory. On 21 October some 150 to 200 PKK fighters attacked an outpost in Yüksekova, manned by a fifty-strong infantry battalion. The outpost was overrun. Twelve were killed and seventeen wounded; in addition eight Turkish soldiers were captured. The Kurdish fighters then withdrew into Iraqi Kurdistan, taking the eight captive soldiers with them; though they later released them unharmed (*Hürriyet*, 4 November 2007). The PKK force was heavily armed – including with a Russian-made Doçka heavy anti-aircraft machine gun (*Hürriyet*, 23 October 2007), as well as RPG-7 rocket launchers and C-4 explosives (*Hürriyet*, 25 October 2007). The stage was now set for the bloodiest fighting in years between Turks and Kurds, as the Turkish military responded by bombing PKK bases on 24 October.

In late October 2007 Turkey's air force again bombed PKK targets inside Iraqi Kurdistan and 300 Turkish troops 'advanced about six miles', killing thirty-four PKK fighters (Tran, 2007). This offensive was supplemented on 28 October by a major operation in Tunceli province involving 8,000 Turkish troops with air support (Tran, 2007). From 16 December an aerial offensive unfolded against PKK camps in Iraqi Kurdistan (MAR Project, 2010). Operation Sun, a major Turkish cross-border offensive, started on 21 February 2008. Up to 10,000 Turkish forces took part in this offensive, supported by 'air assets' (*Hürriyet*, 24 October 2007; *Hürriyet*, 25 October 2007). This was a major offensive designed to remove the PKK threat in Iraqi Kurdistan. A reported total of twenty-seven Turkish soldiers and 724 PKK militants were killed (MAR Project, 2010; Yuksel, 2008). Operation Sun was a total failure, serving only to politically reinforce Erdoğan and weaken the army. Smaller-scale Turkish operations against PKK bases in Iraqi Kurdistan continued (MAR Project, 2010).

PKK attacks continued throughout 2008, with casualties on both sides. During the course of the conflict between 1984 and

September 2008, the Turkish military had succeeded in exacting a heavy toll from the PKK – reportedly killing 32,000 PKK militants and capturing 14,000 (*Hürriyet*, 16 September 2008). One-sided 'ceasefires' had come and gone, but the only result had been a steady increase in bloodshed.

The 2009 'Kurdish Opening'

Such inter-ethnic bloodshed hardly augured well for the prospect of peace breaking out any time soon. Yet the year 2009 opened with the Turkish government permitting Turkey's first ever Kurdish-language television channel, TRT 6, to launch. In addition the state announced plans to rename Kurdish villages that had Turkish names, expand freedom of expression, restore Turkish citizenship to Kurdish refugees and decree a 'partial amnesty' for PKK fighters. Then the pro-Kurdish Demokratik Toplum Partisi (DTP – Democratic Society Party) secured an impressive increase in its vote in local elections held in the Kurdish south-east on 29 March 2009: it polled almost 50 per cent of total votes in the ten provinces where it was successful, winning ninety-nine municipalities (Çandar, 2009: 16; Casier, Jongerden and Walker, 2011: 108, 109). Encouraged by these developments, the PKK chose this conjuncture to announce its sixth unilateral ceasefire, after the *Serok* commanded them on 13 April 2009 to 'end military operations and prepare for peace' (*FM News Weekly*, 2011). The Turkish state's initial response was not positive, as April 2009 also saw a wave of repression directed at the DTP. In the wake of the party's electoral triumph, three DTP vice presidents and around fifty other party activists and supporters were interned in the Kurdish south-east, as well as in Ankara and Istanbul (Casier, Jongerden and Walker, 2011: 106).

Mid-2009 saw the unveiling of the AKP's so-called 'Kurdish Opening', later rebadged the 'Democratic Opening' to appease Turkish nationalists, and subsequently renamed the 'national unity project' (Çandar, 2009: 13). This was the first time since Turgut Özal's hesitant overtures to the Kurds in 1991 that any Turkish government had attempted reconciliation, consultation and negotiation with the Kurds, in a declared effort to wind down the PKK insurgency. President Abdullah Gül declared: 'The biggest problem of Turkey is the Kurdish problem… It has to be solved', adding that the country had a 'historic possibility to solve it through discussions'. The PKK's acting leader at the time, Murat Karayılan, told reporters that the guerrillas were ready to lay down their arms and that, if necessary, the Kurdish nationalist parliamentary Demokratik Toplum Partisi could negotiate in its place (Christie-Miller, 4 August 2010).

Abdullah Öcalan remarked that the PKK's 'ceasefire has started a new era', adding 'What is asked of us is to deepen this process' (Uzun, 2014: 16). He continued:

> We never just took up arms for the sake of it. All we did was to open a road for our nation to freely develop. But we had no other means of struggle to adopt: that is why we had to take up arms and have brought the struggle to this stage. The Kurdish situation is, at heart, a Turkish–Kurdish situation. Our struggle has come to the point of the Turkish public accepting the Kurdish identity; it has seen it necessary to recognise Kurdish existence and solve the problem. (Uzun, 2014: 16)

Unfortunately the process was 'poorly prepared and hastily implemented' on both sides (Jenkins, 2013). The state even failed to produce a legal framework for any PKK fighters laying down their arms. The PKK, for its part, acted with a degree of immaturity, parading a delegation of PKK fighters and their families who had legally entered Turkey:

> A total of 34 persons, of which eight were PKK guerrillas from the Qandil mountains and 26 from the Mahmur refugee camp in Northern Iraq, entered Turkey as a 'peace group' at the border town of Silopi. The group members were welcomed by several ... thousand enthusiastic Kurds making victory signs in a welcoming ceremony organized by the Kurdish legal party DTP. Mayors and parliamentarians from [the] DTP attended the ceremony. (Casier, Jongerden and Walker, 2011: 106 n6)

Everywhere the guerrillas went, they were greeted by mass demonstrations of enthusiastic Kurds – probably encouraged by the PKK, although in truth the demonstrations were spontaneous outbursts on the part of the Kurdish population. Both the state and the PKK were already aware of the latter's high levels of continuing popular support, so the demonstrations were gratuitous. By encouraging (and in some cases organizing) them, the PKK unwittingly gave hard-core Kemalists a stick to break the AKP's resolve, as an ultra-nationalist Turkish mobilization against the incipient peace process gathered force. Broadcast throughout Turkey, the 'welcome home' demonstrations were perceived as PKK victory parades (Gunter, 2012). Protests against a perceived sell-out to Kurdish nationalists occurred in several Turkish cities. 'Terrorists have become heroes', complained Deniz Baykal, then leader of the opposition CHP. The head of the Turkish General Staff, General İlker Başbuğ, added that 'no one can accept what happened' (Güzeldere, 2010; Seibert, 2009).

Ankara had ambitiously hoped that the returning guerrillas would be the start of a flood of PKK militants coming back to Turkey and that this process would culminate in 'the PKK dissolving itself'. But, in the end, the process fizzled out as suddenly as it had begun. The delegation of eight PKK fighters had been promised immunity from prosecution, but this was reversed, and the guerrillas were all arrested under anti-terrorism laws.

A second detachment of PKK returnees (from Europe) did not materialize, as Turkey declined them travel documents (Jenkins, 2013; Seibert, 2009).

Secret negotiations between the Turkish state and the PKK continued behind the scenes after the demise of the 'Kurdish Opening'. These eventually lead to talks in Norway (the 'Oslo Process'), with the state apparently scaling down its offensive operations (Jenkins, 16 January 2013) and the PKK continuing to observe the 'unilateral ceasefire' it had announced in April 2009 (*Milliyet*, 28 May 2009; Uslu, 2009). The Turkish general election of 12 June 2011 meant that the process officially went into limbo (Jenkins, 2013), although the PKK announced the extension of its ceasefire until 15 July, following a request from Abdullah Öcalan (Ciwan, 2013; *Milliyet*, 28 May 2009; Uslu, 2009). The PKK added that the ceasefire might be extended further, until 1 September, dependent upon developments. Unimpressed, General İlker Başbuğ responded that the PKK had only two options: 'laying down its arms or we will take them from their hands' (*Bügün*, 2009; Uslu, 2009).

It did not take much for the promise of peace to be dashed. On 11 December 2009 the Constitutional Court of Turkey (Anayasa Mahkemesi) banned the DTP – some of whose leaders had been interned since April – setting the scene for the party's leaders to be tried later for terrorism. Some 1,400 DTP members were arrested, 900 of whom were held in custody. Then, in late December the Amed Chief Prosecutor's Office issued warrants for the arrest of eighty officials and representatives of the newly formed BDP, a formally legal replacement party for the now illegal DTP. Those arrested included several current or recent Kurdish party mayors – including 'the mayors of Batman, Siirt, Cizre, Amed-Kayapınar, Amed-Sûr, Çınar, Weranşar (Viranşehir), and Kızıltepe, and the former mayor of Dicle' (Casier, Jongerden and Walker, 2011: 107 and n8). In mid-February 2010 a further wave of repression saw the detention of dozens of BDP executive members. All of the DTP/BDP arrestees were charged with membership of the Turkey Council of the Koma Ciwakên Kürdistan, and for 'running municipalities under the direction of the PKK'. A total of 151 Kurdish politicians and activists were eventually charged with 'aiding the PKK' (Casier, Jongerden and Walker, 2011: 107 and nn8, 9; Marcus, 2010).

In response Kurds demonstrated throughout Turkey, resulting in several deaths after the mobilizations were attacked by security forces (*FM News Weekly*, 2011). The PKK certainly participated actively in these actions. Despite the supposed continuing ceasefire, on 7 December the PKK raised the temperature by ambushing Turkish soldiers in Reşadiye, in Central Anatolia, killing seven and wounding three. Taking responsibility for this incident on 10 December 2009, the PKK explained that the attack was perpetrated by a unit acting on its own volition. Contradictorily, however, the PKK statement added that the PKK command centre does not issue orders to assault, and that military units have the right to take the initiative (*Hürriyet Daily News*, 10 December 2009; Arsu, 2009).

2010: *Serok* abandons rapprochement with Turkey

Following a brief period of calm, one Turkish soldier was killed and two others injured during a clash with the PKK in Hakkâri province on 14 March 2010 (*Reuters AlertNet*, 14 March 2010). Another Turkish soldier was killed and a further two wounded on the same day during clashes in Batman province (*World Bulletin*, 2010a). Two PKK militants were killed and three soldiers wounded in Siirt province on the same day (*Kurdish Globe*, 2010). Then, only three days later, on 19 April, two Turkish police officers were killed when suspected PKK fighters opened fire on their police patrol car with automatic weapons in the northern Turkish province of Samsun (*Press TV*, 19 April 2010).

On 1 May 2010 the PKK attacked a patrol of Turkish soldiers in Dêrsim. It then conceded that the ceasefire had totally abandoned. Abdullah Öcalan added a dramatic flourish to this announcement from his prison cell, declaring that he was formally abandoning all attempts at rapprochement with the Turkish authorities, and handing that task to his military commanders (MAR Project, 2010). In a context in which only the *Serok*'s repeated intervention was shown to be effective in preventing the PKK from returning to an ongoing war strategy, this was a calculated move against his Turkish jailers, designed to shake them with the spectre of a return to total war on both sides. The immediate consequence, however, was a further intensification of armed conflict on both sides.

The PKK attacked a naval base in İskenderun on 31 May with 'missiles' (*Today's Zaman*, 1 June 2010). This was followed by clashes on 18 and 19 June (*World Bulletin*, 2010b), and then three further clashes in Hakkâri and Elâzığ provinces. An additional attack in Colemêrg took place on 20 July. All of these confrontations claimed the lives of both PKK fighters and Turkish troops. On 21 July PKK acting leader Murat Karayılan told the BBC that the guerrillas would disarm in return for greater political and cultural rights for Turkey's Kurds through dialogue. 'If the Turkish state does not accept this solution', Karayılan warned, 'then we will declare democratic confederalism independently' (*BBC News*, 21 July 2010).

The Turkish state was now in no mood for dialogue, however. Casualties on both sides had once again been mounting shockingly. The Turkish military announced it had killed a total of forty-six PKK militants during operations over the previous month in the Kurdish south-east (*World Bulletin*, 2010c). Around

100 military personnel had already been killed by this point in 2010 – more than the previous year's total death toll (*World Bulletin*, 2010c).

Then, on 12 August 2010, the PKK seized upon the imminent holy Muslim month of Ramadan to declare a new ceasefire (*AK News*, 2010). This was extended in November up to the Turkish general election of 12 June 2011, even though the PKK later stated that over eighty military operations had been waged against it by the Turkish state during this period.

A PKK raid on a hydroelectric power plant in the Dinar Deresi region of Amed resulted in the deaths of one Turkish soldier and nine PKK fighters on 7 September (*Kurd Net*, 7 September 2010), while a Turkish soldier was killed when an alleged PKK landmine exploded in the Eruh district of Siirt province on 12 September (*Hürriyet Daily News*, 12 September 2010). Then at least nine Kurdish civilians were killed and three others reportedly injured on 16 September, when a roadside bomb exploded under their minibus in Colemêrg (*Al Jazeera*, 2011; Cutler and Burch, 2011). The PKK was blamed for the bombings (*BBC News*, 16 September 2010). However, the PKK denied responsibility for a suicide bomb attack that left thirty-two people injured in Istanbul on 31 October (*BBC News*, 1 November 2010).

Kurdish unrest continued into the New Year. Dozens of young Kurdish protesters, their faces concealed by scarves, throwing Molotov cocktails and stones were dispersed by police using tear gas and water cannon in Istanbul on 16 January 2011. The violence began after a 2,000-strong rally organized to protest against the trial of the 150 Kurdish activists, including many elected officials, accused of links to the PKK (*AFP*, 16 January 2011).

Erdoğan adopted a very hard-line stance on the Kurdish issue in the months that followed, refusing any concessions to PKK demands and stepping up military operations in the Kurdish south-east. In response the PKK once more ramped up its attacks, while denouncing Prime Minister Erdoğan for alleged 'insincerity' (Jenkins, 2013). Peace now looked further away than ever. Hostilities once again escalated on both sides.

Led by their Kurdish deputies and mayors, some 3,000 Kurds filled the streets of Amed on 24 March 2011, demanding their rights and calling for an end to the conflict with the PKK. The authorities banned the demonstration, deploying armoured vehicles to block the protesters. Protesters blocked traffic in protest, chanting 'Kurdistan will be the tomb of fascism' and other PKK slogans. A small group threw firecrackers at police, who unleashed tear gas and arrested five people. Addressing demonstrators, BDP chairman Selahattin Demirtaş demanded the right to education in Kurdish, the release of imprisoned activists, the end of operations against the PKK, and the removal of the electoral threshold of 10 per cent of votes required to enter parliament. 'We shall stay on the streets until the government takes concrete steps for these four applications', vowed Demirtaş (*AFP*, 24 March 2011) 'This decision is ... fascist. We cannot take part in an unfair, undemocratic, election', he declared (*ANF News*, 19 April 2011).

The BDP leader threatened to boycott the legislative elections set for June 2011, after the Yüksek Seçim Kurulu (YSK – High Election Board) banned twelve BDP candidates, including Leyla Zana (*AFP*, 19 April 2011). The authorities' ban on the candidates sparked angry protests by thousands of Kurdish demonstrators in Amed, who pelted riot police with stones, while chanting *Bijî Serok Apo!* (Long Live Leader Apo!). Police responded with tear gas, water cannon and batons. At least five protesters were arrested. Several Kurds were injured in a similar demonstration in Van. Istanbul's Taksim Meydanı (Taksim Square) saw a sit-in by 3,000 pro-Kurdish protestors. Groups of youths attacked subway stations, school buildings and a post office with stones and Molotov cocktails, after police forcibly dispersed protesters. Demonstrators also targeted buses, cars, fire trucks and journalists. The security forces responded with tear gas (*AFP*, 19 April 2011).

New disturbances occurred the following day in Amed, as young protesters battled security forces, while chanting pro-PKK slogans. Several protesters were killed and a number injured. Sixteen demonstrators were arrested. Apparently alarmed by this escalation of events, President Abdullah Gül met on the same day with Selahattin Demirtaş and Parliamentary Speaker Mehmet Ali Şahin (*AFP*, 20 April 2011).

A Kurdish protester was killed and several others injured on 20 April by police gunfire in the small town of Bismil, near Amed, at a rally to protest the invalidation of Kurdish candidates for the June general election. BDP leader Demirtaş accused police of opening fire on demonstrators, killing one and wounding at least four. *Agence France Press* (*AFP*, 16 May 2011) later confirmed this accusation.

Armed incidents once again gradually escalated. Thus, on 1 April, seven suspected PKK guerrillas were killed by a police Jandarma unit near the town of Hassa in Osmaniye province, while trying to enter Turkey from Syria. The Kurdish fighters reportedly fired on the soldiers, who had ordered them to surrender. Six Turkish soldiers were wounded in the clash, one of whom later died (*AFP*, 1 April 2011; 2 April 2011).

A Kurdish protester died when police retaliated after facing an 'intense barrage' of molotov cocktails, stones and fireworks from some 800 protesters in Bismil. The angry demonstration followed the disqualification of several prominent Kurds from running in coming parliamentary elections. A statement from local government officials did not specify the cause of the protester's death. Police made a forceful intervention against demonstrators with tear gas, plastic bullets and water cannon. Protestors shouted *Kîn girţin! Kîn girţin!* (Revenge! Revenge!) and other pro-PKK slogans. Sixteen demonstrators were arrested. A few hours after the incident, youths set fire to the offices of the ruling AKP (*AFP*, 20 April 2011; 16 May 2011).

Before this deadly incident, Demirtaş was scheduled to have that very same evening a meeting with President Gül in Ankara, to find a solution to the issue of invalidation by the electoral authorities of seven nominees on an independent party list. Demirtaş apparently cancelled this meeting following the protestor's death. Once again, a violent incident had undermined a move towards peace. However, Kirdar Özsoylu, vice president of the High Election Board behind the controversial decision, ostensibly taken on account of the criminal records of the would-be candidates, nevertheless tried to calm spirits after the incident: 'I hope that our board will decide in favor of human rights and democratic rights', adding that the YSK would begin reviewing the nominations the next day (*AFP*, 20 April 2011).

At a campaign rally at Bayburt in north-east Turkey on 20 April, Prime Minister Erdoğan denounced what he termed 'vandalism' in the south-east, accusing the BDP of encouraging young Kurds to protest violently and throw molotov cocktails. In Istanbul, BDP supporters had tried earlier that day to close the two bridges crossing the Bosporus to traffic, but police dispersed the group. A roadside bomb exploded on Istanbul's outskirts, slightly injuring two people. Istanbul's governor blamed the PKK for this attack, which may well have been the case, as the organization undoubtedly now wielded tremendous influence among Kurds in the city. The *Apocular* had clearly concluded from the rebuffs to the PKK's ceasefires that only violent struggle would open up the road to resolution of the Kurdish issue. Earlier, Kurdish protesters had stormed the local headquarters of the ruling Justice and Development Party in Bismil, setting it on fire, causing extensive damage but no casualties (*AFP*, 20 April 2011).

On 22 April, the YSK agreed to authorize the applications of six of the seven Kurdish nominees it had initially excluded from the ballot. Several small groups met that evening in Amed, the main city in the south-east, to celebrate peacefully the YSK's decision (*AFP*, 20 April 2011).

Then some thirty-five people, including local leaders of the BDP, were arrested by police early on 25 April in Colemêrg, accused of belonging to the so-called 'urban network' of the PKK, the KCK (*AFP*, 25 April 2011; 4 May 2011). Armed clashes continued to exact a growing death toll, as a peace settlement eluded the two sides (*AFP*, 28 April 2011).

In a spectacular attack on the same day near Kastamonu in northern Turkey, guerrillas using machine guns and grenades ambushed the police escort of Prime Minister Erdoğan, killing one policeman and wounding another. The prime minister was not in the convoy at the time (*AFP*, 5 May 2011). Turkish security sources attributed the assault to the PKK, but the organization did not initially claim the attack. Finally, on 6 May, the PKK claimed the attack, announcing in a statement that the assault 'was made by our members in retaliation for the terror exercised by the police on the Kurdish people', adding that the attack 'targeted police ... not civilians or the Prime Minister' (*AFP*, 6 May 2011).

On 5 May the BDP again threatened a boycott of the parliamentary elections set for 12 June, if Turkish authorities kept arresting Kurdish activists and continued military operations against the PKK. The BDP announced its 'determination to continue to build a democratic and autonomous Kurdistan and organize legitimate resistance to attacks'. Erdoğan rejoined: 'The BDP seeks to achieve its objectives with the support of terrorists' (*AFP*, 5 May 2011).

The BDP is the latest in a series of five pro-Kurdish parties, beginning with the Halkın Emek Partisi (HEP – Peoples Labour Party), which was founded in July 1990. The mere fact that these parties have been established on a non-Turkish basis – on the foundation of Kurdishness – profoundly insults the official Kemalist basis of Turkish society. Each of the predecessor parties was closed down by the Turkish state, accused by Ankara of being tools of the PKK. Members of these parties have been raided by police, pilloried in the media as 'terrorists' – even though the parties have never advocated violence or outright separatism – and imprisoned. It is true that all of the parties have consistently advocated dialogue between Ankara and the PKK. For Turkish ultra-nationalists, that alone is tantamount to acceptance of 'Kurdish separatism'. And the parties' leaders have not endeared themselves to the Turkish public by being photographed with PKK guerrillas and declaring that Abdullah Öcalan is a leader of the Kurdish people (*Hürriyet Daily News*, 22 May 2012).

Yet the fact remains that these pro-Kurdish parties have all secured substantial electoral support in Kurdish regions. In the June 2011 election the BDP increased its number of representatives in the Turkish Assembly by more than one-third, to become the fourth largest party in the parliament. Forbidden by the state from openly supporting the PKK, ordinary Kurds nevertheless flocked to support the BDP, as they did its predecessors.

Arguably, the BDP (like its predecessors) has always been Ankara's best hope as an intermediary with the PKK insurgents. PKK leaders have repeatedly stated that they are willing to accept the BDP playing this role, and the party enjoys a high degree of credibility among ordinary Kurds. Indeed, no other grouping in Turkey – with the exception of the PKK itself – has as much credibility with ordinary Kurds. Hence, despite the AKP's Turkish nationalist base, the government party has no option but to interact meaningfully with the BDP if it wishes to secure a viable, lasting, peace.

Erdoğan's reiterated charge that the BDP are 'terrorists' and his government's excalating attacks on the party bode ill for the chance of a successful, peaceful settlement between Ankara and the PKK. Speaking on the television station Kanal D, veteran journalist Mehmet Ali Birand – who in 1992 published a collection of interviews with Abdullah Öcalan – claimed: 'Erdoğan wants to take the [ultranationalist far right] MHP's votes, so he led with nationalist politics and attacked the Kurds', accusing them of threatening national unity (Birand, 2012). The PKK, meanwhile, 'shows its muscles and demonstrates that it defends its community', he added (*AFP*, 6 May 2011). Meanwhile, Kurdish nationalist icon Leyla Zana declared that, throughout her years of imprisonment by the Turkish state, 'I never stopped believing in the democratic fight. My morale is high. I'm hopeful, and that is my only capital' (*AFP*, 15 May 2011; see also European Parliament, 2009).

Ankara's condemnation of both the PKK and its legal interlocutor the BDP left no option for either of these parties but to resist the government as best it could. And so armed clashes and killings continued – on 7 May 2011 in Nisêbîn (Nusaybin) district (*AFP*, 7 May 2011); on 13 and 14 May in Uludere in Şırnak province and in Hakkâri province (*AFP*, 14 May 2011). Thousands of Kurds – including BDP members – clashed with police in mid-May, in Amed, Siirt and Batman. In Amed protesters threw molotov cocktails at the police. Clashes also took place in Istanbul (*AFP*, 16 May 2011). The PKK was accused of planting bombs in Nusaybin and Cizre in Şirnex the day before a visit by Erdoğan on 23 May and near a police academy in a prosperous Istanbul residential area on 26 May (*AFP*, 26 May 2011).

In a bold step, on 1 June 2011 Erdoğan called for a resolution of the Kurdish conflict at an election rally in Amed, the unofficial 'capital' of Turkish Kurdistan. The prime minster promised the benefit of investment in Kurdish-population regions but made no commitment to the political reforms demanded by Kurdish nationalists. 'We have prepared the ground for a resolution process', Erdoğan told a rally held under the protection of 5,000 police officers. He promised to launch major infrastructure projects for the region, to lift it out of its economic backwardness, including the renovation of the historic centre of Amed; the construction of a new airport; a dam; new hospitals and highways; as well as leisure facilities on the banks of the Tigris, on the city outskirts. The prime minister's speech was punctuated with references to Turks' and Kurds' common Islamic values. He also attacked his party's main competitor in the region, the BDP. 'Taking strength from the PKK, the BDP wants to divide us' (*AFP*, 1 June 2011).

Opportunities for a peaceful settlement had continually arisen during the 1980s and 1990s. The PKK's repeated unilateral ceasefires had met no constructive response from Ankara, which for a long time remained focused on a solely military solution. In this period the military remained dominant in Turkish politics. Even President Özal's hesitant 'Kurdish Opening' could not bear fruit, due to its lack of a legal framework for PKK fighters to lay down their arms and to the PKK's immature response to the initiative.

The BDP made impressive advances during the 2011 Turkish general election of 12 June 2011, winning a record thirty-six seats in the Kurdish south-east. This was even more than the ruling AKP won within the region. Six of the elected BDP deputies were in prison at the time of their election, but the Turkish authorities did not release any of them immediately. It was not until January 2014 that five of the deputies were released, leaving Hatip Dicle still behind bars. Matters worsened when the constitutional court subsequently stripped Dicle of his elected office. Initially released from prison due to his election to parliament in the constituency of Diyarbakır (East), Dicle was subsequently returned to jail by the High Council of Elections. The High Election Board upheld this decision on 21 June 2011 (*AFP*, 22 June 2011; Kurdpress News Agency, 8 January 2014).

Ahmet Türk, president of the Kurdish umbrella organization the Demokratık Toplum Kongresi (DTK – Democratic Society Congress), immediately warned that the decision to strip Hatip Dicle of his office was 'a decision to take Turkey into chaos ... to push our people to an environment of conflict', adding accusingly: 'The state government and judiciary try to block our efforts to create a democratic political base' for a solution to the Kurdish conflict. He called upon the other newly elected Kurdish MPs, supported by the BDP, to again consider boycotting parliament (*AFP*, 22 June 2011).

MP Sefarettin Elçi, a spokesperson for the now thirty-five elected Kurdish MPs (since Hatip Dicle had been stripped of his elected office), denounced the decision to invalidate Dicle's election as a measure of 'manoeuvre and obstruction' that would only prevent a peaceful resolution of the Kurdish conflict. 'We will not go to Parliament as the government and the Parliament have not taken concrete steps to remedy this injustice and provide opportunities for a resolution paving the way for democratic politics', Elçi declared (*AFP*, 23 June 2011).

Six elected Kurdish MPs remained languishing in jail. The Turkish authorities directly responsible for this were clearly obstructing the peace process – but Erdoğan, mindful of not upsetting his own Turkish nationalist electoral base, was in no mood to challenge them at the time. The thirty MPs outside prison now declared a boycott of the Turkish parliament (*AFP*, 13 June 2011; MAR Project, 2011). Meanwhile clashes between security forces and the PKK further intensified in the wake of Turkey's general election. On the day following Dicle's electoral exclusion, a mine exploded beneath a police vehicle in eastern Amed, killing two officers. Turkish authorities were swift to blame the PKK (*AFP*, 22 June 2011). The attack duly raised the hackles of nationalist Turks. Yet more violence was to follow as a peaceful settlement continued to elude the PKK and the Turkish state. On 27 June PKK fighters attacked a military vehicle in Van province (*AFP*, 27 June 2011). The following day three PKK guerrillas were killed in fighting with security forces near the village of Burnak in the Dêrsim region (*AFP*, 28 June 2011). Twenty Turkish soldiers were killed by the PKK in a two-week period in July 2011, as the PKK again intensified its campaign. An estimated ten PKK fighters were also killed during this period (Cutler and Burch, 2011; *AFP*, 15 July 2011).

The old deadly pattern of ceasefire followed by a renewal of hostilities, followed by an ever increasing spiral of violence, was reasserting itself in Turkey's south-east – leading both sides ever further from a peaceful settlement. An armed clash on 15 July in Amed, in which thirteen soldiers were killed and seven wounded in a PKK ambush, especially aroused the ire of Turkish media and politicians. Prime Minister Erdoğan declared that the Turkish army would make the PKK pay 'a high price' for this attack. These losses were the heaviest the army had suffered since October 2008. 'I say openly to the terrorist organization and its extensions they should not expect any good will on our part to actions as malicious', stated Erdoğan (*AFP*, 15 July 2011). He added:

> If they want peace, there is one thing to do: the terrorist organization must lay down their arms. If they refuse to lay down arms, military operations will not cease and the process (reconciliation) will not move. (*AFP*, 15 July 2011)

Turkish soldiers and PKK guerrillas clashed on 22 and 24 July in the Colêmerg and Mêrdînê regions, resulting in four dead soldiers (*AFP*, 22 July 2011; 24 July 2011). It looked as though the situation was running headlong towards a level of conflict not seen since the 1990s. But then it became apparent that attempts at launching a viable peace process had begun behind the scenes. On 20 June 2011 the PKK had set two principal conditions for the renewal of its unilateral truce. These were that Ankara cease all military operations and recognize Abdullah Öcalan as a leading interlocutor in talks to settle the Kurdish question (*AFP*, 20 June 2011). The PKK proposals also included regional autonomy for south-eastern Anatolia, education in Kurdish, and an amnesty for PKK fighters (*AFP*, 2 July 2011; 3 July 2011). Some of the proposals were not new and had already received broad support in repeated pro-PKK demonstrations in Turkey's Kurdish region, such as those demanding the release of Kurdish MPs.

On 27 June 2011 the Turkish daily newspaper *Milliyet* had revealed the existence of three 'protocols' that Abdullah Öcalan had conveyed to the Turkish government. According to Murat Karayılan (also cited in the *Milliyet* report), the proposals included constitutional reforms to grant regional autonomy and education in Kurdish and 'conditions for a complete exclusion of violence and disarmament on the basis of mutual forgiveness'. Karayılan added: 'The official delegation which met Öcalan last month did not reject these protocols. They said they would send them to the state and Government... We expect an answer' (*AFP*, 27 June 2011).

A week and a half earlier, the *Serok* is reported to have said that a 'revolutionary people's struggle' was superfluous, since he was on the verge of concluding an agreement with the Turkish state to form a 'peace council' (*AFP*, 18 June 2011; Karaveli, 2011). The *Serok* was apparently aware that an important new Kurdish initiative was at hand (Özel, 19 August 2011).

On 14 July 2011 the Demokratık Toplum Kongresi declared support for 'democratic autonomy' at an 'Extraordinary Congress' of 850 delegates (many of whom were BDP deputies or mayors) in Amed. This was the new development for peace that Öcalan had been referring to. Parliamentary deputy and DTK chairwoman Aysel Tuğluk conveyed a conference declaration to the media afterwards, stating that the Kurdish people had declared democratic autonomy yet remained loyal to Turkish national unity and respected the country's territorial integrity (Karaveli, 2011; *Hürriyet Daily News*, 15 July 2011; *Today's Zaman*, 14 July 2011). One news report added that the Diyarbakır Prosecutor's Office – immediately suspicious – responded to the DTK initiative by launching an investigation into the conference's final declaration (*Today's Zaman*, 14 July 2011).

The DTK had earlier, in December 2010, at a conference in Amed, presented a draft outline of its 'Democratic Autonomous Kurdistan Model'. Nevertheless, advocacy of democratic autonomy was very different to the PKK's own founding objective of a pan-Kurdish state animated by Marxist–Leninist dogmas. Yet, as this book has shown, the PKK (especially its *Serok*) has a vast capacity for adaptability, and has been moving towards its current position since the 1990s. And the legal Kurdish parties inspired by the PKK – such as HEP, HADEP, the

Demokratik Toplum Partisi and the present-day BDP – have all demonstrated a similar capacity, evolving their programmes as the PKK moderates its own line, just as they organize militant street demonstrations at precisely the same times that the PKK returned to intensified military struggle at various junctures. These parties are organizationally independent of the PKK, yet manage to mirror its moods and policy changes.

One of the BDP's political predecessors, the Demokratik Toplum Partisi (DTP – Democratic Society Party) went to great lengths to prove that it supported the principle of a unified Turkey. The DTP's Aysel Tuğluk has referred in an article to a *Misak-ı Milli* (National Pact) between Turks and Kurds in Turkey, affirming that Turks and Kurds are each other's best ally. The article evokes the unity of Turks and Kurds against 'imperialism' (Tuğluk, 27 May 2007). In the present period, the Demokratık Toplum Kongresi (DTK) is a legal platform for Kurdish NGOs and political organizations in Turkey. Interestingly, Aysel Tuğluk is a leading member of the DTK. In this capacity he told a Turkish daily newspaper in mid-2011 that his party remained loyal to the national unity of Turkey, respected the country's territorial integrity and based its advocacy of 'democratic autonomy' on 'democratic national principles' (*Today's Zaman,* 20 July 2011).

The Brookings Institution's Ömer Taşpınar conceded at this time that 'Kurdish nationalism, as a political force', was 'alive and well across Turkey'. Taşpınar, a Kemalist intellectual, counsels Turkish nationalists to realize that for 'millions of Turkish Kurds' the PKK and Öcalan are 'heroic symbols of rejection of decades of forced assimilation under the Kemalist republic'. He adds that 'Turkey's Kurdish minority has now much higher aspirations than 15 years ago', as evidenced by 'demands for decentralization and federalism bordering on autonomy' (Taşpınar, 2012).

By the end of July 2011, however, Öcalan was once again despairing of the peace initiative succeeding, declaring that his dialogue with the Turkish government was 'finished'. Interestingly, the *Serok* this time blamed intransigence on both sides in the conflict (the government and the PKK) for this failure, declaring: 'Both parties use me for their own interests. I am ending this intermediary role... There can be no peace talks under the current conditions' (*AFP*, 29 July 2011).

Six Turkish soldiers were killed and three others injured in clashes with the PKK in late July and early August 2011 (*AFP*, 30 July 2011; 1 August 2011). Two policemen died from a mine explosion (*AFP*, 7 August 2011) and another was shot dead by an 'unidentified masked assailant' (*AFP*, 8 August 2011). On 9 August yet another police officer was killed and another injured in a shoot-out between the guerrillas and the Turkish military, which also saw the death of a PKK fighter (*AFP*, 9 August 2011). Then, on 17 August 2011, eight Turkish soldiers and a village guard were killed and eleven soldiers wounded in a PKK ambush in Çelê (*AFP*, 17 August 2011).

The rising casualty toll among security force personnel and policemen infuriated Turkish nationalists, and the AKP government felt compelled to resort to sterner measures. On 17 August Turkish warplanes hit sixty PKK positions in the Iraqi mountains (*AFP*, 18 August 2011). This was the first time in over a year that the Turkish military had struck alleged PKK bases in northern Iraq by air (*Al Arabiya*, 2011).

Politicians and the Turkish military had already announced plans to consider a complete reorganization of the military and police effort against the PKK, to be discussed at a forthcoming meeting of the Milli Güvenlik Kurulu (MGK – National Security Council) on 17 August 2011. Proposed measures included the deployment in combat zones of special police units and fully professional military troops (*AFP*, 18 August 2011). After meeting for almost five hours on 18 August 2011, the MGK drew up a 'new strategy' for dealing with the PKK. Erdoğan in fact endorsed even tougher measures than those foreshadowed by the military, citing especially the bloody 17 August PKK ambush as his justification. Over forty policemen and soldiers had recently been killed by the PKK (*AFP*, 18 August 2011). The prime minister declared 'a new era' in Turkey's military confrontation with the PKK, warning that 'those who do not deviate from terrorism will pay the price' – which was understood to be addressed to Kurdish politicians close to the PKK (*AFP*, 18 August 2011).

That evening, Turkish F-16 fighter planes commenced six consecutive days of bombarding PKK targets in Iraqi Kurdistan. A statement by the Turkish army on 29 August claimed that these raids had resulted in the intense bombardment of thirty-eight targets, with between 145 and 160 guerrillas killed and over 100 injured, while insisting that due care had been taken to avoid civilian casualties (*AFP*, 29 August 2011). A Human Rights Watch statement issued a few days later, however, claimed that many of the areas attacked in the Turkish raids 'were not used by armed groups, but were inhabited by civilians' (*AFP*, 2 September 2011).

Peace now looked less likely than ever. 'We are entering an era where the language of war and violence will prevail', wrote popular columnist Soli Özel in the daily *Haber Türk*. Özel warned of the consequences of such an upsurge in violence: 'The most dangerous thing is to leave in despair Turks, Kurds, the majority of people who live in this country, even at every opportunity they show with their votes they cannot achieve anything else but terror and war' (Özel, 2011).

PKK spokesperson Ahmed Denis threatened a 'war' if the raids continued (*AFP*, 22 August 2011). The PKK did not wait long to respond, launching deadly new attacks on security forces (*AFP*, 28 August 2011). On 27 August thousands of Kurds from six provinces initiated a protest march to the Turkish–Iraqi border in opposition to the Turkish military's ongoing campaign in Iraqi Kurdistan. Yıldırım Ayhan, a BDP deputy to the Van assembly, was killed when police dispersed the protest in the town of Çelê, after a tear-gas canister penetrated his chest (*AFP*, 28 August 2011).

On 29 August the PKK announced a three-day truce to honour the three days of *'Eid al-Fitr* following the end of the Islamic holy month of Ramadan. PKK spokesperson Dozdar Hammo warned that PKK fighters 'would defend themselves against any Turkish attack' (*AFP*, 29 August 2011). However, violence continued in Turkish Kurdistan, as two soldiers, two policemen and two militiamen were killed in three clashes with the PKK in Amed and Colemêrg on 2 and 3 September (*AFP*, 4 September 2011).

The conflict continued to expand, as new fronts were added. Thus, concurrent with the Turkish military campaign against the PKK, in the same region Iran's Army of the Guardians of the Islamic Revolution (Sepāh-e Pāsdārān-e Enqelāb-e Eslāmi – Revolutionary Guards for short) were at this time pursuing an offensive against the Iranian Partiya Jiyana Azad a Kurdistanê (PJAK – Kurdistan Free Life Party), which is the main armed Iranian Kurdish nationalist movement and a PKK affiliate. The Kurdish people, it will be recalled, straddle the borders of Iran, Iraq, Syria and Turkey – countries that have long been regional rivals.

The Kurdistan Regional Government (KRG) in Northern Iraq comprises political elements (organized in the Kurdistan Democratic Party and the Patriotic Union of Kurdistan) that are no strangers to betrayal. Each has clashed militarily with other Kurdish nationalist groups (including each other) and could do so again. They permit both the PKK and the PJAK to maintain military bases inside KRG territory for diverse reasons – including the difficulty of ejecting these groups in military terms and the potentially unbearable scandal within their own constituencies were they to eject fellow Kurdish nationalists.

Since 2006 the PJAK has waged sporadic guerrilla war against Tehran. Its struggle has figured in relations between Iraq and Turkey, both of which have their own concerns about the PJAK's armed operations in the light of their own perceived interests. The Kurdish authorities in the KRG in Northern Iraq would like to be independent of Iraq, if they could manage it, but to achieve this they need US support. This backing is potentially endangered by the PJAK's operations on the Iran–Iraq border. Having active in the region an armed group that it considers to be a PKK proxy does not amuse the US. Turkey concurs, not wanting to have solved its own Kurdish problem only to face a group with an identical ideology in the same neighbourhood that shares, as it currently does, PKK munitions in the Qandil mountains (Wilgenburg, 2010; Cagaptay and Eroglu, 2007; Sehirli, 2000: 420–21).

On 3 September 2011 the PKK announced that it had decided to lend strong support to the PJAK against the Iranian offensive in Iraqi Kurdistan. 'We will now fight alongside the PJAK fighters against the attacks of Iranians trying to enter Iraqi Kurdistan, particularly in the region of Qandil', PKK spokesperson Dozdar Hammou told *AFP*. Iran's Revolutionary Guards confirmed in a statement that it had been waging operations against the PJAK on the border with Iraqi Kurdistan (MAR Project, 2010; *AFP*, 3 September 2011).

On 5 September the PJAK announced a ceasefire, to enable it to redeploy its forces from Iran to join the PKK's conflict with Turkey (Cagaptay and Eroglu, 2007). Eight simultaneous PKK attacks on military outposts and police stations near Çelê (Çukurca) and Gewer on 19 October killed twenty-six Turkish soldiers, injuring twenty-two others. Around 100 'Kurdish rebels' allegedly participated in the attacks, according to Turkey's state-run TRT television (*AFP*, 5 September 2011; *RT/Reuters*, 2011; MSNBC, 2011).

On 7 September PKK fighters kidnapped two village guards and two civilians near Beytüssebap in Şirnak province (*AFP*, 8 September 2011). Less than a week later, on 12 September, five people were killed and ten soldiers and policemen injured when the PKK reportedly attacked a police station and barracks in Şemzînan, a town of Hakkâri province. The PKK is said to have launched four simultaneous attacks in the Şemzînan area (*AFP*, 12 September 2011).

As the PKK had predicted in late August (*AFP*, 22 August 2011), Turkey now announced it was considering a further ground incursion against its forces in Northern Iraq. The PKK attacks in Şemzînan had enraged Turkish nationalist opinion and were duly cited by the government as its justification for this action. Prime Minister Erdoğan convened an emergency meeting with his ministers of the interior and defence and the army to discuss options. The Turkish army's forces had already concentrated on the border with Iraq during recent weeks (*AFP*, 13 September 2011).

As this threat was being discussed in the Turkish media, the Turkish government admitted on 15 September 2011 that it had engaged in secret direct negotiations with the PKK. The announcement was the cause of much consternation among sections of the Turkish media, and extreme Turkish nationalists in the state seized the opportunity to accuse the head of intelligence, Hakan Fidan, of treason. Officials from the Milli İstihbarat

Teşkilatı (MİT – National Intelligence Organization), together with Mr Fidan (acting as Erdoğan's emissary), had met several times with PKK leaders in Oslo.

Claiming that some 120 people had been killed in clashes and attacks by the PKK since mid-June, Erdoğan blamed the breakdown of negotiations on the alleged upsurge in PKK attacks (*AFP*, 3 October 2011), with Ankara once again threatening a ground attack on PKK bases in Iraqi Kurdistan. Turkish warplanes had already conducted a total of fifty-eight attacks on PKK targets there during August and September (Çandar, 2013a; *AFP*, 15 September 2011; *Pravda*, 2011). The PKK, predictably, blamed the government for the talks' collapse, accusing it of delaying tactics at the negotiations and then forsaking the few promises it made once it secured the June 2011 elections with 50 per cent of the votes (Çandar, 2013a). Another opportunity for peace had been lost.

More violence was the inevitable consequence of this breakdown. A Turkish soldier was killed and two others were injured in clashes with Kurdish rebels on 17 September in a rural area of Bingöl province. Police arrested 122 people in the Istanbul city centre the following day, for attempting to participate in a demonstration opposing military operations against the PKK. Protesters also objected to Abdullah Öcalan being unable to meet his lawyers for almost two months. Police prevented protesters from gathering, while police helicopters flew overhead, monitoring the situation (*AFP*, 18 September 2011). Denied any means to redress their grievances by the Turkish state, Kurkish nationalists grew steadily more frustrated, with 'armed struggle' – however fruitless it had proven to be – seeming to many the only option available.

Armed clashes between the security forces and the PKK now occurred on an almost daily basis. On 20 September a bomb explosion in Kızılay, in downtown Ankara, killed three people and injured fifteen others, two of whom later died in hospital. This attack was eventually claimed by the Teyrêbazên Azadiya Kurdistan, however, and denounced by the PKK, which described it as 'reprehensible', adding that it 'undermined the legitimate demands of the Kurdish people'. Turkish authorities once again alleged that TAK was a PKK affiliate (*AFP*, 24 September 2011; *AFP*, 14 October 2011).

Later the same day, an assault on a police academy in Siirt killed four civilians and one of the attackers (*AFP*, 20 September 2011). Following this operation, on 24 September the PKK leadership ordered 'all guerrilla units to be more careful in their preparations' to avoid civilian deaths. Two Turkish soldiers were killed and three others were wounded in fighting late on 22 September in Çatak, in Van province. A policeman injured on 22 September in another attack, in Amed, died a few days later. All attacks were attributed to the PKK by the authorities (*Al Jazeera*, 2011; Cutler and Burch, 2011).

On 21 September the Turkish military said it had hit 152 PKK targets in Iraq by air in almost sixty sorties since 17 August. 'All targets were shelled with acuity and were destroyed' said an online statement, adding that rebel movements would be 'closely monitored' and that air strikes would continue 'if necessary' (*AFP*, 21 September 2011).

The atmosphere became immensely more deadly on 21 September, when Erdoğan revealed that he had asked the United States to locate US Predator drones to strike PKK positions in Iraqi Kurdistan. The prime minister had met briefly with the US president. President Obama 'told me that the United States is prepared to give us any support in the fight against terrorism', reported Erdoğan. He added that the United States would continue to provide Ankara with 'real-time information' on PKK activities in northern Iraq (*AFP*, 21 September 2011; *Kurd Net*, 21 September 2011). In late October 2011 the Pentagon announced – subject to congressional approval – the sale of three AH-1 Super Cobra attack helicopters to Turkey for $111 million. On 14 November a Pentagon spokesman announced that the US military had relocated four unarmed Predator drones, formerly based in Iraq, to the US/NATO Air Base in İncirlik in Turkey, to support Ankara against the PKK (Zanotti, 2012: 22). US material support for the Turkish military was nothing new, of course, given that Turkey hosts a web of US military bases on its soil and is a member of NATO. Nor was there anything novel in strong political support for Ankara against the PKK. Washington's decision to provide powerful direct military assistance to the Turkish military against the PKK reflected the former's rising concern with the PKK's entrenchment in Iraqi Kurdistan, which the Americans considered ran contrary to their own interests in the same region – especially in the light of their military drawdown from Iraq (Zanotti, 2012: 22).

Prime Minister Erdoğan disclosed on 23 September that co-operation with Iran was being considered against the PKK in Northern Iraq. He added that Turkey was 'already engaged in sharing information' on the PKK with Iran. The prime minister called on the PKK to relinquish its weapons if it wanted to avoid a new ground offensive against its bases in Northern Iraq (*AFP*, 23 September 2011). However, six Turkish soldiers were killed and eleven others wounded the following day in an attack on a small barracks in the village of Belenoluk, near Pervari, in Siirt province, also attributed by authorities to the PKK. Three PKK fighters were also reportedly killed in the clashes (*AFP*, 24 September 2011; *AFP*, 25 September 2011).

On 28 September the thirty-five BDP MPs of the Turkish parliament re-elected at the June 2011 elections suddenly announced their decision to end their boycott of that institution. As shown earlier, this decision came at precisely the time when the government and media alike were attributing an upsurge in government/PKK violence to Kurdish rebels. Plans for a military operation against PKK bases in Northern Iraq were being openly threatened. BDP co-chairman Selahattin Demirtaş told a press conference: 'We felt the need to make a change in attitude and to defend peace against war … we decided to participate in the parliament.' He accused the AKP government of wanting to thwart efforts for a resolution of the Kurdish conflict by ordering mass arrests of Kurdish activists across the country in recent months. Erdoğan responded on the day of the Kurdish MPs' initiative by accusing the BDP of collusion with the PKK and of 'profiting from' the atmosphere of violence. The prime minister called on Kurds to 'resist' the PKK (*AFP*, 28 September 2011). BDP deputies duly returned to the assembly in early October, where they were sworn-in (*AFP*, 1 October 2011).

The violent atmosphere continued to build relentlessly. On 29 September PKK spokesperson Ahmed Denis claimed that Turkish warplanes carried out new raids that day against PKK bases in Iraqi Kurdistan. Denis also stated that a number of individuals had been 'arrested' by the PKK in Turkey, including military officials, a mayor and twelve teachers. The PKK accused them of alleged 'crimes' against the Kurds. Asked about the laws that could be applied against them, Denis replied: 'We have our own laws… We respect rights and our laws do not provide for the death penalty.' The PKK spokesperson gave no further details of the 'arrested' individuals. He added that Turkish warplanes had bombed the areas of Khuwa Kork Khnera and Zap (north-west of Erbil and north-east of Dohuk) for two hours (*AFP*, 29 September 2011). Two soldiers fighting the PKK were killed on the same day in Beytüssebap in Şirnak province, bordering Iraq, where a group of PKK fighters attacked a security forces unit, injuring three soldiers (*AFP*, 30 September 2011).

The focus moved to the Turkish parliament on 1 October, when President Abdullah Gül declared that one of its 'main tasks' was to draft a new constitution – to be ultimately approved by a referendum (*AFP*, 1 October 2011). This potentially momentous step heralded the possible dawn of a new chance for Turkish/Kurdish peace, since Kurdish rights were high on the agenda for consideration of the new draft constitution (*AFP*, 1 October 2011). Stressing that the current constitution 'does not meet the aspirations of the Turkish people', Gül argued for a more liberal text based on Western standards of democracy, without sacrificing the existing text's republicanism, especially its secularism. Despite its supposed 'Islamist' roots, the AKP has always committed itself to secularism and republicanism. Gül's emphasis on the non-negotiable nature of these aspects was intended to mollify extreme Turkish nationalists, who might suspect an Islamist conspiracy behind the proposed constitutional reform process.

The AKP government announced the goal of a new constitution by mid-2012, with the perspective of achieving this through political consensus. The government did not possess the necessary two-thirds majority for constitutional reform, although much agreement existed in the parliament on the need to change a constitution inherited from a military coup in 1980. So the AKP sought agreement with opposition parties. A Constitutional Reconciliation Commission (CRC), comprising members from each parliamentary party, was established in September 2011. However, the process effectively collapsed in November 2012, when the four parties presented rival reform proposals.

At first glance, it appeared that the Turkish state did not regard the PKK as a potential interlocutor in this discussion, since *AFP* revealed that the Erdoğan government was still preparing to launch a ground operation in Iraqi Kurdistan – with the PKK claiming that new air raids on its bases in Northern Iraq had already begun (*AFP*, 30 September 2011; *AFP*, 1 October 2011). On 3 October the prospect of peace was briefly revitalized, however, when Prime Minister Erdoğan declared that a revival of talks with the Kurdish rebels was not excluded, adding that dialogue with the PKK might possibly resume (*AFP*, 3 October 2011).

Meanwhile, operations against the PKK by the Turkish state continued at all levels. On 4 October police across Turkey arrested almost 150 people suspected of links to the KCK and the PKK. The arrestees joined the over 2,500 Kurds already imprisoned, accused of 'links with rebels' (*AFP*, 4 October 2011). Moving the focus of its renewed offensive to Iraq, on 5 October the Turkish parliament approved the one-year renewal of the authorization to carry out raids against PKK bases in Iraqi Kurdistan (*AFP*, 5 October 2011). The PKK responded harshly to Turkey's military response in the wake of these clashes. Spokesperson Ahmed Denis said on 19 October that Turkey was liable to be hit 'harder' if it conducted military operations outside its borders. He promised: 'We will not allow them to lead a military incursion into Iraqi Kurdistan. If they conduct this raid, they will be unable to get out.' As it turned out, however, Turkey was soon to succeed in achieving precisely that.

The PKK also responded within Turkish Kurdistan, and armed operations by both sides occurred in Hakkâri, Siirt, Adana and Bitlis provinces (*AFP*, 9, 13, 14 October 2011; *Al Jazeera*, 2011). On 16 October a bomb exploded at Şeyhan in Adana province, as police attempted to disperse 'a banned demonstration' of PKK supporters; it injured four policemen and two civilians (*AFP*, 16 October 2011). More significantly, twenty-four Turkish soldiers were killed and several more wounded in PKK attacks carried out simultaneously later the same day against police Jandarma posts in eight localities in Çelê and Gewer. The Turkish army launched ground and air operations in the night in retaliation. Observers claimed that these fatalities represented the second highest army death to date (*AFP*, 19 October 2011).

According to Ahmed Denis, fighting between the two sides began when Turkish soldiers tried to cross the Iraqi border hunting for PKK guerrillas. 'What happened was not planned by the PKK', he added. Denis continued: 'The Turkish air force bombed several areas of Northern Iraq heavily and later staged land operations.' According to him, the PKK killed 100 Turkish soldiers as well as injuring many others, and seized large quantities of ammunition. He added: 'The battle continues in some areas and there is bombing by fighter jets and helicopters.' Another PKK spokesperson, Dozdar Hammo, claimed that five PKK fighters were killed on 18 October.

On the day following the simultaneous PKK attacks of 18 October 2011 in south-eastern Turkey, President Abdullah Gül echoed the words of his prime minister in July (*AFP*, 15 July 2011), promising 'very great' revenge on the PKK. The remarks came after Turkish security forces said they had killed fifteen 'Kurdish militants', in the wake of the alleged PKK attacks. Turkish security forces now launched their long-threatened incursion inside Iraq, involving 'multiple attacks along the border' (MSNBC, 2011). Sounding very much like a 1980s' Kemalist leader, the president addressed reporters:

> No one should forget this: those that inflict this pain on us will endure far greater pain; those that think they will weaken our state with these attacks or think they will bring our state into line, they will see that the revenge for these attacks will be very great and they will endure it many times over. (*RT/Reuters*, 2011; MSNBC, 2011).

Prime Minister Erdoğan reported that Turkish elite troops had entered Iraqi territory to hunt down Kurdish assailants, 'as permitted by international law'. Hundreds of Turkish commandos penetrated 4 kilometres into Iraq to prevent the rebels retreating to their bases in the mountains. Turkish military operations by combined ground and air forces continued until 27 October (*AFP*, 19 October 2011; *AFP*, 27 October 2011). On 31 October BDP deputy chairperson Meral Danış Beştaş accused the Turkish army of using chemical weapons during this operation (*Press TV*, 29 December 2011). Curiously, this accusation was not denied by the Turkish military until 8 December, some five weeks later (*AFP*, 8 December 2011), with perhaps even the Turkish general staff being wary regarding what some of its units might have done. German chemical weapons experts later confirmed that the Turkish army had almost certainly used chemical weapons (Uzun, 2014: 15).

Turkish military operations against PKK fighters in the Hakkâri region as well as in Iraqi Kurdistan continued on 21 October. Turkish fighter planes and helicopters engaged the PKK during the night on both sides of the border, involving some 10,000 troops in the whole operation (*AFP*, 21 October 2011). The Turkish army continued its offensive on 22 October for the third consecutive day, causing forty-eight deaths in PKK ranks in the space of two days, (*AFP*, 22 October 2011). Operations continued on 23 October. Then on 24 October twenty tanks and thirty military trucks reportedly entered Iraq from the village of Siyahkaya in Silopi province, before heading towards PKK bases located in the Haftanın valley (*AFP*, 24 October 2011).

The PKK responded forcefully, as best it could. Police in Amed deployed water cannons to scatter stone-throwing protesters, as the bodies of twenty-four PKK fighters killed in a military operation arrived at a mortuary in Malatya (*Reuters*, 29 October

2011). An unnamed security source told *AFP* that a female PKK suicide bomber attacked the provincial headquarters of the ruling AKP on the same day in Bingöl, killing two persons, including herself, and injuring ten others (*Reuters*, 29 October 2011; *AFP*, 29 October 2011).

On 12 November Turkish transport minister Binali Yıldırım accused the PKK of hijacking a small Turkish ferry in the Sea of Marmara for over twelve hours. He said that four or five members of the PKK's military wing the HPG took possession of the ferry *Kartepe* with eighteen passengers on board, including five women, four crew members and two trainees. 'There are no demands', claimed the minister. One hijacker claimed to be in possession of a bomb and told the ferry captain that he wanted this to be reported by the media, according to the mayor of İzmit, Karaosmanoğlu İsmail. Later, however, this hijacker was found to have only a mock bomb after security forces who stormed the vessel at dawn on 12 November killed him. It was also discovered that he was the sole hijacker. All the hostages were unharmed, according to the Istanbul governor Hüseyin Avni Mutlu (*AFP*, 12 November 2011). The PKK has not claimed responsibility for this stunt. If it were responsible, it would indicate the PKK's increasing desperation to reach international opinion with its message.

Iran's Ministry of Foreign Affairs had already condemned on 20 October what it termed the 'terrorist' activities of the PKK. Tehran pledged to 'work with the Turkish Government on security issues to prevent such actions from occurring' (*AFP*, 21 October 2011). On the following day, Turkey's foreign minister Ahmet Davutoğlu revealed that Iran had agreed to fight together with Turkey against both the PKK and Iran's PJAK, in a 'common action plan until this terrorist threat is eliminated'. Turkey thus brought to fruition the cooperation with Iran envisaged by Erdoğan the previous month (*AFP*, 21 October 2011). Iran's foreign minister Ali Akbar Salehi, and Massoud Barzani, president of the autonomous region of Iraqi Kurdistan, claimed on 29 October that the 'PJAK issue' had been settled by Tehran, following the conclusion of an operation beginning in July (*AFP*, 29 October 2011).

In a massive operation across the country on 22 November, Turkish police arrested more than seventy people accused of KCK membership. Abdullah Öcalan's lawyers, as well as BDP members, were among those arrested (*AFP*, 22 November 2011).

The government, however, was determined to combine repression of Kurdish politicians considered close to the PKK with gestures towards the Kurds more generally. On 23 November Prime Minister Erdoğan addressed one of the primary sources of Kurdish animosity towards Turks, when he presented a historic apology to members of his ruling AKP on behalf of the Turkish state for the murderous repression of the 1937–38 rebellion in Dêrsim, which many had attributed to the Kurds, due to the PKK's denial of the separate ethnic identity of the Zaza people (White, 2000: 49).

The Zaza-speaking Alevi tribes of Dêrsim rebelled against Ankara from March to November 1937 and from April to December 1938, led by the Alevi cleric Sayyid Riza [Seyt Rıza]. These rebellions triggered a process of repression that forced the exodus of tens of thousands of Dêrsimli Alevis. 'Dêrsim is one of the most tragic and painful events of our recent history', observed Erdoğan. 'I apologize and I apologize'. Referring to an official document of the time, the prime minister cited a total of 13,806 killed by air and ground bombardment, followed by abuses and summary executions in the province of Dêrsim (*AFP*, 23 November 2011). Unfortunately, a member of the prime minister's party had proposed renaming Sabiha Gökçen International

Airport after Mustafa Kemal Atatürk's adopted daughter, who had actively participated as a pilot, bombing Dêrsim (*AFP*, 23 November 2011).

The armed clashes between the army and the PKK and its suspected supporters continued unabated. On 15 December Turkish soldiers stormed a house in Çay, in Bingöl province, killing eight alleged PKK fighters (*AFP*, 15 December 2011). Then twenty-one PKK fighters were killed in six days of fighting with the Turkish armed forces, beginning on 15 December, in Görese in Diyarbakır province. Turkish ground troops, supplemented by helicopter gunships, were responsible for killing between fifty and seventy guerrillas, according to estimates (*AFP*, 21 December 2011).

On 30 December the PKK called the Kurdish population of Turkey to an 'uprising', following the apparently accidental death of thirty-five Kurdish smugglers in an air raid by Turkish F-16s at the Iraqi border on 28 December. Erdal Bahoz, an HPG cadre, announced: 'We urge the people of Kurdistan, especially in Hakkâri [Colemêrg] and Şirnak [Şirnex], to show their reaction against this massacre and to hold accountable the perpetrators.' Thousands of angry Kurds ensured that the funerals of the dead villagers were a demonstration against the Ankara government. A long convoy of cars honking their horns denounced Prime Minister Erdoğan, calling him a 'murderer'. Many of the Kurds were convinced that the accidental killings were deliberate. 'It is impossible that were killed by mistake. Soldiers were 150 metres away and within sight', stated a local named Mehmet from Robozik (Ortasu) village, from which most of the victims originated (*AFP*, 29 December 2011). Erdoğan expressed regret at the 'unfortunate and distressing' air raid killings of civilians, conveying his condolences to relatives of the victims. On 2 January 2012 the deputy prime minister, Bülent Arınç, promised that the government would pay reparations to the families of the slain Kurds (*Al Jazeera*, 2012).

Tension continued to build on the day following the funerals, when two PKK fighters were killed on 31 December in Amed when they threw grenades at police who had ordered them to surrender after attacking their position (*AFP*, 31 December 2011a). Already enraged by the deaths of the thirty-five Kurdish civilians, hundreds of Kurds took to the streets of Amed. Some protesters threw stones at police, who responded with water cannon and tear gas. Ten protesters were arrested (*AFP*, 31 December 2011).

The year 2011 thus ended as it had begun – with bloody violence on both sides. As the year drew to a close, it seemed that nothing could prevent Turkish Kurdistan descending into a deepening bloody cycle of violence.

Armed hostilities continued into 2012, although initially at a lower rate than in the recent past. No major incidents are recorded for January 2012. The Turkish military clashed with the PKK on 9 February, killing thirteen alleged PKK fighters, while two other guerrillas were wounded and one Turkish soldier was killed. Turkish warplanes hit back on 11–12 February with overnight strikes on suspected PKK targets in the Zab and Hakurk areas of Iraqi Kurdistan (*Al Arabiya*, 2012).

PKK fighters killed policemen on 25 May and 12 June in Kayseri and Istanbul respectively (*Today's Zaman*, 29 June 2012). The violence was now obviously becoming increasingly senseless. Casualties continued to pile up on both sides, but neither a military solution nor a viable peace process appeared to be any closer.

This reality called out for bold steps to resolve the stalemate. Throughout June and August 2012 heavy clashes erupted in Hakkâri province, when the PKK military leadership ordered a temporary abandonment of standard guerrilla war tactics, by waging a 'frontal battle' with the Turkish army for the Kurdish town of Şemzînan. Roads leading to the town from Iran and Iraq were blockaded by the PKK. PKK rocket launchers and Russian-made DShK heavy machine guns were positioned on high ground in preparation for an assault on Turkish motorized units that the PKK anticipated would be sent to secure Şemzînan. Refusing to take the bait, the Turkish military reportedly destroyed the guerrillas in air attacks, supplemented by long-range artillery salvos. On 11 August the military declared victory, claiming to have killed 115 PKK fighters at the cost of six soldiers and two village guards (MAR Project, 2010).

The decision by PKK military leaders to eschew standard 'hit and run' guerrilla war tactics in this instance is incomprehensible logically, as they could not seriously have believed that they had the capacity to keep possession of Şemzînan. The only explanation seems to be that the decision-makers simply did not know what to do next: ceasefire after ceasefire had failed, and a return to all-out war was only leading to greatly increasing PKK casualties. Their acquiring of some heavy weapons (quite possibly from Iran) also probably played a part. Given the number of PKK fighters and heavy munitions involved, it is unlikely that one or two local commanders alone made this decision. It must have been made rather by the central military leaders, in consultation with the PKK political leadership. As such it must be seen as indicative of their high degree of disorientation at this point.

The bloodshed continued after this carnage. Some fifteen suspected PKK guerrillas were killed in Hakkâri province and two soldiers died in a mine explosion on 19 August alone (Şahin, 2012; Cakan, 2012). Then, on 19–20 August, a car full of explosives exploded close to a police station in Gaziantep province, killing nine civilians (four of whom were children) and wounding fifty-six (Cakan, 2012; *NTV–MSNBC*, 2012). With this attack the number of civilian casualties since 2007 reached sixty-five, including twenty-three children (*Anadolu Ajansi*, 2012). The carnage was far from over, however.

Turkey responds by bombing PKK bases in Iraqi Kurdistan

Turkey responded to these attacks with six days of intense bombing of PKK bases in the Qandil Mountains. On 23 August Turkish authorities claimed to have killed as many as a hundred PKK fighters in these air raids. Professor Gokhan Bacık of Zirve University commented that the bombing might have been assisted by US intelligence. Despite reports of civilian casualties and condemnation from the president of autonomous Iraqi Kurdistan, Prime Minister Erdoğan declared that his government had 'run out of patience', and vowed to continue the attacks on the PKK (Christie-Miller, 2012). The Turkish state's bombing campaign thus appeared to indicate a decisive move back to military methods for dealing with the PKK.

The year 2012 was shaping up to be the most deadly in the conflict between the PKK and Ankara since 1999. Nearly 800 people died in the conflict between June 2011 and 2 September, including some 500 PKK fighters, more than 200 security personnel and 85 civilians, according to estimates by the think-tank International Crisis Group (*Guardian*, 3 September 2012; Tezcür, 2013: 69). Clashes and deaths continued unabated throughout September (*Radikal*, 2012; *CNN Türk*, 2012; Watson and Comert, 2012).

The Koma Ciwakên Kurdistan reported no fewer than 400 incidents of shelling, air bombardment and armed clashes during August 2012. Erdoğan claimed in mid-September that, 'Within the last month, in the operations executed throughout the region, about 500 terrorists were eliminated' (Watson and Comert, 2012;

Yesim, 2012; *BBC News*, 17 September 2012). Veteran observer Hugh Pope told *CNN*:

> We're seeing the longest pitched battles between the army and the PKK. [W]e're seeing a wide-spread campaign of kidnapping, suicide bombings and terrorist attacks by the PKK. They're very much on the offensive and unfortunately this is matched by much harder line rhetoric on both sides. (Watson and Comert, 2012)

A letter from Aysel Tuğluk, the BDP MP for Van, was published in the daily *Taraf* on 20 September, making concrete suggestions for stopping the fighting and advancing in the direction of peace. She suggested that the Turkish state end Öcalan's solitary confinement, release '8,000 KCK friends' and accept the status of autonomous administration for Turkish Kurdistan. She recommended that, in return, the PKK declare a ceasefire and become partners with Turkey, 'working together toward the democratic and free future of the region' (*Taraf*, 2012). *Hürriyet Daily News* responded positively, noting that the BDP MP was merely advising Turks how to avoid worsening Turkish–Kurdish relations in Turkey. 'In short, she was sending the message: "You are forcing us; you are pushing us to partition. We are separating"' (*Hürriyet Daily News*, 19 September 2012).

However, in mid-September 2012 forty-four Kurdish journalists appeared in court in Istanbul to face terrorism charges. Many of them had been remanded in prison since their arrest the previous December (Watson and Comert, 2012). In October 2012 several hundred Kurdish political prisoners went on hunger strike demanding better conditions for Abdullah Öcalan and the right to use the Kurdish language in the education and justice systems. The hunger strike only ended after the *Serok* ordered his fighters to stop after sixty-eight days (*BBC News*, 21 March 2013).

On 4 December 2012 Prime Minister Erdoğan indicated that he might be prepared to repeat the methods of his predecessors in the early 1990s in dealing with the challenges presented by legal Kurdish parliamentary parties, by putting them on trial on terror-related charges, accusing the BDP as a whole of being the political wing and the tool of the PKK. To do so, he would have to cancel pro-Kurdish lawmakers' parliamentary immunities. Interestingly, President Abdullah Gül stated his disapproval of this suggestion, and was joined in this by over thirty other AKP colleagues. Gül – whose popularity continued to grow, even as Erdoğan's declined – perceived that the prime minister was going too far and wished to insulate himself from popular distaste at this move. Erdoğan responded fiercely, openly threatening the dissidents with expulsion from the party. The *Hürriyet Daily News* commented that the lack of political channels to help solve the Kurdish question, were the BDP to be made illegal, would make a peace settlement with the PKK very difficult – 'if, of course, the government still has such a will' (*Hürriyet Daily News*, 5 December 2012). As the year progressed, peace seemed an increasingly less likely prospect.

As has been seen, the deadly pattern that has long plagued the Kurdish–Turkish conflict in Turkey – wholesale bloodletting followed by fruitless peacemaking, which produces even worse bloodletting – continued to reassert itself throughout the period examined in this chapter. To fully understand events in the period described above, it is necessary to examine the role of the Kurdish diaspora in the conflict.

The Kurdish diaspora's role

Many of the Kurds from Turkey living in Europe have lived there for several decades, arriving in waves in the 1970s, 1980s and 1990s in response to tumult and oppression in their homeland (Kaya, 2012: 157). Living in the diaspora, they encountered their fellow Kurds from other parts of putative Kurdistan, especially

Iraq – evoking an increasingly 'pan-Kurdish' identity, which allowed them to see themselves simultaneously as Kurds from a particular sector of Kurdistan and as part of the larger entity of Greater Kurdistan. Observing this, Martin van Bruinessen refers to the '"deterritorialization" of the Kurdish question', due to the combined effects of mass migration and globalization (van Bruinessen, 1998: 12).

Naturally, Kurdish immigrants from Turkey did not land in Europe bereft of identity. Feelings of cultural, economic and political subordination in their homeland had already come together within many of them as a Kurdish identity politics that constantly seeks a coherent Kurdish national identity. Kurdish nationalism seemed 'to offer a framework to construct a narrative of a unique Kurdish identity that needs to be restored by "going back" to one's history and origin' (Eliassi, 2013: 84).

These feelings never departed the hearts of the older generations in the earlier waves of Kurdish mass migration from Turkey. Aware that they were now living in a quite different environment, however, they generally limited themselves to cultural Kurdish activities. Any Kurdish organization that was established in this earlier period was tiny (Kaya, 2012: 159). Not wanting to cause trouble for themselves in their new lands – which they feared would have lasting consequences for their children – they were content at first to allow themselves to be described as 'Turkish'. Their children, in the meantime, were already becoming culturally integrated into the countries of migration.

Events in Turkey changed all that. The 1971 and 1980 *coups d'état* in Turkey ejected many leftist activists and intellectuals from Turkey, several of whom were Kurds. Landing in the diaspora, they formed political groups and community organizations. Different perspectives initially competed, as Turkish leftists also called the Kurds to their fold, evincing support for Kurdish rights. Some of the same Kurdish political groups that competed for Kurds' support in Turkey also emerged. But the emergence and growth of the PKK in Turkish Kurdistan soon convinced the majority of Kurds to support the organization. The PKK sent as many as 7,500 organizers to facilitate this politicization process (Kaya, 2012: 163; van Bruinessen, 1998: 8 n12). It was the politicization of Kurdish migration by the PKK that ensured that diaspora Kurds in Europe and elsewhere ceased regarding themselves in any sense as 'Turks' (White, 2004; Kaya, 2012: 160, 162). As Zeynep N. Kaya explains, 'Activities of the PKK among the diaspora offered a sense of identity, meaning and confidence to the second generation of guest workers, especially in Germany' (Kaya, 2012: 163).

The diaspora Kurds were providing vital support for the PKK. Observing that the PKK was successfully raising large sums of money and mobilizing Kurds for protests across Western Europe, Turkey was quick to explain that the PKK was forcing Kurds to support the organization with extortion, threats and acts of violence (Ministry of Foreign Affairs Turkey, 2014; Australian National Security, 2014). However, most contributions were in fact voluntary. Furthermore, the large numbers of youth recruited as guerrillas, technical and other skilled specialists, as well as organizers and diplomats, demonstrated the level of support of these diaspora Kurds for the PKK.

It is due to the high level of Turkish Kurdish diaspora support for the PKK that the latter was able to produce prodigious publications in several languages, open television stations and mobilize around 50,000 Kurds for important demonstrations (van Bruinessen, 1998: 8–9; 2000: 19). The PKK's hard work in the diaspora provided 'a sense of identity, meaning and confidence to the second generation of guest workers, especially in Germany' (Kaya, 2012: 163). PKK diaspora militants' widespread use of the

Internet and other modern communication methods transformed them into 'long-distance Kurdish nationalists', carrying out their activities in a 'transnational realm' (Kaya, 2012: 160). The Kurdish question continued to be 'deterritorialized'. The diaspora activists had been inspired by the rise of the PKK's militancy in Turkish Kurdistan. The diaspora militants' activities, in turn, reverberated in the hearts of their compatriots back home, reassuring them that they were not isolated, and that support was building for their cause in Europe.

Europe's Turkish Kurdish diaspora watched the steady ratcheting up of Turkish state violence against Turkey's Kurds with growing consternation. No longer isolated from their homeland by virtue of being in Europe, diaspora Kurds followed political developments in Turkey closely, especially those concerning the country's Kurds. The PKK's successful insertion into the Kurdish diaspora gave it an increasingly formidable supporters' network throughout Western Europe. Importantly, the failure of the PKK's efforts towards a peaceful settlement infuriated the diaspora, which was now strongly influenced by the organization.

Indeed, Turkey's preference in the 1980s and 1990s for ruthless military force to solve its Kurdish problem had the opposite effect to that which Ankara intended, as the Kurds forced from Turkish Kurdistan into the diaspora were compelled by circumstances to overcome their differences, as a consequence of which many were integrated 'into more inclusive, non-territorial Kurdish networks' (van Bruinessen, 2000: 21). However, this development also facilitated the deterritorialization of Ankara's war on Kurdish nationalism.

The PKK leadership evolved a network for leading the deterritorialized Kurds, linking the diaspora to the PKK via the Confederation of Kurdish Associations in Europe (KON-KURD), which is based in Brussels. Pro-PKK Kurdish associations in

Australia, the United States and Canada are also connected to KON-KURD (Gunter, 2011: 167). However, a pan-Kurdistan body, the Kongra Netewiya Kurdistan (KNK – National Congress of Kurdistan) now acts as an umbrella organization for the PKK diaspora as a whole, comprising representatives in Europe, the Middle East, North America, Australia and Asia, together with representatives of political, religious and cultural institutions, intellectuals and non-Kurdish ethnic groups from all over Kurdistan (Akkaya and Jongerden, 2011: 159 n13).

Ankara was not complacent in the face of these developments and showed itself increasingly capable of working directly with Germany and France regarding these groups, especially against PKK supporters. Nevertheless, building on its successful multi-state mobilizations to 'save Öcalan' when the Kurdish leader briefly sojourned in Europe, by 2010 the PKK had attained a sophisticated organizational and propaganda apparatus in Europe. The Turkish state countered this by providing evidence to European states claiming that the diaspora organizations included terrorists. Turkey signed a broad agreement against terrorism with France in 2011. The PKK had already been classified as a terrorist organisation by the European Union in May 2002.

Until 2012 European PKK supporters did indeed include a number of organization members, who at that point acted as though they were still in Turkey. In other words, when devising their political strategies and seeking to lead the diaspora, they paid little attention to the very different, liberal-democratic states in which they now lived. Their only concern was that the PKK and its perspectives were under attack in Turkey. Like the PKK in this period, on occasion they resisted these attacks using violent means. In this struggle, the diaspora leaders believed that such violence was justified. The Turkish state seized on this approach and used it to secure joint action by European governments against the PKK's members and supporters in the diaspora.

Exactly as in Turkey, each attack by either side (the pro-PKK diaspora or one of the European states) produced retaliation. Thus, six alleged PKK members were indicted in Paris in December 2010 by the anti-terrorist judge Thierry Fragnoli for conspiracy in connection with and financing of a terrorist organization (*AFP*, 5 June 2011). This set the tone for mobilizations by PKK supporters and members in Europe during the period of the PKK's violent upsurge of 2011 to 2012 in Turkey. Particularly notable events of that period included disturbances in two parts of France, following the arrest of two men accused of being PKK leading cadres 'without reason' on 4 June 2011 in Evry, in the southern suburbs of Paris. In a remarkable (but hardly unprecedented) display of its ability to instantly mobilize supporters, some fifty PKK supporters soon assembled on the street and directed projectiles at police, who called for reinforcements. As Kurdish protestors' numbers doubled, they continued to hurl projectiles at police, who retaliated with rubber bullets and tear gas (*AFP*, 4 June 2011).

Behind this incident was a crackdown by French authorities on the PKK's organizing in France. Pressured constantly by Ankara to act against the PKK's deterritorialized militants on its own soil, the French state (along with other European states with large Kurdish populations) was now concerned that the deterritorialized war between Turks and Kurds was both harming its own relations with Turkey (an important strategic partner) and damaging its security. Part of this concern flowed from the emergence and growing electoral successes of far-right political parties, which, capitalizing on economic instability, were prospering by targeting the influx of immigrants (including the highly visible Turkish Kurds). European Union states now determined to snuff out the burgeoning transnational war on their soil.

Pro-PKK Kurds continued to clash with police in France. Searching for PKK cadres at a Kurdish Cultural House, police in northern France clashed with PKK supporters on 4 June 2011, leading to arrests (*Libération*, 2011; *AFP*, 4 June 2011). But that was not the end: just as in Turkish Kurdistan itself, one incident led to another. Hundreds of local Kurds mobilized to battle police, with order not being restored until four hours after the initial arrests (*Libération*, 2011; *AFP*, 4 June 2011). Thousands of Kurds protested the following day in Evry and in Arnouville, where some demonstrators brandished flags bearing the image of Abdullah Öcalan (*Fdesouche*, 2011; *AFP*, 5 June 2011). At a follow-up demonstration in Paris up to 3,000 protesting Kurds likewise waved Kurdish flags and portraits of Öcalan (*AFP*, 11 June 2011).

The arrests in both Val-d'Oise and Evry had followed 'an investigation conducted for several months by the anti-terrorist sub-directorate (SDAT) on the instructions of the anti-terrorist prosecutor of Paris', Interior Ministry spokesperson Pierre-Henry Brandet later claimed (*Libération*, 2011). Seven Kurds were subsequently indicted for supposed 'conspiracy in relation to a terrorist enterprise' and for allegedly financing terrorism. One of the arrested Kurds was also charged with attempted extortion and wilful violence. Five of these Kurds were subsequently imprisoned (*AFP*, 9 June 2011).

Then, perhaps not coincidentally, on 20 June 2011 the trial opened in Paris of eighteen Kurds who had been arrested in France in February 2007. All stood accused of acts of terrorism and of financing the PKK's activities. They were also charged with being active members of the PKK; the French state claiming that they had financed guerrilla attacks in Turkey and laundered money obtained from drug trafficking. The defendants included Ali Rıza Altun, Nedim Seven and Atilla Balıkçı, accused of being respectively the representative of the PKK in Europe, the organization's 'secretary' and its 'treasurer' (*AFP*, 20 June 2011). A further four Kurds were subsequently arrested for PKK membership in Marseille and Paris following police raids and accused of financing terrorism and conspiracy in relation to a terrorist enterprise (*AFP*, 20 September 2011).

French interior minister Claude Gueant signed a broad agreement on terrorism in Ankara on 7 October 2011, aimed mainly at the PKK. He stated that in 2010 and 2011 respectively, thirty-eight and thirty-two PKK members had been arrested on French soil. The signing took place only three weeks before the French court was due to reach verdicts in the trial of eighteen Kurds of Turkish nationality, referred to above (*AFP*, 28 September 2011; *AFP*, 7 October 2011). More Kurds were arrested in the following weeks, after France's Central Directorate of Internal Intelligence (DCRI) raided several premises in Bordeaux (*AFP*, 15 October 2011).

Sentences were finally handed down in Paris on 2 November 2011 for the eighteen Kurds arrested in 2007. Seventeen of the defendants received prison sentences ranging from one to five years (two of which were suspended), for alleged acts of terrorism and for financing the PKK. One sentence was accompanied by a ban from French territory for ten years. Presented as active members, if not leaders, of the PKK, they were found to have participated in the financing of attacks in Turkey. The court was unable to prove charges of money laundering from drug trafficking. One defendant was acquitted (*AFP*, 2 November 2011). The court also ordered the closing down of the Ahmet Kaya Kurdish Cultural Centre.

Protests by pro-PKK Kurds continued to flare up in France (*AFP*, 30 December 2011; *Hurriyet Daily News*, 6 October 2012).

In Germany, meanwhile, security authorities arrested two suspected PKK recruiters on 18 July (*AFP*, 19 July 2011). The PKK also remained active elsewhere in Europe, conducting protests notably in Vienna on 17 October (*AFP*, 17 October 2011) in Amsterdam (*AFP*, 30 October 2011) and in Strasbourg (*AFP*, 23 November 2011).

The PKK's successful establishment in the Kurdish diaspora gave it an increasingly formidable supporters' network throughout Western Europe. These diaspora Kurds provided vital support for the PKK, raising large sums of money and mobilizing Kurds for protests across Western Europe. Initially evoked by the rise of the PKK's militancy in Turkish Kurdistan, these deterritorialized militants' activism reassured their compatriots back home that they were not isolated, and that support was building for their cause in Europe. The pro-PKK diaspora's proudest period was its successful organization of multistate mobilizations to 'save Öcalan' when the Kurdish leader briefly sojourned in Europe. Building on this, by 2010 the PKK attained a sophisticated organizational and propaganda apparatus in Europe. These Kurdish activists are well informed and follow political developments in Turkey closely, especially those concerning Turkey's Kurds. The failure of the PKK's past efforts for a peaceful settlement infuriated the diaspora, and it has protested in large numbers on the streets of Western Europe. The same diaspora will not remain passive in the face of provocations from Turkish nationalist extremists aimed at derailing the new peace process.

Breaking the deadly pattern?

This chapter has demonstrated the utterly contradictory nature of the PKK/Ankara peace process. After peaking in the 1980s and 1990s, the PKK's armed struggle against the Turkish state went into abeyance for a period, before again growing visibly bloodier. The reasons for this deadly pattern are no mystery. Both Turkish governments and the PKK (and its wider movement) have exhibited the capacity to think outside of their respective boxes. The AKP, for instance, has grasped the necessity to speak directly to Turkey's Kurds; yet, partly due to its being blinded by short-term electoral concerns, it has been unable to accept for many years that this necessitated interacting meaningfully with the BDP. While talking of peace, the AKP persecuted the BDP.

A viable peace settlement requires the building of trust on both sides. The precondition for this is the abandonment by protagonists of ways of thinking and acting that, by their very nature, make the agreements that must be reached by all concerned practically impossible. This has proved very difficult, on both sides, for many years. The PKK has offered Ankara several unilateral ceasefires, but all have been ignored, as the deadly pattern continued to reassert itself. (The 2009 'Kurdish Opening' is a partial exception to this trend, since the Erdoğan government did seek a peace settlement of sorts with the PKK. However, as shown earlier, the latter behaved immaturely at the time, demonstrating it was not yet capable of securing a lasting peace, while the government of the day, for its part, was unable to break the grip of the Turkish military on affairs of state.)

In the face of repeated failure to resolve the conflict, events have tended to quickly spiral out of control. Kurds protesting on the streets have met fierce repression, and so their demonstrations turned into increasingly violent confrontations with the authorities. Concluding that only violence could resolve the Kurdish issue the PKK has spoken darkly of 'political genocide against the Kurdish people'. The unilateral ceasefire called on 13 August 2010 was formally abandoned on 28 February 2011 by the PKK, which recommenced attacking Turkish military targets. Abdullah Öcalan formally ended all peacemaking moves with the Turkish State in mid-2010, stating that this was now the job of his military commanders. Although this was an attempt to alarm the authorities with the menace of total war, Öcalan's initiative simply intensified the violence on both sides.

Öcalan did not abandon the possibility of a peace process, however. In mid-2011 both he and the DTK announced support for Kurdish 'democratic autonomy', within the boundaries of the Turkish state. Convinced that this proposal had been ignored, Öcalan declared at the end of July that this dialogue was 'finished'. Unfortunately, he was correct, as attacks on the PKK in Turkish and Iraqi Kurdistan became even more intensive. Then, though, even as a new Turkish offensive was waged against PKK bases in Iraqi Kurdistan, the Turkish government admitted in September 2011 that it had been engaging in secret direct negotiations with the PKK. Yet this initiative looked like failing altogether after just a few short weeks, and clashes reached very high levels of intensity.

Growing increasingly anxious as all its efforts brought it no closer to a viable peace settlement, the PKK became more and more desperate during 2011 and 2012, when the armed conflict returned to levels approaching that of the 1980s and 1990s conflict. Ankara exacerbated the problem by resorting to solely military methods and seeking assistance from the United States in pursuing this approach.

Nevertheless, surprising new developments were to emerge at the end of 2012, following behind-the-scenes activity, raising hopes for the possibility of a viable peace process succeeding.

FIVE

The move towards peace

A viable peace process was the very last thing that most people were expecting as the year 2012 ended. The terrible bloodshed of the preceding twelve months especially had sickened a great number of Turks and Kurds alike in Turkey, and most saw no reason why this would be likely to decrease in scale in the near future. In reality, events behind the scenes were about to create a stunning opportunity for peace, as the PKK prepared to announce its complete abandonment of guerrilla activity.

31 December 2012: peace negotiations announced

In the midst of the heightened state of bloodletting, on 31 December 2012, Prime Minister Erdoğan stunned Turkey by admitting that secret peace negotiations had been taking place with Öcalan in Imralı prison. Of course, the very fact that these negotiations had been happening for some time proves that the incipient peace process had been proceeding at the very same time as the conflict between Ankara and the PKK had reached a new level of bloodshed. The explanation for this apparent paradox is Erdoğan's realization that he needed to achieve the resolution of a number of threatening historical issues – any one of which could explode and jeopardize both the peace process and his own government.

Nevertheless, broad public support for the peace process was apparent as soon as Erdoğan revealed that the intelligence organization MİT had been conducting discussions with Abdullah Öcalan. The International Crisis Group commented: 'The talks, which enjoy wide political support, may offer a genuine opportunity to end Turkey's long-standing Kurdish conflict.' Peace and Democracy Party representatives were permitted to visit the PKK leader for the first time, further lifting Kurdish expectations in the emerging peace process. Öcalan told his visitors that the period of armed struggle was now ended (International Crisis Group, 2013).

This opportunity had been a long time coming. The ceasefire that the PKK had launched on 1 September 1998 led directly to a decrease in violence between the PKK and Turkish security forces. This enabled the Turkish state to end Emergency Rule in the provinces of Colemêrg and Dêrsim on 30 July 2002. This was extended in 30 November 2002 to Diyarbakır and Şırnak – the last two remaining provinces under Emergency Rule (Gunes, 2012: 465). However, Ankara still failed to respond positively to the PKK/Kongra-Gel offer of a lasting peace settlement. On 1 June 2004 Kongra-Gel therefore formally ended the ceasefire. All previous PKK/Kongra-Gel unilateral ceasefires had met the same sorry end, for the reasons explored in the previous chapter – the failure of protagonists to abandon ways of thinking and acting that made a viable peace agreement practically impossible.

A total of 32,000 PKK militants were killed and 14,000 captured between 1984 and 2008. Some 5,560 civilians died and 6,482 Turkish soldiers were killed during the same phase (*Hürriyet*, 16 September 2008). The war has cost Ankara over $300 billion. Hundreds of thousands of Kurds have been displaced (Pope, 2013; Schmid, 2012; Traynor and Letsch, 2013). In the eighteen months following the collapse of the 2009–11 'Kurdish Opening' alone, almost 900 people had been killed and 8,000 Kurdish political prisoners taken into detention. To an increasing number of people involved on both sides of this conflict, the sheer senseless horror of the loss of human life was now becoming apparent. The scale of the human carnage began to gradually educe qualitative changes in thinking. The bloody military and political stalemate now convinced 'senior figures on both sides' to accept the impossibility of securing a thoroughgoing military or political victory (Pope, 2013; Schmid, 2012; Traynor and Letsch, 2013). At the same time, a year without elections gave Erdoğan the political space he needed in order to obtain a peace settlement, before his predicted run for Turkey's presidency in mid-2014 (Pope, 2013).

The prime minister's adviser on Kurdish affairs stated on 4 January 2013 that the government's goal was a 'final settlement' with the Kurds. The fact that the same spokesperson added exactly one week later that military operations against the PKK would continue until it disarmed (International Crisis Group, 2013) does not contradict anything that has been said about the current peace process – which is, in any case, highly contradictory. The AKP government must at all times maintain a difficult and often convoluted posture in the peace process – continuing to pose as the implacable, active opponent of 'PKK terrorism' and upholder of the values of the 'Turkish nation', while also promoting a peaceful but genuine compromise with the Kurds of Turkey.

As may be expected from such a complex agenda, the peace process did not advance without difficulties, but in fits and starts, with setbacks and roadblocks. As long as Ankara made positive gestures towards the Kurds, however, the peace process went forward. Such gestures include the government passing a law on 25 January allowing defendants to speak Kurdish in court at will, and a Diyarbakır court on 31 January acquitting ninety-eight Kurdish mayors of terrorism-related charges. Kurds warmly appreciated this. Over a million Kurds who gathered to listen to the *Serok*'s peace message in Amed in both Kurdish and Turkish on 21 March 2013 were permitted by security forces to sing, dance and wave pro-PKK banners with images of Öcalan (Dalay, 2013; *Associated Press*, 2013). Other goodwill gestures included the government's decision in early January 2013 to allow Öcalan to watch television and to permit Kurdish movement leaders to visit him in prison (Pope, 2013).

An opinion piece by İhsan Dağı in *Today's Zaman* talked up the prospects for lasting peace, noting that both Abdullah Öcalan and the BDP were assets in implementing a future peace deal. The op-ed piece added: 'Öcalan is an aging man and in an era of post-Öcalan Kurdish politics it will be impossible to find or create a leader like him to make peace with' (Dağı, 2013). This opinion certainly has much merit. The PKK leader has relentlessly pushed both his own party and the AKP government towards the most hopeful peace initiative of the entire conflict in Turkey. Abdullah Öcalan admits that his party has committed terroristic deeds at times in the past, but now does not condone these. It is he, more than any other individual in the PKK, who has been responsible for persisting with unilateral ceasefires, even though these have usually been fruitless. On the other hand, his party also contains leaders and cadres who have demonstrated the opposite dynamic – reneging on ceasefires and returning to the path of all-out war. It is a measure of Öcalan's leadership abilities that he has been able to reverse such dynamics, despite being confined to a prison cell.

Furthermore, relations between Iraqi Kurdistan and Ankara have improved appreciably, allowing Turkey to emerge 'as the only regional ally and balancer vis-à-vis Baghdad'. This cordial relation is likely to continue and prosper, given that Iraqi Kurdistan is a prized market for Turkey and a probable energy provider. It is a strategic partner because of the Iraqi Kurds' deteriorating relationship with both Baghdad and Syria's al-Assad regime. Mutual 'strategic and economic interests' make it increasingly probable that the KRG would help facilitate the PKK/Ankara peace process (Dağı, 2013).

By February 2013 Öcalan had called for prisoners to be released by both sides. In response the PKK freed eight Turkish soldiers and officials it had held captive in Iraqi Kurdistan (*BBC News*, 21 March 2013). Peace was clearly back on the agenda.

Turkish responses to the Turkish/Kurdish peace process

Milliyet columnist Kadri Gürsel cites three forces that have opposed the AKP government since 2002: 'the prime minister, the prisoner and the preacher' (cited in Dombey, 2013a). This observation also neatly captures the powers that must be secured for the peace process to succeed. The evolving stances of 'the prisoner' (i.e. Abdullah Öcalan) have been discussed in earlier chapters. The responses to the peace process of the prime minister and his chief opponents both within and outside the state are considered in the present chapter. The power politics reviewed here, it will be shown, relates directly to an attempt to return Turkey to its previous status as a praetorian state under direct military tutelage. The factors driving this conspiracy derive in large part from fears of rapprochement between Ankara and the PKK.

The AKP in power

As a party of so-called 'moderate political Islam' the AKP is an unusual – but not unprecedented – government in modern Turkey. The Republic of Turkey was founded on 29 October 1923, with Mustafa Kemal Atatürk as its first president. Atatürk comprehensively dismantled the Ottoman Islamic Caliphate, outlawing religion in all spheres of public life, with secularism and virulent Turkish nationalism becoming the new state's first principles. It took over four and a half decades for political parties inspired by Islamic values to reappear in Turkish public life. Despite this success, these parties have all been stalked perpetually by the threat of judicial abolition – if not removal by the Kemalist military apparatus. These parties have also often been important players in the politics of Turkey's Kurdish region and therefore factors in the PKK/Ankara peace process. Indeed, the Kurdish issue has been a constant factor prompting powerful opposition by sections of the Turkish state.

The Adalet ve Kalkınma Partisi led by Prime Minister Erdoğan derives from deeply conservative Islamic organizations – some of which were closed by the Kemalists for supposedly planning to establish an 'Islamic state'. One of these predecessor parties, the Refah Partisi (RP – Welfare Party), led by Necmettin Erbakan, became the junior partner in a coalition on 28 June 1996 with the arch-secularist Doğru Yol Partisi (DYP – True Path Party) (Yeşilada, 1999: 123–4). The Genelkurmay (military general staff) of the Türk Silahlı Kuvvetleri (TSK – Turkish Armed Forces) exerted mounting pressure on the coalition. In the face of this, perhaps, Erbakan sought to broaden his base in Turkey's Kurdish region. The Erbakanists – in all their various incarnations —struck a real chord in Turkish Kurdistan, consistently polling 'well above the national average' in that region during the 1970s and 1980s (van Bruinessen, 1991: 22).

Kurdish nationalist votes had in fact become crucial to Erbakan's political project, as legal Kurdish parties were outlawed or heavily repressed, and electoral support for them was transferred to the RP (Barkey and Fuller, 1998: 101–7; see also Gunter, 1997: 85, 87). However, the Kurdish question was also the RP's undoing. In late July 1996 the RP attempted to explore seriously the possibility of a peaceful settlement in the war between the Turkish military and the PKK. Taking advantage of the PKK's unilateral ceasefire since mid-December 1995, Erbakan held secret meetings with the Islamist writer İsmail Nacar, who had been chosen as an intermediary by the pro-Kurdish Peoples Democratic Party (HADEP) (*Sabah*, 4 August 1996; *AFP*, 4 August 1996). HADEP was the predecessor of the present-day Peace and Democracy Party. Erbakan met directly with HADEP leaders (*Reuters*, 5 August 1996) and, the daily *Sabah* claimed, was also in contact with PKK leader Abdullah Öcalan (*Sabah*, 4 August 1996).

Less than forty-eight hours after receiving a friendly visit from two senior military officials, Erbakan was repeating the mantra of the Kemalists: 'We will not sit down at the table with terrorists. We will not give one inch in our struggle with terrorism. We will not surrender our insistence on a united state' (*Wall Street Journal*, European edition, 9 August 1996). Within days of this statement, Erbakan was talking about fighting the PKK militarily again (*Reuters*, 7 August 1996).

Meanwhile, the military-dominated Milli Güvenlik Kurulu continued to warn Erbakan to diverge from what the generals believed were challenges to the generals' Kemalist agenda, but Erbakan refused to change course. The military soon moved painfully close to direct physical confrontation with the RP. Faced with a full-blooded military coup, the Erbakan/Çiller coalition resigned in June 1997. Abdullah Gül, RP's deputy chairman (and later president of Turkey under the AKP government) endorsed the interpretation of these events as a 'post-modern coup d'état' (Çandar, 1997).

As the RP faced imminent proscription by the Supreme Court, the Fazilet Partisi (FP – the Virtue Party) succeeded the RP in late 1998 (Yeşilada, 1999: 124). The issues causing concern to the generals were many, but a key worry of the ultra-Kemalists was that the FP might also attempt to deal with the PKK, after its chairman, Recai Kutan, spoke of recognizing 'some of the rights of Turkey's Kurdish identity' (*Turkish Daily News*, 13 August 1998). Some of the party's leaders formed a new party, the Adalet ve Kalkınma Partisi (AKP – Justice and Development Party), in August 2001 (*Milliyet*, 17 December 1998).

The AKP received 34.17 per cent of votes in the 3 November 2002 Turkish general elections, winning 66 per cent of the parliamentary seats, due to the electoral threshold that disregards parties polling less than 10 per cent of the vote (Tezcur, 2011). The first AKP government was formed in November. Unusually for an Islamic-tainted ruling party, the AKP remained in power following the 2007 and 2011 general elections and even achieved overall domination of the municipalities in the 2004 and 2009 local elections (Tezcur, 2011). In the March 2014 municipal elections the AKP polled a six-point increase over its 2009 results.

The AKP's consecutive electoral successes enabled it to introduce measures that greatly facilitated its peace process with the PKK, by removing obstacles that had stymied its predecessor parties – despite the tremendous concern that this generated within the Kemalist military and judicial establishment. In contrast to its timid predecessor parties, the AKP responded to predictable pressures from the Kemalist judicial establishment and military brass, by making concerted efforts to neuter these institutions (Tezcur, 2011). The Genelkurmay now lacked the ability to veto government policies and was now unable to impose policies that identified groups (such as the Kurds or their political representations) as 'internal enemies' (Tezcur, 2011).

The abolition of the generals' judicial immunity exposed them to prosecution. Beginning in 2007, the AKP instituted a string of criminal investigations that identified highly placed officers in what became known as the so-called Ergenekon conspiracy (discussed below) against the AKP government. By September 2011 over 15 per cent of all generals were in prison (Tezcur, 2011).

In the face of – and in response to – a web of interlocking conspiracies centred in the Turkish military to allegedly overthrow bloodily the elected AKP government, Turkey voted positively in a constitutional referendum on 12 September 2010. The constitutional amendments placed new limitations on the authority of the military and its personnel, including: introducing civilian trials of members of the army who are accused of violating the constitutional order; subjecting decisions of the high military council to judicial review; and lifting the judicial immunity granted to the leaders of the 1980 coup. The amendments gave Turkey's legislature and government enhanced power in judicial appointments, thus ending the protection of the senior judiciary, and thereby hampering the generals' ability to sway judicial decisions. The reform also weakened the traditional partnership between the CHP, the military and the senior judiciary.

After the endorsement of the 2011 general election – and with its constitutional reforms already in hand – the AKP imposed restrictions that precluded the promotion of generals hostile to the government. Summing up, one can agree with Tezcur's assessment that the AKP succeeded in consolidating its authority over the presidency, the high judiciary and the armed forces (Tezcur, 2011). However, a series of financial 'scandals' in late

2013 undermined these achievements significantly. These are examined below. To make sense of the events, however, it is first necessary to grasp the reality of Turkey's deep state, which originated in the Cold War, and which has impacted heavily on Turkey's Kurds.

Turkey's deep state

Numerous sources attest to the existence of secret armies in many Western European countries from the onset of the Cold War (Ganser, 2005b: 69; Senate of Belgium, 1991). In 1974 the then Turkish prime minister, Bülent Ecevit, exposed a so-called *kontrgerilla* (counter-guerrilla) force operating independently of the military command. In 2005 former President Süleyman Demirel confirmed that the 'deep state exists, and it is the military', adding that the deep state could take over the state as a whole in times of crisis (*NTV–MSNBC*, 2005). Discussing Demirel's admission, Merve Kavakci suggests that the deep state has infiltrated vast sectors of the state (Kavakci, 2009). Prime Minister Recep Tayyip Erdoğan agrees, affirming that the deep state 'does exist' (Erdoğan, on Kanal 7 television, 26 January 2007). Maureen Freely asserts that the deep state is 'Turkish shorthand for a faceless clique inside the Turkish state'. She adds that, while Turkey's deep state may be based in the army, it is also connected closely with the Milli İstihbarat Teşkilatı, the judiciary and the mafia (Freely, 2007: 20; see also Celik, 1999).

Debate on the extent of Turkey's deep state (*derin devlet*) continues to rage in Turkey. Some blame the deep state for the military coups of 1971 and 1980, while some also allege that the *derin devlet* has been mobilized against the PKK (Celik 1999; Dundar, 2006). Abdullah Öcalan alleges that a deep-state unit attempted to take over the PKK (*Sunday's Zaman*, 2008).

Interestingly, many now assert that some alleged PKK armed attacks were actually perpetrated by deep-state forces (see Esayan, 2013: 34). In one notorious incident on 24 May 1993, for instance, thirty-three unarmed soldiers were allegedly executed by the PKK in Bingöl. PKK advocate Adem Uzun casts suspicion on claims that the PKK was responsible for killing these soldiers, and Abdullah Öcalan has requested an independent inquiry into the incident (Uzun, 2014: n3 & 17).

Three members of the Turkish armed forces were subsequently scapegoated in connection with this incident for alleged negligence of duty. A series of appeals by the soldiers failed to resolve their case, although the file in the case mysteriously went missing. Şemdin Sakık, a former PKK commander – known also as 'Parmaksız Zeki' – alleges that the military formed a group called the Doğu Çalışma Grubu (DÇG – East Working Group) in eastern Turkey back in the 1990s, which he charges with numerous illegal activities, including the killing of the thirty-three soldiers in Bingöl. Perhaps not coincidentally, the attack occurred at a time when the then-president, Turgut Özal, was working for a peace settlement with the PKK, which had declared a ceasefire. The attack ended the ceasefire (Cihan, 2012).

Discussing the 'clandestine operations of the Turkish deep state' Serdar Kaya cites the activities of the Jandarma İstihbarat ve Terörle Mücadele (JİTEM – Gendarmarie Intelligence and Counter-terror Unit), which he names as 'allegedly responsible for thousands of extrajudicial executions and assassinations of PKK sympathizers and supporters' (Kaya, 2009: 103; Jenkins, 2009: v).

İsmet Berkan claims that in late 1992 a section of Turkey's military formed an ultra-right-wing group involving mafia boss Abdullah Catlı and senior police officers, aspiring to physically liquidate the Kurdish problem permanently (Berkan, 1996). Thousands of Kurds died in extrajudicial killings and some

3,500 Kurdish villages were burned to the ground (McKiernan, 1999; Cengiz, 2011). Numerous independent reporters assert that the nucleus of this secretive armed force was the ultra-rightist Nationalist Action Party (Bayart, 1982: 111–12; Erdem, 1995; Kürkçü, 1996: 5; Zürcher, 1995: 276; van Bruinessen, 1996; 8; Panico, 1995: 170ff.). In the 1960s Alparslan Türkeş established the Komünizm İle Mücadele Dernekleri (KİM – Association for Struggling with Communism), and a crypto-fascist political front the Milliyetçi Hareket Partisi (MHP – Nationalist Action Party), both of which have worked closely with the *derin devlet*. An investigation by Ankara's deputy state attorney into possible connections between KİM, MHP and the deep state found that all were complicit in massacres and assassinations during the 1970s. The deputy state attorney, Doğan Öz, was himself assassinated on 24 March 1978 (*Türkiye*, 2008; Ganser, 2005: 237).

Turkey's deep state has always been rigidly Kemalist. By definition, therefore, it is deeply secularist, anti-communist and anti-Kurdish nationalist. But that has not prevented it utilizing both leftist and (after 1980) many Islamic forces to achieve its aims. Ahmet Şık writes that the *derin devlet* appoints people to interact with the leaders of groups it wishes to make use of. 'Be respectful of Atatürk and we'll help you' these Muslims were told. Both sides have 'mutual interests', despite some of their final goals diverging (Şık, 2013: 4). This is because all of the groups – the leftists as well as the Islamic forces – are nationalists. The most significant Islamic grouping working with the deep state has been the organization of Muhammed Fethullah Gülen. Osman Nuri Gündeş asserts that during the 1980s Gülen worked with the ultra-right anti-communist groups in Turkey supported by both the CIA and the Turkish deep state (Gündeş, 2010). Gülen is a notable nationalist who was politicized and trained in the Cold War fight against communism. The Gülenists are known to have infiltrated Turkey's Ministry of the Interior, its police force and its Ministry of Justice (Şık, 2013: 4).

The contemporary intervention of Turkey's *derin devlet* against the PKK became apparent in Paris in early 2013, in a provocation apparently aimed at derailing the PKK/Ankara peace process. On 10 January three prominent PKK members – Sakine Cansız, Fidan Doğan and Leyla Söylemez – were shot dead in a northern district of the French capital. French police immediately began investigating a connection with Turkey's National Intelligence Organization (Milli İstihbarat Teşkilatı, or MİT). The provocation provoked a mass resurgence of PKK supporters onto the streets of Western Europe.

The killings had every mark of a meticulously planned intelligence operation. Tenants in nearby offices heard no shots; a silencer was used to muffle the sound (Yetkin, 2013). But which intelligence service orchestrated the assassinations? *Spiegel Online* voices 'suspicions' that 'there may be Turkish intelligence links to the slayings'. It adds that Germany's domestic intelligence agency, the Bundesamt für Verfassungsschutz (BfV) 'curtailed its cooperation' with Turkey's intelligence organizations, due to these suspicions (Diehl, Gezer and Schmid, 2014).

Yet this scenario raises an even bigger issue: why would the Turkish state assassinate the PKK's Sakine Cansız and her comrades in the middle of peace negotiations? Does this indicate that Ankara's declared commitment to the peace process is a sham? The likely answer to this question is that the government remains committed to the process, but that other sectors of the state – Turkey's notorious *derin devlet* – have never accepted it. President Abdullah Gül urged calm, saying that time was needed to reveal the truth concerning the murders. Prime Minister Erdoğan suggested that the attack could be a provocation from forces who do not want a peace solution to the Kurdish/Turkish conflict. He added, however, that the killings 'could be an internal feud' (*Hürriyet Daily News*, 11 January 2013).

Tantalizing revelations emerging after the assassinations in Paris name Ömer Güney, a Turkish citizen, as the primary suspect in the murders of the three PKK militants. A video has emerged of Güney at the crime scene, watching French police investigate the killings (Dickey, 2013). On 13 January 2014 a close associate of Güney released an audio recording, allegedly made covertly by Güney but only to be released in the event of misadventure on his part. The recording is apparently of Güney planning with MİT the murders of Cansız and her comrades. French police arrested Güney on 17 January 2013 (*EKurd Daily*, 13 January 2014).

In addition to this, a secret document dated 18 November 2011, supposedly signed by a high official of MİT, Uğur Kaan Ayık, and countersigned by other high MİT officials, O. Yüret, S. Asal and H. Özcan, has come to light. Entitled 'Ref: Sakine Cansız, Codenamed Sara', the document purports to report information from an agent – code-named 'Legionnaire' – on Sakine Cansız, a PKK founding member. The document claims that 'Legionnaire' met with MİT in Turkey in order to plan Cansız's assassination. The document states that €6,000 was paid to 'Legionnaire' for the assassination's preparation. Güney apparently made several trips to Turkey in 2012 (ANF, 2014; *Pariscinayeti*, 2014; YouTube, 2014).

France's interior minister Manuel Valls declared that the killings were 'without doubt an execution' (*The Province*, 2013; Dilorenzo, 2013). A statement by the Koma Ciwakên Kürdistan responded to the assassinations: 'As a matter of fact, these murders couldn't have taken place without the support of intelligence services' (Kurdistan Democratic Communities' Union, 2013).

Hundreds of Kurds quickly gathered outside the Kurdish centre where the three militants were killed. On 15 January

Pro-PKK activists carried coffins representing the three dead Kurdish women through the streets of the Paris suburb of Villiers-le-Bel. An estimated 10,000 members of France's Kurdish community attended the ceremony. Waving Kurdish flags, the demonstrators chanted 'We are the PKK' (*Deutsche Welle*, 2013). Some 700 Kurds also demonstrated on the streets of Berlin, carrying posters of the three dead women. One group carried a sign reading: 'Women are murdered, Europe is silent'. Some 200 people stood in sub-zero temperatures outside Stockholm's French embassy, chanting 'Long Live the PKK' and 'Turkey, Terrorists' (Yackley, 2013a). On 17 January thousands of Kurds gathered in Amed for the funeral of the three PKK members (Cheviron, 2013). In an impressive display of organization, demonstrators in Turkey and in France carried the same full-colour portraits of the slain activists. The PKK and its supporters across Turkey and Western Europe had reasserted their strength in the face of a perceived provocation, without letting themselves be drawn back into a shooting war. The provocation had failed.

Turkey's *derin devlet* has a proven track record of staging anti-Kurdish provocations at critical political junctures. Whether it was centrally involved in the assassinations of the three PKK militants in Paris will only be definitively proven over time. In the meantime, further provocations from Turkish forces opposed to the PKK–Ankara peace process could occur, before peace is achieved. Sinan Ulgen, a former Turkish diplomat, observes: 'Unfortunately, we are bound to see acts designed to derail this process and I think this [the slayings of Cansız, Doğan and Şaylemez] is act one' (Landauro and Parkinson, 2013).

The prime minister and the preacher

By any account, Fethullah Gülen has immense political influence in Turkey (Cetinkaya, 1996, 2004, 2005, 2006, 2007, 2008a,

2008b, 2009). Several police commissioners and security personnel take orders from him (Yanardağ, 2006, cited in Sharon-Krespin, 2009). His organization, Hizmet, has 600 schools and an estimated 6 million adherents globally (Oda TV, 2010), making it the largest Islamic organization in the world. Gülen's former right-hand man Nurettin Veren admits that Gülenist 'graduates' include governors, judges, military officers and government ministers. Veren adds: 'They consult Gülen before doing anything' (*Kanaltürk*, 2006, cited by Sharon-Krespin, 2009).

Gülen has many devotees in the AKP and is assisted by his movement's massive holdings in the media, financial institutions, banks and business organizations. When entering the state bureaucracy, Gülenists are required by Hizmet to sign a letter of allegiance to Fethullah Gülen. These state officials, including provincial governors, make startling statements of allegiance to Gülen. One governor, for instance, vows 'duty of all kinds' to Gülen. A high-ranking official in the Istanbul University Faculty of Law promises 'a lifetime of obedience'. Another bureaucrat addresses Gülen reverently: 'I kiss your foot' and undertakes to perform any requested services for Gülen 'where you want, the way you want…' The letter-writers frequently express the desire for 'martyrdom' in Gülen's service (*Gündem*, 2014).

Gülen has lived in the United States since 1997. Interestingly, former CIA officers were among the conspicuous references in Gulen's green card application (Edmonds, 2011). He has always openly exhibited the greatest hostility to the PKK. Yet, according to Hizmet supporter İhsan Yılmaz, 'Fethullah Gülen very clearly announced that he supports the peace process' (Yılmaz, 2013). Nevertheless, in a speech on 24 October 2011 entitled 'Terör ve Izdırap' (Terror and Agony), Gülen rhetorically 'supplicates' God:

> O God, unify us (*Allahim birligimizi sagla*), and as for those among us who deserve nothing but punishment (*o hakki kötektir bunlar*),

> knock their homes upside down (*Allahim onlarin altlarini üstlerine getir*), destroy their unity (*birliklerini boz*), burn their houses to ash (*evlerine ateş sal*) may their homes be filled with weeping and supplications (*feryad ve figan sal*), burn and cut off their roots (*köklerini kurut, köklerini kes*) and bring their affairs to an end (*işlerini bitir*). (Popp, 2013; Abu Khalil, 2014)

'Gülen calls here for the killing of 50,000 people', observes journalist Çiler Fırtına chillingly (Fırtına, 2011).

The Gülenists deny this account now – although it is interesting that there is now no archival copy of Gülen's 2011 original speech on their own websites. Yet even the Gülenists admit that in the speech Gülen 'suggested that there should be military operations targeting PKK members' (*Today's Zaman*, 31 August 2012). And Gülen sympathizer Max Farrar concedes regarding Gülen's stance that 'He does, however, say that those Kurds who use military methods in support for their claim for independence should be met with an overwhelming military response by the Turkish state' (Farrar, 7 November 2012).

A pro-PKK source asserts that Gülen contends:

> let us say there are 15,000 or 50,000 of them. So [addressing the Turkish state], you have around … a million intelligence personnel. I don't want to mention them all by name but you have several intelligence organizations; you are member of NATO; you are involved in cooperative projects with a number of international intelligence organizations… So, use these projects and programs and localize, identify and triangulate every single of them and then kill them all one by one… (Soleimani, 2011)

Gülen's tirade caused quite a stir in Turkish Kurdistan. He appeared to realize that he might have gone too far. A further article on his official website stressed that Gülen had not cursed all the Kurds, only the PKK. Yet even this version – the video of which features very obvious cuts at all the crucial points – contains a toned-down segment of a passage from the original speech in which Gülen calls for the destruction of the PKK by the Turkish military. Thus, Gülen asks God: *birliklerini boz, evlerine ateş sal, feryad u figan sal, köklerini kes, kurut ve işlerini bitir* (destroy their unity, burn their houses to ash, dry their roots and bring their affairs to an end). Gülen's audience can be clearly heard on the recording vocally approving his rhetorical supplications to God (fgulen.com, 2012; Gülen, 2011).

In February 2012 the Istanbul prosecutor attempted to question MİT boss Hakan Fidan – an 'Erdoğan confidante' – about alleged 'links' to the PKK. The pro-Gülen media supported the prosecutor's fanciful initiative. Erdoğan viewed the move as a direct political attack on him. Around the same time he apparently began demoting suspected Gülenist police chiefs. The special-authority courts, supposedly controlled by Gülenist judges and prosecutors, were eliminated (Akyol, 2014: 2–3; Gursel, 2013). Over the following twelve months the deepening conflict between the Gülenists and the AKP government evolved into an open war, with Gülen himself apparently comparing the government to a dictatorial 'Pharaoh' (Gursel, 2013).

Gülen's Hikmet movement is yet to show its real power in Turkey, for the simple reason that he has never mobilized all his supporters in an all-out push for power. He is an extremely cautious player – but one who has never lost sight of his goal of a Turkey reorganized along lines dictated by him. His most significant power plays are only now being uncovered. They include alleged complicity in a military coup plot – 'Ergenekon' – to overthrow the AKP government.

Ergenekon

The Ergenekon conspiracy highlights those state institutions – primarily the high judiciary and the military hierarchy – that must remain neutralized if peace between Kurds and Turks is to prosper in Turkey (Tezcur, 2011). This intrigue also demonstrates how Turkey's deep state, the Gülenists and the generals have colluded to derail the PKK/Ankara peace process.

Since the establishment of the Turkish Republic in 1923, Turkey's Kemalist armed forces have considered themselves its guardian. 'Kemalism' – the praetorian political doctrine that began with Kemal Atatürk himself – asserts that the military has both the right and the responsibility to intervene in affairs of state at critical junctures, in order to guarantee the system's continuance (White, 2000: 130). The Ergenekon coup plotters' principal planning document explicitly evokes the armed forces' responsibility to protect Turkey's secular Kemalist nature (*Taraf*, 2010). The AKP's accession to power in 2002 allegedly provoked senior military officers to draw up an elaborate scenario in 2003 – entitled *Balyoz* (Sledgehammer) – involving the creation of a strategy of tension. *Balyoz* aimed to create widespread fear, to manipulate public opinion into supporting a military coup (*Taraf*, 2010). It has to be remembered that Turkey is no stranger to such plots. Turkish *kontrgerilla* used the same approach to justify the 1980 military coup, racking up public hysteria about 'separatist terrorism' (Ganser, 2005a). According to the extensive documentation seized by Turkey's Counterterrorism Department, *Balyoz* explicitly states that its model is a strategy to generate tension leading up to a coup (Young Civilians and Human Rights Agenda Association, 2010: 34; *Taraf*, 2010).

Combatting so-called Kurdish 'separatism' was never the only objective of the Ergenekon conspirators, who were at least equally concerned about the rise of Islamic religiosity in Turkey (Altunişik, 2005; Sakallioğlu, 1996: 231–51; Saktanber, 2002) and the potential ramifications this might have for the demise of their beloved secular state – but the Kurdish question remains a central concern, nevertheless. For this reason, key conspirators have included senior figures in key paramilitary bodies tasked with liquidating the PKK – the Jandarma İstihbarat ve Terörle Mücadele and the Özel Harp Dairesi (ÖHD – Special Warfare Department) (Mavioglu, 2008; *Hürriyet Daily News*, 15 January 2009).

Even before taking power, Erdoğan was well aware of the fate of previous so-called 'Islamist' governments in Turkey at the hands of the Kemalist military establishment and appears to have been determined not to share his predecessors' fate. Accordingly, soon after the first AKP government assumed office on 14 March 2003, it began undermining the military's autonomy and political power, using the cover of reforms demanded by the European Union as part of Turkey's accession to EU membership.

The government established oversight and control of military extra-budgetary spending and removed military representatives from the Radio and Television Supreme Council (RTÜK) and the Council of Higher Education (YÖK), where they supposedly protected Turkey from 'Islamism' and 'Kurdish separatism'. More significantly, the number of military officers on the National Security Council (MGK) was drastically cut from five to one and a civilian secretary-general imposed on it. In addition, the MGK lost its executive authority and was ordered to submit its annual budget to the prime minister. The military was outraged, but was nevertheless compelled to comply, due to the enormous public support – up to 77 per cent – for the EU reforms (Cook, 2010). The AKP government later abolished the heinously unjust state security courts that had been used by its predecessors to persecute Kurds on the pretext of 'fighting terrorism', and drew up a draft constitution that would subject the military to civilian control.

In April 2007 the military tested its declining strength, threatening to intervene should AKP co-founder Abdullah Gül become president. Prime Minister Erdoğan responded with a snap general election, winning 47 per cent of the votes – a landslide win in Turkish terms. Gül became president in August 2007, with the military powerless to prevent it. His enemies within the state responded in March 2008, when the public prosecutor charged the AKP with being 'a centre of anti-secular activity'. The party was found guilty, but the Constitutional Court decided not to ban the party or its leading members from politics (Cook, 2010). But everything changed when a chest of twenty-seven grenades was discovered in an apartment in Ümraniye, prompting intense police and judicial activity. A web of conspiracy was found, beginning with retired junior officer Oktay Yıldırım, who had originally placed the grenades in the apartment, but leading to the top of the Genelkurmay (Esayan, 2013: 30).

The Turkish military establishment now endured serious sustained attacks. Police soon uncovered a document entitled *Ergenekon-Lobi* (Ergenekon Lobby), which laid out the first 'detailed accounts' of a terrorist network. The document was discovered on alleged conspirators' personal computers – including that of a retired member of Turkey's Özel Harp Dairesi, Muzaffer Tekin. Tekin confessed to complicity and in turn implicated Fikret Emek, also a retired ÖHD member. Police raided Emek's residence and found long-range weapons, hand grenades, explosives and bomb-making equipment. Police then discovered three further arsenals across Turkey (Esayan, 2013: 30–31).

Hundreds of suspects were detained by the Counterterrorism Department of the Turkish National Police. Some forty-nine generals, admirals and former Turkish navy and air force commanders were charged with plotting a coup against the government (Cagaptay, 2010). In early 2012 the retired former leader of the MGK, General İlker Başbuğ, was arrested for his alleged role in Ergenekon. Başbuğ was specifically charged with 'gang leadership' and seeking to remove the government by force

(*National Turk*, 2012). Several four-star generals (including Şener Eruygur, Hurşit Tolon and Özden Örnek) were then arrested for co-leading the conspiracy – marking the first occasion that coup plotters have faced judicial sanction in the history of the Turkish Republic (Esayan, 2013: 39, 40). Those accused of plotting to overthrow the government and of membership of a terrorist organization also included the former chief of military staff, retired general İlker Başbuğ (Esayan, 2013: 29).

The biggest consequence of all these events is that the military has lost its aura of untouchability, to the extent that the AKP government was able to cancel the longstanding Protocol on Cooperation for Security and Public Order (EMASYA) in 2010, under which the military assume control of law and order in the event of a governmental breakdown – giving it the legal framework for military intervention (Taspinar, 2010; Park, 2010).

A new protocol became law in mid-2013, allowing governors to call for military units in the event of social incidents in a province. This supposed 'civilian' version of the EMASYA protocol permits military units to intervene in a social incident if demanded by a governor (Zibak, 2013). Other regulations and bylaws can still be deployed by the Turkish military if it wishes to intervene directly in politics – such as Article 35 of the army's internal service regulations, which allows it to 'protect' the state from Islamic 'fundamentalism' and Kurdish 'separatism' (Taspinar, 2010). Nevertheless, the abolition of EMASYA has enormous symbolic value, displaying publicly the decline of the military's once unassailable position of power and respect.

The chief prosecutor of Erzincan, İlhan Cihaner, was arrested on 17 February 2010 for allegedly being an player in the Ergenekon plot. In retaliation, the chief prosecutor of Erzurum – who had ordered Cihaner's arrest – was then dismissed by the ultra-Kemalist Hâkimler ve Savcılar Yüksek Kurulu (HSYK

– Supreme Board of Judges and Prosecutors). Accusing the HSYK of undermining the Ergenekon prosecutors, the AKP swiftly restructured the HSYK, rationalizing this as a requirement if Turkey were to satisfy the process of accession to the European Union (Park, 2010).

The military fought back against the arrests of alleged military coup plotters, apparently attempting to influence legal proceedings, alleging a conspiracy against the military. This followed an appellate court's decision to uphold 237 convictions, with prison sentences of up to twenty years for complicity in the 'Sledgehammer' plot, in October 2013. The court also released a number of the jailed defendants (Peker, 2013; 2014). A handful of the generals caught up in the Ergenkon trials appealed to the European Court of Human Rights (ECtHR). The ECtHR ruled that the Ergenekon network was 'a criminal organization working to overthrow the government' – the identical verdict reached by Istanbul's 13th High Criminal Court (Esayan, 2013: 37). Markar Esayan concludes that the Ergenekon network was clearly 'no ordinary criminal organization but a concise strategy that the country's old elite class formulated to cling onto power' (Esayan, 2013: 35–6).

On 17 December 2013 a massive corruption scandal broke, which many see as retaliation against the AKP for its nobbling of the military establishment. Pre-dawn raids targeted eighty-nine people, some of whom are Erdoğan's closest associates. The sons of the interior minister and the economy minister were formally charged with bribery and corruption, as were prominent businessmen and a banker (*Daily Star*, 21 December 2013).

Gareth Jenkens suspects that Gülen supporters are behind the corruption investigations: 'The movement wants to intimidate Erdoğan' (Popp, 2013). Referring to these allegations, Erdoğan declared in early 2014 that members of the judiciary were 'seeking to smear innocent people'. 'They call it a big corruption operation', he added, asserting that 'unfortunately, there's a gang that is establishing itself inside the state' (Peker, 2014). He also described it as 'a dirty plot against the national will' (*Daily Star*, 21 December 2013), nothing less than a 'judicial coup' (*Daily Star*, 12 January 2014). 'This conspiracy eclipses all other coup attempts in Turkey. It is a virus bent on taking power' Erdoğan told AKP MPs in mid-January 2014 (Parkinson and Albayrak, 2014; *Kurdish Info*, 2014). Erdoğan alleges that Gülenists in the police and judiciary were plotting to force him from office, by creating a 'parallel state' within the bureaucracy (Parkinson and Albayrak, 2014). Abdullah Öcalan saw the United States' hand in the rise and fall of the Ergenekon conspiracy, commenting:

> Those who were detained in the Ergenekon case are professional soldiers who had been trained by the US since the 1960s as intelligence and counter-guerilla officers. The US told them, 'You screwed up!' and later threw them out with the garbage. (Öcalan, cited in Gürbüz, 2014)

Several observers believe that a power struggle between Erdoğan and Fethullah Gülen is behind the corruption charges (Rodrik, 2014; Akyol, 2014: 2–3). Dani Rodrik – generally a fierce opponent of Erdoğan – concedes that 'the Gülenists' campaign is evidently guided by ulterior political motives and that Erdoğan rightly questioned the prosecutors' motivations' (Rodrik, 2014). If the Gülenists are behind the corruption allegations, the AKP faces a truly formidable opponent. As stated earlier, Gülen's organization wields influence in the judiciary and police. This was almost certainly Erdoğan's justification for his sackings and transfers within the police force and the judiciary.

Turkey's AKP national government had already profoundly antagonized the military establishment and fascist elements organized in Turkey's 'deep state', when Erdoğan irretrievably infuriated these formidable foes by negotiating with Abdullah Öcalan. The prime minister, his party and his government now faced the combined wrath of leading forces in the military, the deep state, fascist organizations and Fethullah Gülen's Hizmet network – with its millions of adherents within Turkey, including an additional two million sympathizers strategically placed in the police force and the Ministry of Justice. For its part, Turkey's deep state was only acting consistently, of course, given that it has sabotaged every attempt by the PKK and (less frequently) Ankara for a peace settlement.

Peace: reality or illusion?

The secret peace negotiations that came to light in December 2012 are the best hope yet of an end to the conflict between Ankara and the Kurds in Turkey. Abdullah Öcalan announced a new ceasefire and broad public support for the peace process was apparent. Of course, all previous PKK ceasefires have ended in failure, but both sides now seem to accept that one or the other achieving military or political victory cannot resolve the conflict.

The current peace process is due, above all, to the PKK leader ceaselessly pushing both the PKK and the AKP towards settlement. It is Abdullah Öcalan who has been responsible for persisting with unilateral, usually fruitless, ceasefires. But his party also contains leaders who have shown a capacity to return to all-out war, and the ascendancy of these men remains a possibility if the peace process seriously falters.

The AKP government prefers peace through a genuine compromise with Turkey's Kurds, but must at all times maintain a difficult and often convoluted posture in the peace process – representing itself as the implacable, active, opponent of 'PKK terrorism' and upholder of the 'Turkish nation', while also promoting reforms to keep the peace process alive.

Real hope exists for lasting peace, but the current process remains highly contradictory. Turkey's responses to the Turkish/Kurdish peace process have especially been mixed. The AKP government remains haunted by the fate of its predecessor 'Islamist' parties, at the hands of the Kemalist military establishment and its fascistic 'deep state' – which has sabotaged every previous attempt at a peace settlement. But the government has worked hard to neuter both the military establishment and the strongly Kemalist high judiciary. Ankara has also taken on the *derin devlet* directly, ending the generals' judicial immunity and jailing senior military figures implicated in the planning for the bloody Ergenekon coup.

The Kemalist military retaliated against Ankara's curbs, with crucial assistance from Fethullah Gülen's shadowy Hizmet – apparently unsuccessfully. Even an attempt to provoke the PKK and its supporters across Turkey and Western Europe into a return to lethal violence failed, due to the PKK's strong leadership of Turkey's Kurds. Indeed, the provocation allowed the PKK to reassert its strength with dignity. Further provocations from Turkish forces opposed to the PKK/Ankara peace process could occur, nevertheless – especially due to machinations by Gülen's Hizmet, which Erdoğan's government has also taken specific steps to curb. It is still unclear whether the measures taken are sufficient to permit the establishment of peace. Nevertheless, it seems that Prime Minister Erdoğan has managed to overcome daunting foes, in the military, the deep state, fascist organizations and the Hizmet network's operatives in the police force and the Ministry of Justice, and managed to subdue them.

SIX

Democratic confederalism and the PKK's feminist transformation

The PKK's ability to transform itself from a classical guerrilla organization inspired by Marxism–Leninism to one seeking a peaceful resolution of Turkey's Kurdish problem rests directly upon the organization's capacity to undertake radical ideological innovation. The present chapter reviews the PKK's ideological journey from striving for an independent Marxist–Leninist Kurdistan to the current position of advocating 'democratic confederalism' by peaceful means. The PKK's equally astonishing feminist transformation is also examined.

From independent Kurdistan to 'democratic confederalism'

Shortly before his capture, the PKK leader successfully focused global attention on Turkey's Kurds – a people of whom the world was largely unaware until then. Turkish government attempts to portray Abdullah Öcalan as a monster were partially undermined by his remarkable transformation of the Partiya Karkerên Kurdistan from a nationalist movement of 'primitive rebels' (with a Marxist–Leninist heritage of sorts), pursuing 'national liberation' via 'armed struggle', to a thoroughly 'modern' movement pursuing 'peace' and even 'democratic confederalism'.

Since Öcalan's capture it has become commonplace to read that he turned from violence only under pressure from his Turkish captors. That is not true; the move away from 'armed struggle' began earlier, with the first PKK unilateral ceasefire in March 1993. Indeed, the PKK contemplated bringing an end to its armed activities before Öcalan's capture curtailed this political evolution.

A PKK unilateral ceasefire began on 1 September 1999 on Öcalan's orders from his prison cell.

Confined in his island prison, the Kurdish leader struggled to end the conflict through his leadership. But Öcalan was by now determined not to repeat the mistakes of the past, and looked for new solutions. In 2005, faced by the reality that over two decades of bloody struggle had seen the political awakening of the Kurds but had not yielded an independent Kurdish state, Öcalan wrestled with the conundrum of the way forward for his movement and his people.

Encountering in prison the writings of the theorist of radical municipalism Murray Bookchin, Öcalan became enthused with the latter's notion of 'democratic confederalism' (*Ideas and Action*, 2 March 2011). Öcalan believes that democratic confederalism offers a way to establish Kurdish national rights, while sidestepping the elusive, bloodstained goal of Kurdish statehood. 'Whereas Marx accepted the nation-state, I do not', he indicated in 2010. The *Serok* continued: 'The reason for the crisis in Europe is the nation-state structure and its mentality' (Öcalan, 2010b). Consequently Abdullah Öcalan initiated debates on democratic confederalism among Kurds. As Joost Jongerden notes, this represented a real 'paradigm shift in [Kurdish] politics' (Jongerden, 2012: 4).

Democratic confederalism maps out a system of popularly elected administrative councils, allowing local communities to exercise autonomous control over their assets, while linking to other communities via a network of confederal councils (Jongerden, 2012: 3; Wood, 2007; Özmaya, 2012).

Bookchin's contribution to this system of community organization is to highlight its societal aspect. In its most developed form, confederalism becomes full-blown 'autonomy', which places 'local farms, factories, and other enterprises in local municipal hands', and in which 'a community … begins to manage its own economic resources in an interlinked way with other communities'. Control of the economy is not in the hands of the state, but under the custody of 'confederal councils', and thus, 'neither collectivized nor privatized, it is common' (Bookchin, 1990, cited in Jongerden, 2012: 3–4). Bookchin, who says he realized long ago that the proletariat is not going to take power anywhere (Biehl, 2012), has in practice transposed the notion of rule by a network of workers' councils (soviets) to the 'post-proletarian-centred' context, by replacing workers with ordinary people.

Öcalan may have discovered this system in the writings of Murray Bookchin, but his advocacy of 'democratic confederalism' is not as novel as might first appear. The concept is arguably the practical working out of a much older concept that arose first in the international Marxist movement in the late nineteenth century under the rubric of 'cultural-national autonomy' or 'national cultural autonomy' (NCA). It is not clear whether either the PKK leader or Murray Bookchin were aware of this controversy among Marxist scholars, but it nevertheless provides a compelling theoretical framework for understanding Öcalan's advocacy of democratic confederalism.

The debate on NCA within the international workers' movement began in the Austrian Social Democratic Party and was led by that party's leading intellectuals (the so-called 'Austro-Marxists'), most prominent of whom were Otto Bauer and Karl Renner. The Russian Bolsheviks polemicized fiercely against them (Löwy, 1976: 87–8; Lenin, 1963b: 503–7, 1964: 34; Stalin, 1913). Other leading Austro-Marxists included Max Adler, Karl Renner and Rodolf Hilferding. Their prescriptions regarding what we know today as NCA were intended to resolve the complex problems of minorities in the Austro-Hungarian Empire (see Bottomore and Goode, 1978: 1–44), but they resonate eerily with the contemporary Kurdish problem as well.

Renner (1918) urged the adoption of overlapping jurisdictions as a means of solving the problems of minorities. He did not accept that 'nations' and 'states' should necessarily be identical, considering that this set up two competing and mutually deleterious dynamics. For, when a majority culture establishes a nation-state, minority cultures are in practice compelled to live in it as if they were members of the majority culture. Inevitably, this produces a separatist territorial dynamic, as minorities seek their own 'self-determination'. Crucially, Renner separated territorial jurisdiction from cultural affiliation, thus allowing space for self-government and collective responsibility in certain spheres. This approach also simultaneously defused national struggle, by sidestepping the territorial imperative for national groups. More recently, theorists of NCA in academia have focused discussion on the option of 'non-territorial cultural autonomy' as an alternative to the old 'national cultural autonomy'.

Transformation into an autonomist movement of democratic confederalism

Öcalan had already concluded that 'real socialism' (Stalinism) and national liberation movements had failed due to their congenital statism. He now told the movement he headed to restructure itself on the basis of the principles of autonomy and democratic confederalism. Between 2005 and 2007 the PKK created the Koma Komalên Kurdistan (KKK – Council of Associations of Kurdistan), later renamed the Koma Ciwakên Kürdistan (KCK – Kurdistan Communities Union), as the umbrella organization of all bodies affiliated to the PKK in Kurdish communities in Turkey, Iran, Iraq, Syria and the diaspora.

Following a lead from Turkish authorities, the Turkish media immediately labelled the KKK/KCK 'the urban extension of the PKK' (İstegün, 2011). *Today's Zaman* journalist Aziz İstegün disagreed, pointing out that the PKK was actually 'just a piece of the overarching KCK, a fragment of the whole'. By forming an alternative to the official organs of justice, management and politics in Turkey, Syria, Iran and Iraq, the KCK 'provides a roof under which its supporters can gather'. The KCK has reportedly 'spread out to cities, towns, neighborhoods, streets, village organizations, communes and homes' (İstegün, 2011; see also Akkaya and Jongerden, 2011: 159 n12).

With the aim of organizing itself from the bottom up in the form of assemblies, the Koma Ciwakên Kürdistan advocates radical democracy, presenting this as an alternative to the nation-state. This is 'self-determination in a new form, namely, based on the capacities and capabilities of people themselves' (Jongerden, 2012: 4). KCK is thus 'a movement which struggles to establish its own democracy, neither grounded on the existing nation-states nor seeing them as the obstacle' (PKK, 2005, cited in Jongerden, 2012: 4).

The practical organizational framework of the KCK is set out as an agreement between its participants, *sözleşme*, also known as 'the Constitution of Kurdistan'. This envisages the KCK as a 'democratic, social and confederal system' with members and its own judiciary, which 'tries to gain influence on central and local administration'. The KCK is seen as an umbrella organization for the Kurds in all parts of putative Kurdistan (Democratic Turkey Forum, 2012).

The Istanbul Special Authority Public Prosecutor's Office has produced a number of charts that purport to show the KCK's democratic confederalist structure. Given that the PKK's sworn enemies produced these, they cannot be considered completely trustworthy, but they are interesting nevertheless. The charts claim that, in addition to its central and provincial leaderships, the KCK also has a 'justice commission', a 'social area', a 'political area', an 'ideological area', a women's movement and a 'financial area'. There are assemblies for each region, as well a 'democratic town assembly'. Five councils exist to represent the Kurds living in Turkey, Iraq, Iran, Syria and in countries other than these. In addition to the PKK, included are its affiliated political parties in other parts of Kurdistan and its armed wing the HPG, as well as civil society organizations. All the councils mentioned previously are represented in a 300-member KCK parliament, called Kongra-Gel (the name was briefly used for the PKK, but it now describes a much more significant entity) (Democratic Turkey Forum, 2012; *Haber Türk*, 2011; *Prohayat*, 2014; T.C. İstanbul Cumhuriyet Başsavcılığı, 2011–12).

Kurdish engineer Ercan Ayboga suggests that 'there are [democratic confederal] assemblies almost everywhere' in Turkish Kurdistan. He claimed that some assemblies even exist in Istanbul. Assemblies are at a number of levels. Ayboga describes the structure at the most basic grassroots levels, in which the neighbourhood assemblies in each local community choose the delegates that constitute the city assembly – which is the next level. For 'decisions on a bigger scale', he continues, 'city and village assemblies of a province come together'. The Demokratık Toplum Kongresi (DTK – Democratic Society Congress) is the next level up (Biehl, 2011). The DTK brings together all Kurds within Turkey: 'It consists of more than five hundred civil society organizations, labor unions, and political parties – they make up 40 percent of its members; 60 percent of its members are delegates from village assemblies' (Biehl, 2011).

This bottom-up model can be represented as follows:

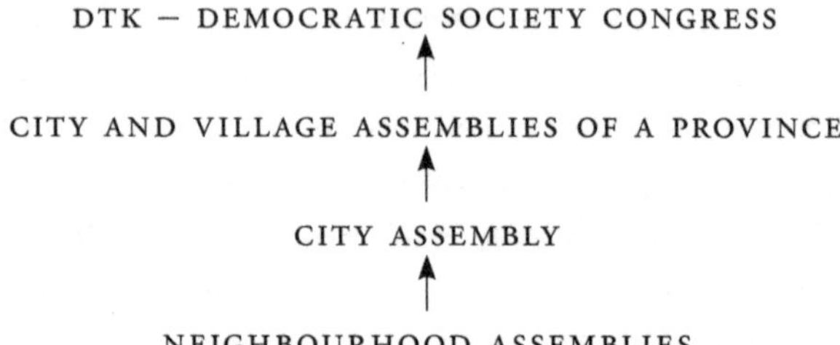

Ayboga claims that in Hakkâri and Şırnak provinces – where 'the people don't accept the state authorities' – 'two parallel authorities' exist, with the democratic confederal structure being more powerful in practice (Biehl, 2011). However, repression of the KCK has taken a heavy toll, and Ayboga admits that 'the assembly model has not yet been developed broadly'. He gives reasons for this: 'in some places the Kurdish freedom movement is not so strong. Almost half of the population in Turkey's Kurdish areas still do not actively support it. In those places there are few or no assemblies' (Biehl, 2011).

An investigation by a group of German leftists who visited Turkey's Kurdish areas and interviewed many Kurds attempting to put democratic confederalism into practice reveals that KCK/PKK supporters attempting to build the new autonomist structures inside the shell of the old society are expending an enormous amount of energy. The authors admit that the Kurds have not yet managed to build stand-alone structures that are completely independent of the Turkish nation-state, although the existing democratic confederal structures do demonstrate a potential counter-power to that state (Tatort Kurdistan, 2013).

Repression of the KCK

Beginning on 14 April 2009 (İstegün, 2011) the Turkish state arrested thousands of those centrally involved in the KCK experiment, due simply to the fact that its inspiration was the PKK (Human Rights Watch, 2012). The KCK detainees included around 190 elected mayors and municipal councillors (Gursel, 2013). It is noteworthy, however, that of the almost 8,000 people imprisoned on charges of being KCK members, 5,000 were workers and activists of the legal Kurdish Peace and Democracy Party (BDP) (Gursel, 2013). The arrestees were charged with 'membership of PKK front organizations' (Jenkins, 2010).

Trials of the accused began in 2010, resulting in a handful of detainees being released. Courts resolved fairly quickly that the KCK was to be regarded legally as the political branch of the PKK (*Today's Zaman*, 28 February 2012). Both Turkish and international human rights organizations heavily criticized the trials (İnsan Hakları Ortak Platformu, 2011).

The PKK and women

The PKK's attitude to its women militants has always differentiated it from other Kurdish parties. Yet the theoretical stance and practice of the *Apocular* on this question have continued to undergo the most radical evolution.

When it began life as an orthodox Marxist–Leninist party, the PKK initially adopted the thesis of Marx's closest collaborator Friedrich Engels, which located the emergence of social classes in society in the appearance of private property, following the break-up of the initial 'primitive communist' human communities

(Engels, 1884). According to Engels's book *The Origin of the Family, Private Property and the State*, the essential precondition for this social inequity was the 'world historical defeat of the female sex'. He continued:

> The man took command in the home also; the woman was degraded and reduced to servitude, she became the slave of his lust and a mere instrument for the production of children. (Engels, 1884)

Women now occupied a 'degraded position' and Engels denied emphatically that this position was changing with time. This subjugation could only be overcome with the disappearance of society based on social classes. Basing himself heavily on Lewis Henry Morgan's *Ancient Society* (1877), Engels accepted the latter's assessment that 'the exclusive supremacy of the man shows its effects first in the patriarchal family' (Morgan, 1877: 474, cited in Engels, 1884). He argued that women under capitalism remained oppressed in their relations to men, since marriage is a form of exclusive private property, declaring: 'Within the family he is the bourgeois and the wife represents the proletariat' (Engels, 1884).

In Engels's analysis, economic deprivation created by capitalist industrialization forced women into capitalist production as workers. As economically exploited wage slaves (proletarians), just like their husbands – although they were paid for their labour as little as half what their spouses earned – women were condemned to depend on their husbands. Unequal at work and unequal at home, women under capitalism were thus doubly oppressed.

The PKK adapted this analysis at its foundation, recognizing that Kurdish women were oppressed, first, as Kurds by colonialism, and then also as women (Rygiel, 1998: 117; *Isku*, 1997). In the PKK's understanding, Turkish colonialism connives with Kurdish feudalism to keep women ignorant and tied to the home (*Isku*, 1997). Abdullah Öcalan himself compared women's oppression in Kurdish society to Kurdistan's national oppression, calling for a 'double liberation' (McDonald, 2001: 148).

According to the PKK's 1995 programme, women in Kurdish society are acknowledged as being 'excluded from social life, often do not attend school' and are 'kept away from political life'. Internalizing their subordinate role as colonized subjects, they find their slavery 'normal'. '[B]ought and sold like a commodity', they are 'exchanged for money and viewed as property' (*Isku*, 1997). The PKK repudiated 'the slave-like suppression of women', declaring that a 'national, independent, democratic society, ruled by the people, must be established' (PKK, 1995), in which

> All forms of oppression against women will be stopped, and the equal status of women and men in the society will be realized in all areas of social and political life. Women, who possess an enormous social revolutionary dynamic, will be mobilized towards this aim. (PKK, 1995)

A congress of PKK women had been held in late 1992. One controversial decision made at this meeting was to seek to change the internal PKK regulation prohibiting fighters from being married. Denouncing this as 'liquidationism', Abdullah Öcalan ruled that the congress's decisions were null and void (*Zagros Newroz Aryan Kurdistan*, 2012; *Isku*, 1997). There was a further International Kurdish Women's Conference on International Women's Day, 8 March 1994 (Rygiel, 1998: 117).

On International Women's Day 1995 in Metina on the Turkish–Iraqi border, the first official Congress of PKK Women was held. The Congress elected a 23-member executive, which subsequently founded the Tevgera Jinen Azadiya Kurdistan (TJAK – Kurdistan Women's Freedom Movement). The TJAK later changed its name to the Yekîtiya Jinen Azadiya Kurdistan (YJAK – Association of Free Women of Kurdistan). The current name of the PKK women's association and army is Yekîtiya Jinen Azad (YJA STAR – the Free Women Units). 'STAR' is a melding of the name of the pagan goddess Ishtar and the Kurdish word *sterk*, meaning star. Öcalan explains: 'For me, Ishtar is *Star*. In fact, *star* in Kurdish is *sterk*. *Star* means star in the European languages.' The origins of the word are Kurdish, from Mesopotamia, according to Öcalan, who tells women to become goddesses, promising 'that new (and respected) [desexualized] boundaries of female identity are closely associated with the refusal of any other love than that of the homeland' (Öcalan 1999: 34–5). He emphasizes that women's respectable participation in the liberation movement is wholly dependent upon women developing an ardent love for their homeland, and fighting for it (Çağlayan, 2012: 17, 19). Rapperin Afrin, a commander of the YJA STAR women's army, explains that the Yekîtiya Jinen Azad acts independently within the PKK, adding: 'The women's movement is the most dynamic part of the PKK. We are aware that without the liberation of women a liberated society cannot be developed' (Dolzer, 2013).

By 2008 independent reports emerged citing a total figure of 10,000 PKK fighters – of whom between one-third and one-half half were women (Marcus, 2007: 173; *CNN*, 2008; Taylor-Lind, 2010). The growth in female recruitment surged following the *Serok*'s decision to speak out boldly in support of women's rights (Marcus, 2007: 173).

The PKK's feminist transformation

From the early 1990s Öcalan began averring that the Kurdish movement's 'basic responsibility' is to 'liberate women'. He criticised the PKK for its failures towards women, continually complaining – to cite Aliza Marcus's account – that Kurdish women 'were treated like slaves, their lives governed and restricted by their fathers, brothers, and other male relatives' (Marcus, 2007: 173). Öcalan insisted that the PKK's revolutionary fight would be impossible without the presence of Kurdish women 'who had broken with the prejudices of traditional life', becoming imbued with an immediate sense of their own worth (Marcus, 2007: 173).

As increasing numbers of women joined the PKK and its military wing, PKK ideologues, and even some of the party's supporters, claimed that women in the organization confronted opposition from men wanting to maintain their positions of power in the party. Such men, it was asserted, did not accept women as commanders, hindering the development of independent women (*Isku*, 1997).

The PKK 1995 programme explains that, in order to break down gender roles solidified by centuries, women 'had to be on their own', so they could believe in themselves and develop strength and willpower. The independent women's army thus 'represents the strength and power of women; they are here to learn self-confidence to take responsibility and power' (Kurdeng, 1995; Arbeiterpartei Kurdistans, 1995, cited in *Isku*, 1997). Even before then, in 1993, Abdullah Öcalan had declared the objective of forming a PKK women's army. The PKK's Fifth Conference resolved:

> Eventually, an independent Women's Army of women fighting in the ARGK will be created, and women's units and command structures will be developed to the point where they can operate independently. (Kurdeng, 1995)

From 1995 separate units of female guerrillas were formed, which had their own headquarters. The Yekîtiya Jinên Azadiya

Kurdistan was founded at this time. From late 1992 the PKK was reportedly organizing suicide operations, principally conducted by its women fighters, in Tunceli, Adana and Sivas (*Hürriyet*, 13 August 1997). One of the most famous of this series of suicide bombings was the operation on 30 June 1996 in which Zeynep Kınacı (Zilan) blew herself up in a Dêrsim military parade of Turkish soldiers who were singing the Turkish national anthem. Zilan's attack reportedly killed ten Turkish soldiers and seriously wounded a further forty-four (PKK, 1996; *Zagros Newroz Aryan Kurdistan*, 2012).

The Turkish state contemptuously dismissed Zilan and her comrades as mere 'women terrorists' (Republic of Turkey, 2011). Suicide operations are by definition brutal for all involved. The PKK explains this event:

> After Turkish Military Intelligence attempted an assassination of Kurdish leader Abdullah Öcalan in Syria, Zeynep Kınacı (Zilan), took the decision to avenge this attempt and to also protest against the Turkish regime's savage and 'dirty war' against the Kurdish people in Turkey that was being hidden from the outside world. (PKK, 1996)

The PKK justified such operations with the same logic that informed its engagement in political violence, such as guerrilla attacks upon military targets: the Kurds of Turkey faced genocide and the humiliating denial of their identity by the Kemalist state apparatus. Some analysts believe that emotional states such as humiliation can indeed explain the recourse to suicide terrorism (Fattah and Fierke, 2009: 24). Of course, suicide bombings often target civilians, an act more difficult for organizations to justify. However, as Jonathan Fine explains, the PKK's suicide attacks targeted government and military installations, instead of populated areas. He adds: 'Suicide bombing was never a major component of its terrorist operations; it launched only fifteen suicide attacks between 1995 and 1999, some of which were particularly deadly' (Fine, 2008).

The first PKK suicide attack in the mid-1990s took place in the midst of considerable state brutality against Kurdish victims, not only in terms of lives lost but also the complete destruction of countless Kurdish villages, resulting in some 4 million people becoming homeless. Paul Gill observes that in 1995 the Turkish army claimed it had killed more than 1,100 PKK guerrilla fighters in Iraqi Kurdistan alone. He notes that 'Some analysts posit that the first suicide bombing by the PKK, occurring in early 1996, was a response to this' (Gill, 2013: 86).

Of the fifteen PKK suicide bombings that took place between 30 June 1995 and 5 July 1999, fourteen of the suicide bombers were women, none of whom was older than 27 (Ergil, 2000: 82–3; Beyler, 2003; Zedalis: 2004: 2). Leyla Kaplan was the youngest of the bombers, being only 17 years of age, in June 1996. The first female PKK suicide bomber was apparently pregnant (Zedalis: 2004: 2). Clara Beyler argues that women's entry into combat operations and suicide attacks meant that they 'would not be defined as a man's subordinate anymore'. In contrast to the very limited domestic role that traditional Kurdish society offered them, the PKK provided them with a 'productive' role for the first time (Beyler, 2003; Ergil, 2001: 105–14, 118–28). Thus, Dogu Ergil argues, 'young Kurdish women began to look to the PKK not only for ethnic liberation, but for their own emancipation as well.' Furthermore, as women they were less suspicious to security forces, making them attractive to the PKK for these operations (Ergil, 2001: 83–4). The PKK carried out suicide operations from the mid- to late 1990s. The bombings peaked with the brief violent wave of PKK attacks following Abdullah Öcalan's capture in February 1999, before stopping with the reimposition of the ceasefire.

PKK women's organizations

Rengin, who commands a female battalion, joined the PKK at the age of 14. She says she enlisted to fight for both Kurdish and women's rights: 'We want a natural life, a society that revolves around women – one where women and men are equal, a society without pressure, without inequality, where all differences between people are eliminated' (*Truthhugger*, 2008). The fighter continued:

> Women grow up enslaved by society. The minute you are born as a girl, society inhibits you. We've gone to war with that. If I am a woman, I need to be known by the strength of my womanhood, to get respect. Those are my rights. And it was hard for the men to accept this. (*Truthhugger*, 2008)

Expounding the *Serok*'s concept, the PKK publication *Serxwebûn* avers that in present-day Kurdish society a woman's relationship with a man results in her brain and heart being 'locked in a dungeon', inducing in her a 'slave personality', instead of allowing her to develop freely. The article notes Öcalan's call for men with all forms of 'slave personalities' to resolve their contradictions with the female identity, relating to women based on freedom and equality. Truth and beauty are thus revealed principles for men. *Serxwebûn* concludes that 'every man and woman' should be responsible for the fight against women's slavery in 'all areas of society', in order to successfully organize the democratic Kurdish nation's 'mentality and institutions' (*Serxwebûn*, 2012).

By 1997 there were reportedly some 5,000 women in the women's army, while 11,000 women continued to fight in mixed units. By this time the women's army had its own commander-in-chief, as well as its own plans and actions. A decision of the PKK National Women's Congress in March 1995 agreed that PKK women should create their own infrastructure (education, health care, military structure, and so forth) (*Isku*, 1997).

The Fifth Congress of the PKK (8–27 January 1995) encompassed a substantial elaboration of the party's position on the 'women's issue'. Conference delegates included an unprecedented 63 women out of a total of 317 present. The conference discussion stressed the role of women's participation in the revolution, reaching detailed decisions (APS/Central Committee of the Kurdistan Workers' Party, 1995).

If Kurdish women can be released from their oppression as women, argues the PKK's 1995 analysis, 'this will ensure the development of social equality and freedom in the true sense' (*Isku*, 1997). Nevertheless, unlike most of the parties that had been dominated by pro-Kremlin Marxism–Leninism, the PKK did not assume 'that the revolution will automatically be accompanied by the liberation of women'. The PKK considered that in order for that to happen women needed to have their own independent basis in autonomous institutions, and fostered the creation of these organizations. The women's associations associated with the PKK are now coordinated by one overseeing body, the Koma Jinên Bilind (KJB – High Women's Council). There also exist an affiliated women's party, the Partîya Azadîya Jin a Kurdistan (PAJK – Party of Free Women in Kurdistan), grassroots mass organizations, the Yekitiyên Jinên Azad (YJA – Unions of Free Women) as well as YJA STAR, the women's guerrilla army, discussed above (Koma Jinên Bilind, 2011; Jongerden and Akkaya, 2013: 165 n7).

As already noted, in 1995 the PKK declared that the function of the PKK women's army was to facilitate women becoming confident in their own strengths and in their ability 'to take responsibility and power', despite centuries of patriarchal oppression (Kurdeng, 1995; Arbeiterpartei Kurdistans, 1995, cited in *Isku*, 1997). In a book edited by Nesrin Esen, Öcalan argues that the existence of all-male armies is indicative of women's oppression and the reality that Kurdistan must overcome this inequality if it is to be free (Öcalan, 2002). The *Serok* argues that the way to begin this was the creation of the PKK's women's army.

Handan Çağlayan's (2012: 8) Western feminist analysis implies that Öcalan's advocacy of women's liberation was from the start targeted at winning the freedom of Kurdish women from the constraints of the traditional Kurdish family, in order to secure their active participation in the Kurdish national movement. Nevertheless, Çağlayan also concedes that Öcalan fundamentally subverted traditional Kurdish notions of women's role and place in society (2012: 8–10). Öcalan redefined Kurdish (and Middle Eastern) conceptions of 'honour' (signified by the Arabic term *namus*), which requires a woman to be obedient, faithful and modest. As Dilek Cindoğlu (2000) argues, women's virginity in the region is far from being the relatively minor, purely personal question it has become in the West, being a virtual social phenomenon there. Öcalan radically switched the focus of *namus* from concern for the protection of women's bodies to concern for the defence of the Kurdish homeland. The *Serok*'s redefinition of *namus* was successful – being accepted by ordinary Kurds – enabling women to freely leave home and to actively participate in demonstrations (including violent clashes with security forces) and join the PKK (Çağlayan, 2012: 8–11).

The party resolved to actively recruit women to its ranks, so that by the end of the 1990s some 30 per cent of members were women. In the party's guerrilla camps, these women 'worked, trained, and fought on equal terms with the Kurdish men, sometimes becoming camp commanders'. Moreover, equal participation by women in the party's rank and file apparently challenged 'the male dominated power structures so present in the rest of Kurdish society' (McDonald, 2001: 148).

Surbuz, a young PKK guerrilla when she joined the PKK in 1993, told a British journalist in 2007:

> There is a lot of pressure in Middle Eastern society, in Kurdistan especially, on women from the father, the mother and the brothers… Mothers and sisters, they are made to live in the man's house. I do not want to be like that. (Haynes, 2007)

Many young women decided to join the PKK in order both to break out of patriarchal oppression and to escape the violence of Turkish soldiers (Rote Zora, 1995). Rote Zora, a leftist/feminist German terror cell that carried out several bombings of its own between 1977 and 1995 in West Germany, cites a young female PKK guerrilla from the mid-1990s: 'At home, my father gave the orders, and when he wasn't there, my brother did. In the guerrilla, I can decide things for myself, perhaps even become a commander!' (Rote Zora, 1995). Certainly, some observers suggest that many Kurdish women see the party as the mainspring for both national and women's liberation (*Isku*, 1997; McDonald, 2001: 148; Ergil, 2000: 83).

Women have been a part of the PKK's fighting force since the insurgency began in 1984. At first the Turkish army did not take the women fighters seriously, claims Surbuz (*Truthhugger*, 2008). However, she observes,

> Then they realised that the women are as tough if not tougher than the men… After this the soldiers stopped distinguishing between the male and the female fighters. I think they are now more afraid of the women because the women are more disciplined and they will never surrender… We will either kill or be killed… For me it is freedom, success or death. It is simple. (*Truthhugger*, 2008)

Çağlayan (2012: 23) emphasizes the PKK's feminist reorientation and its determined efforts to recruit women fighters and promote the importance of gender equality within the Kurdish movement – including at the organizational level. Writing from a PKK base in Iraqi Kurdistan, journalist Deborah Haynes reports that women 'play a crucial role in the PKK', adding:

> The best women fighters are also able to climb up the ranks to positions of command, with the 'self-defence' armed wing of the PKK operating an obligatory 40 per cent female quota. (Haynes, 2007)

She observes:

> Treated as equals by their male counterparts on the battlefield as well as in the political arena, women fighters are trained to use Kalashnikovs, grenades and other weapons before being dispatched in mixed and single-sex units. (Haynes, 2007)

Deniz Gökalp (2010) notes that PKK women possess agency in the organization, based on their political consciousness and aptitude for striving for national, social and gender justice. Early in the twenty-first century, however, women remained 'largely absent in the upper echelons of party power' (McDonald, 2001: 148). However, this began to very quickly change, and Kurdish women are now 'prominent in the PKK's leadership council' (Yildiz, 2013). The PKK elected two new joint leaders at a conference held between 30 June and 5 July 2013: in place of Murat Karayılan, the conference selected Cemil Bayık and a woman, Besê Hozat. The conference – convened to consider the PKK's political and organizational structures – also agreed to increase the proportion of female party members to 40 per cent (Kurdpress New Agency, 2013; Shekhani, 2013).

The PKK's radical reorientation on the 'woman question' involved fundamental rethinking within the organization. This extended to a complete remaking of the PKK's Median national myth. Identification with the ancient Medes as the mythical ethnic predecessors of the modern Kurds (Wahby, 1982: 2–3;

Minorsky, 1986: 438–86; White, 2000: 14) is utilized by almost all Kurdish political parties. Yet the PKK alone has been successful in exercising this discourse. The *Apocular* not only linked the Kurds to the Medes, but extended the story to the 'patriotic' resistance of the Median/Kurdish blacksmith Kawa and thence to the PKK's contemporary struggle (Sayın, 1998: 96–8). The Kawa parable was thus established as a central PKK foundational myth.

By the late 1990s, however, the PKK began replacing the Kawa parable with another ancient myth – that of Ishtar the goddess. Both stories stress the modern Kurds' unbroken connection with ancient Mesopotamia, thereby rationalizing an unbroken historical national myth of Kurdish identity. The Ishtar myth adds a new dimension, however: a 'historical period and structure in which women were active' (Çağlayan, 2012: 2).

The patriarchal domination of men over women was denounced. Women were urged to be independent: 'Do whatever you need to do for self-determination as a sex' (Öcalan, 2000: 120, cited in Çağlayan, 2012: 13). Meanwhile men were ordered to cease their patriachal domination. Öcalan advocates (ethically) 'killing the man', which he asserts is 'the fundamental principle of socialism'. This means that one strives 'to kill power, to kill one-sided domination' (cited in Sayın, 1998: 61, and Çağlayan, 2012: 17). The *Serok* told men that they were 'the main problem' – they exercise dominance over women to prove their manhood – and that 'This is a dominion of crude power; I found it foul and I shattered it' (Öcalan, 1999: 30, cited in Çağlayan, 2012: 13). Çağlayan (2012: 12) argues that Zilan's 'suicide protest' in 1996 was the crucial catalyst that transformed the PKK's 'constitutive myth' from the symbolism inherent in the nationalist self-sacrificial liberation parable of the male Kurdish 'Kawa the blacksmith' to a legend now based wholly within Kurdish womanhood; in the new myth, the 'liberators' mission' is assigned to women. Zilan was thus elevated not only to the pantheon of martyrdom, but also to the status of goddess (Çağlayan, 2012: 16) by Öcalan, who declared: 'When Zilan's identity was revealed, old manhood was entirely dead' (Öcalan, 1999: 108).

As goddesses, the *Serok* implies, women fighters in the movement are both superior to men and the bedrock of the movement. Öcalan elaborates that the Yekîtiya Jinen Azadiya Kurdistan stands for 'the attainment of the highest possible sentiments for one's country. This means that even if everyone gives up on their country, YJAK continues the struggle' (Nurhak, 2013). This stands in stark contrast to the conception of national liberation advocates, of which Franz Fanon (1965) is the paradigm. Fanon famously asserts that colonialism renders colonized men impotent. In a manner radically at odds with that of the PKK leader, he thus conceptualizes the anti-colonial struggle as 'men reclaiming their manhood' (Çağlayan, 2012: 6).

PKK deputy commander Mustafa Karasu summed up in mid-2000 the PKK's evolving understanding of women's role in the Kurdish revolution. Basing himself on Abdullah Öcalan's recent teachings, Karasu wrote in the party organ *Serxwebûn* that women in the Soviet Union had achieved significant gains in economic, political and social life – in fact, 'the most advanced bourgeois-democratic rights'. Due to a certain 'narrow approach', however, there was a 'lack of freedom and democracy in the Soviet Union', he insisted. Therefore, he argued, a 'new approach' to the 'women's question' was formulated by the PKK and Chairman Apo (Karasu, 2000).

This comprehensive approach involves women and men striving together for the national democratic revolution, Karasu and Öcalan assert, since the feminist approach of women fighting by themselves is inadequate for the achievement of such a revolution.

Nevertheless women must be in the front line of the 'national democratic revolution', to solve the considerable theoretical problems (Karasu, 2000). (Interestingly, Karasu here still uses the obsolete terminology of 'national democratic revolution' that Stalin misappropriated from Marx, although he appears to have otherwise absorbed his leader's evolved teaching on the role of women in the Kurdish national movement.) 'The leadership given to the liberation of women by the PKK and Chairman Apo is very important and goes beyond the contributions developed by the women's liberation movement', states Karasu. He asserts that the PKK's approach overcomes the shortcomings of the former Soviet paradigm, adding that his party's approach is relevant for women globally (Karasu, 2000).

Karasu insists that 'the most basic measure' of the Kurdish revolution's achievements is the transformation in Kurdish women: 'Women of the PKK's movement see themselves as a force for the liberation of not only women but of all of humanity' (Karasu, 2000). He concludes:

> The PKK martyr Zilan (Zeynep Kınacı) was a model who undermined male domination. The actions of women comrades, the real owners of the struggle for freedom and revolution, add to the spirit of the PKK, deepening the understanding of revolutionary freedom. Women's issues not only concern woman but men also. (Karasu, 2000)

Of course, the new women's movement that has emerged over the past dozen or so years throughout Turkish Kurdistan is not just based in the PKK's own organizations – although the PKK apparently does have significant influence over the movement. The Demokratik Özgür Kadın Hareketi (DÖKH – Free Democratic Women's Movement), for instance, was founded in 2003. It organized the '1st Middle East Women's Conference' jointly with the Demokratık Toplum Kongresi (DTK – Democratic

Society Congress) between 31 May and 2 June 2013 in Amed. The DTK is a legal platform for Kurdish NGOs and political organizations in Turkey (Tatort Kurdistan, 2013: 127; Association for Women's Rights in Development, 2013). The Conference, organized around the slogan 'Woman, Life, Freedom' (*Jin, Jiyan, Azadi*), managed to arrive at common standpoints on 'racist nation-state structures, the hegemonic capitalist system, and problematic approaches to women by religions and political Islam which are instrumentalized by tyrannical powers' (Association for Women's Rights in Development, 2013).

The principal force in the DÖKH appears to be the BDP, and both the DÖKH and the BDP are heavily influenced by Abdullah Öcalan's politics of feminized democratic autonomy. When a small group of German radical leftists journeyed to Turkish Kurdistan in 2011 they spoke with elected members of the municipal government in one region. One city councillor told the German collective: 'Democratic Confederalism [autonomy] means that the society is organized by women, that the society's mentality is changed, and that taboos are broken' (Tatort Kurdistan, 2013: 127). Gülbahar Örnek, the mayor of the Sûr municipal council, told the Tatort collective that projects organized with the municipality's assistance teach women 'what Democratic Autonomy is' (Tatort Kurdistan, 2013: 131).

A radical transformation

The PKK began its political and ideological existence as a classical guerrilla organization whose ideological axis was a variant of Marxism–Leninism, with the perspective of an independent Kurdistan carved out of the Turkish state by 'people's war'. By 1993 it was showing signs of change, when it quietly dropped the demand for an independent Kurdish state and began speaking about Kurdish autonomy – without fixing the form that this would take. As we have seen, Abdullah Öcalan later theorized this as 'democratic confederalism', leading to self-managed Kurdish autonomy within the borders of the Turkish state, after encountering the radical municipalism of Murray Bookchin.

The year 1993 also saw the beginning of a leap in female recruitment, following the *Serok*'s decision to speak out boldly in support of women's rights and his declaration regarding formation of a PKK women's army. The PKK's intriguing feminist transformation since then is no less astounding than its evolution towards the perspective of democratic confederalism. The rapid theoretical and practical feminist transformation of the PKK testifies to its deep commitment to this new world-view. But it does not necessarily follow that traditional Kurdish society will accept this 'women's revolution' for itself, simply because it agrees with the PKK about Kurdish nationhood.

In the name of repudiating 'the slave-like suppression of women', the PKK has transformed itself into a feminist movement. This has been done by encouraging women to believe in their own strength and abilities, through forming their own autonomous organizations at every level of the PKK movement. So far, this feminist project has been highly successful within the PKK itself, but there is no indication that it has affected traditional societal values – especially in the rural areas that comprise most of Kurdistan, which largely continue to be bound by customary Islamic standards regarding the value of family life and women's role within this. The PKK could well face resistance to its modernist notions of women's emancipation in the future from traditional Sunni Kurdish Muslims. The very secular PKK might not be aware of it, but most women in conservative Kurdish society value their traditional role. To them it seems very strange when the PKK tells them that their values are 'backward' or 'colonialist'.

SEVEN

Coming down from the mountains

The PKK emerged from racist provocation, Kurdish economic under-underdevelopment, as well as from Turkish leftism and Kurdish 'primitive nationalism'. A more or less orthodox 'guerrilla Marxist' organization emerged, founded on orthodox Marxism–Leninism. At first quite small and unsophisticated, it has blossomed over time to become a pan-Kurdish political formation, with affiliated organizations in Europe, North America and Australia, capable of mobilizing many thousands onto the streets of Turkish Kurdistan, and in some of Turkey's cities, as well as in Europe. In Turkish Kurdistan it has eclipsed all its rivals and gained mass support.

The PKK's charismatic leader Abdullah Öcalan has evolved the party's ideology, so that Marxism is now largely sidelined in the organization, which now mobilizes its affiliates and supporters to struggle peacefully for 'democratic confederalism'. Perhaps most surprisingly of all, the PKK has been guided by its imprisoned *Serok* to become a feminist party, in which women and women's self-organization and leadership are prized above all.

It has been shown that a leader of an 'inspirational' type (such as Öcalan) generally symbolizes his national group's conviction that it is a 'great' people. He must regularly demonstrate his ability for this greatness to be realized, by finding new ways forward, thus continuing to inspire followers. So far, against tremendous odds, Öcalan has achieved this. Even after he was captured by his enemies, Öcalan continued to personally symbolize the aspirations of his supporters, while still seeking ways to energize and motivate them, in a very flexible manner. Through their warm personal relationship with their *Serok*, his members and supporters have come to believe that they were already, in a sense, 'liberated', or at least 'experiencing' Kurdistan.

From terrorists to legitimate rebels?

Though serving life imprisonment, Abdullah Öcalan is still considered to be the organization's leader. The present author has suggested (White, 2000: 213–16) that his physical absence, together with his crucial failure to designate a successor, created the possibility of serious internal disputation inside the PKK in the future. That is indeed what has occurred.

A leadership council, initially comprising Osman Öcalan (the *Serok*'s brother), Cemil Bayık, Nizamettin Taş, Murat Karayılan, Duran Kalkan and Mustafa Karasu, took over the running of the movement, but soon 'split into hardliner and reformist camps', as the party initially spun downwards in a spiral of crisis (Cagaptay and Koknar, 2004; see also Mango, 2005: 55). After the *Serok*'s capture, it transpired, PKK 'militants were physiologically and psychologically defeated, and the organization came to the point of dissolution' (Dönmez and Enneli, 2008: 4).

In 2004 Nizamettin Taş, Shahnaz Altun and Osman Öcalan split from the PKK, establishing a new political organization, the Partiya Welatparezen Demokraten Kurdistan (PWDK – Patriotic and Democratic Party of Kurdistan), together with fourteen other cadres, including another leader, Kani Yılmaz, and some thirty fighters. The trio accused Abdullah Öcalan of being a 'despot comparable to Stalin or Hitler', claiming that he ordered the murder of a number of dissidents. They also condemned him for giving up the historical goal of his party – the independence of Kurdistan – following his capture. Osman Öcalan further denounced the PKK as a terrorist organization (Dönmez and Enneli, 2008: 4; Cagaptay, 2007; *Turkish Daily News*, 17 September 2004).

Abdullah Öcalan responded to the split by urging Osman Öcalan and his group to return to the Kongra-Gel, assuring them of protection. At the same time, he heavily criticized Cemil Bayık, Rıza Altun, Duran Kalkan and others (Hevidar, 2004). In the event, the PWDK venture was unsuccessful, and Osman Öcalan duly reconciled with the PKK (Cagaptay, 2007). However, he split from the organization again, and henceforth remained politically inactive. Cemil Bayık's continuing authority rests very much upon his ability to successfully embody the *Serok*'s charisma.

It was clear at the time of Öcalan's capture that the violent conflict between Ankara and PKK militants would become immeasurably worse in the immediate future. Indeed, there are still observers who insist that 'Weapons in the hands of militant cadres and mountain cadres' (*Dağ kadrolarının elindeki silahların ve bu militan kadroların*) will determine the fate of all the PKK's projects (Kaya, 2012). The soundness of this position remains to be seen. But what is clear is that Öcalan's ability to lead his movement and his people to a peaceful resolution of the Kurdish conflict in Turkey rests upon a number of factors. The first of these has already been dealt with: Öcalan's continued ability to function as the *Serok*. Three other factors could prove crucial: (i) the continuing impoverishment of Kurdish eastern and south-eastern Turkey; (ii) the effects of the Arab Spring on the Kurdish national movement in Turkey; and (iii) the PKK's ability to maintain its new path of avoiding bloodshed and revenge.

Economic factors

Kurdish nationalist activity is the practical manifestation of a whole complex of contradictions, including certain types of religious feeling, inter- or intra-tribal tensions, inter-ethnic pressures, and economic issues arising from modernization. Of these, economic pressures seem to be particularly important, in turning 'on' or 'off' other factors.

Over the past thirteen years, Turkey's central authorities have continued to allow the country's Kurdish region to remain 'under-underdeveloped' while effectively excluding the Kurds themselves from citizenship. Yet the contemporary Kurdish national movement arose among Turkey's Kurds due to worsening impoverishment following Turkey's economic 'modernization'. Turkey continues to struggle with the process of economic development. The economic crisis of 2008–09 was the country's fifth in thirty years (Uygur, 2010: 1). The economy recorded the sharpest quarterly GDP decline of the last three decades, at –14.3 per cent. The unemployment rate averaged 10.7 per cent between 2005 and 2014, reaching an all-time high of 16.1 per cent in February of 2009, according to the Turkish Statistical Institute. The number of unemployed persons totalled 2.8 million in February 2014. The non-agricultural unemployment rate was 12.1 per cent, and the youth unemployment rate hit 17 per cent (Trading Economics, 2014c).

It is extremely difficult for countries running a large external deficit to avoid subsequent stresses (*The Economist*, 4 April 2012). Turkey's external debt reached 43 per cent of GDP in 2010, falling slightly to 40 per cent in 2011. Between 1989 and 2013, Turkey's external debt averaged US$1.54 billion, reaching an all-time high of US$3.73 billion in September of 2013 (Trading Economics, 13 February 2014b). Inflation remains high – at 7.75 per cent in January 2014 (*Trading Economics*, 13 February 2014a) – making it difficult for the government to repay debts, especially if interest rates need to be raised, which is likely, and could precipitate a serious economic crisis, with worrying implications for internal stability (Uygur, 2010: 3). A large current-account deficit makes Turkey vulnerable to a shift in global market sentiment (*The Economist*, 2013).

Veteran observers are only too aware that these pressures are being felt most keenly in the Kurdish region. Nurcan Baysal argues that 'armed conflict and forced migration' have combined to cause people of the region to be 'utterly pessimistic' about their future (Baysal, 2008). Baysal adds: 'During the AKP Government, the situation in eastern and south-eastern Anatolia has worsened in terms of the rates of poverty, unemployment and education-training' (Baysal, 2008). A small number of Turkey's industrialists and merchants (including a number of wealthy AKP supporters) have earned huge incomes from massive industrialization and growth in trade. Meanwhile the Kurdish east and south-east remain under-underdeveloped and Kurds there have been steadily impoverished due to inflation. In such circumstances, social unrest was inevitable (Amarilyo, 2012: 3–4).

On 16 April 2010 brick workers in eleven factories in Amed staged a wildcat strike over their low wages. The strike spread spontaneously and lasted for six days, until the workers succeeded in securing a 28 per cent pay increase (*Libcom.org*, 22 April 2010). The following year, workers in Amed defied a heavy police presence (including an overhead helicopter) to march on International Workers' Day (May Day) on 1 May 2011. The march was convened in Amed by the trade-union confederations KESK, DİSK, TMMOB, Türk-İş and TTB (Kahraman, 2011: 182). In Wan, 460 municipal workers staged five one-day strikes in 2013, seeking the right to belong to their trade union. On 7 July the city council agreed that nine workers who were sacked after ten days would return to work and that the workers' trade-union rights would be upheld (Uluslararası İşçi Dayanışması Derneği, 2013). It seems certain that further workers' strikes will occur in this region, due to its deepening economic distress.

On the other hand, there is some hope for economic justice. The peace process has already resulted in some positive economic benefits for the Kurds. Thus, in 2012 alone,

> over 500 new investment applications were made in eastern Turkey. As violence has stopped, more corporations and entities are becoming interested in investing in the region. According to the Minister of Economy, from June 2012 to June 2013 5,126 domestic Investment Incentive Certificates worth TL68.5 billion were issued. This created employment opportunities for 187,478 people. (*Sabah*, 30 January 2014)

Unfortunately, most Kurds in south-eastern Anatolia are yet to experience the benefits of such investment. The Five Year Development Plan for the period 2007–13 'assigns no priority to the region in terms of development and indicates no specific effort to eliminate regional development disparities' (Baysal, 2008). Since 1985 several economic packages for the region have been launched, but most investment goes to the Güneydoğu Anadolu Projesi (GAP, or Southern Anatolia Project). GAP will supposedly create up to 3.8 million new jobs in the region and increase local agricultural yields (GAP, 2006). Yet GAP will not be the economic and political salvation that Ankara continues to promote it as. GAP consists of several massive projects centring on energy production, which involves the irrigation of 17,000 square kilometres of Kurdish land, affecting Adıyaman, Gaziantep, Urfa, Merdin, Amed and Siirt.

Some local Kurds will undoubtedly benefit from the project – but not those in the direst need. Flooding is displacing entire villages. And, while compensation is paid to the owners of flooded land, this ignores the sharecroppers who cultivate the land, who receive only small sums for their houses. This has provoked new migration to the western part of Turkey. Irrigation from the project has therefore tended to have only negative social and economic effects on inhabitants of rural Turkish Kurdistan. Already suffering chronically stunted development long before GAP was even envisaged, the region has been unable to capitalize upon it economically or in terms of industrial development. Energy produced through GAP will therefore tend to flow to the west of Turkey, not to Turkish Kurdistan (Franz, 1989: 187–98). And right from the start, workers employed on the project have come from outside the Kurdish region (Kafaoğlu, 1991: 44–5). Representing not so much a modernization of Turkish Kurdistan as a further modernization of the west of Turkey, GAP is of little direct economic benefit to the inhabitants of Turkish Kurdistan.

A 'Turkish Spring'?

A so-called 'Turkish Spring' erupted in May 2013 in Istanbul's Taksim Gezi Park, and quickly spread through the country. However, this movement – although potentially significant— represents a very heterogeneous attempt to extend democracy. In reality it is no Turkish Spring, for the very obvious reason that it is not an uprising aiming at the revolutionary overthrow of a dictator. It is a potentially significant moment but it represents at most an attempt to reconstruct citizenship and unleash democratic identities (Sadiki, 2013). Having experienced this brief moment of rebellion against perceived autocracy, it is not impossible that this diverse movement might resurrect itself against any future anti-democratic putsches – including ones that seek to destroy the possibility of peace between Turks and Kurds.

It might also be argued that the eventual collapse of Syria's al-Assad regime 'could possibly turn the "Arab Spring" into a "Kurdish Spring" in Turkey with the help of the PKK', using a newly liberated Syrian Kurdish autonomous region as the springboard (Noi, July 2012: 23). Öcalan might not support such a development, but the experience of the 1990 *serîhildan* in Turkish Kurdistan has shown that Turkey's Kurds are now quite capable of acting autonomously in emergent circumstances, when the *Serok* is unable to provide leadership. In such circumstances, the PKK's Hêzên Parastina Gel fighters would inevitably be drawn into the conflict. Then, just as in 1990, the PKK would declare that it had initiated the uprising, in order to assume its leadership. This assertion would contain a grain of truth: without the PKK's almost three decades of political, cultural and military struggle, Turkish Kurds would not have developed consciousness of their Kurdish identity.

Return to armed conflict?

On 8 February 2014 Abdullah Öcalan emphasized to visiting BDP MPs three immediate objectives for the faltering peace process: the implementation of a legal framework for the negotiations, the formation of third-party oversight bodies, and a permanent commission to oversee the negotiations under eight general headings. 'If the AKP does not take a step now the political cost will be very heavy from their perspective. In the past those who did not solve the Kurdish problem disappeared', Öcalan is reported to have said (*Kurdistan Tribune*, 2014). The Turkish government, for its part, continues to declare its support for the peace process. On the other hand, it failed to punish members of the military who shot and killed unarmed civilians in Yakacık in Amed's Lice district on 29 June 2013 and in Gewer on 6 December 2013 (*ANF News*, 29 June 2013; *Hürriyet Daily News*, 7 December 2013). The state claims that the Yakacık victims were hit by ricochets from warning shots, after protestors rather than the soldiers opened fire (Karaca, 2013; Democratic Turkey Forum, 2013). In Gewer, Kurds who rushed to the local hospital where the shooting victims were being treated were alarmed when special operations teams surrounded the building with armoured vehicles. Police teams also threw tear-gas canisters into the hospital, having broken the windows and doors with their guns. The governor of Hakkâri later released a statement claiming that two men were accused of attacking police at the demonstration with heavy weapons and explosives, forcing the police to respond (*Efendisizler*, 2013).

For the moment, Öcalan's extraordinary 'democratic confederalism' project has captivated his supporters and the movement's membership. If the peace process does not result in any tangible progress towards this goal, his reputation could be seriously weakened and the PKK could once again resort to its Kalashnikovs, RPGs and M16s. History shows that this is a possibility. The outbreak of the spontaneous 1990 *serîhildan* in Turkish Kurdistan was arguably a warning sign that the Kurdish population was dissatisfied with the efforts of Öcalan and the PKK. It is likely that the PKK (or at least its Hêzên Parastina Gel fighters) would consider that there was no other option – if it wishes to retain popular Kurdish support – but to resume 'armed struggle', should the *Serok*'s 'democratic confederalism' project be perceived to be failing.

Despite numerous unsuccessful ceasefires, and an estimated 45,000 deaths, the PKK abandoned armed struggle on 31 December 2012, in the sincere hope of securing a lasting peace.

Turkish responses to the Turkish–Kurdish peace process in the past were – with some notable, partial, exceptions – negative, due to the crushing weight of the state's Kemalist praetorian ideology. Atrocity has been heaped upon bloody atrocity by the Turkish military in Turkish Kurdistan. Abdullah Öcalan admits that the PKK has also been guilty of atrocities against innocent people, but such instances are few compared to the Kemalist military's deeds.

It is obvious that the current peace process is highly contradictory. Overwhelming Kurdish support for the process was apparent when Öcalan's peace message in Amed was read out to over a million of his supporters on 21 March 2013 (Dalay, 2013). Yunus Akbaba, an analyst with Turkey's SETA Foundation, argues that the peace process continues not only due to support from political actors such as the AKP, the PKK and the BDP, but also because of 'the push of public will'. Political analysts have also drawn attention to strong public support for the process. Opinion polls indicate that Turkey-wide support for the peace process stands at 70 per cent (Ünal, 2014).

Nevertheless, in order to succeed the Serok's bold scheme requires Turkey to accept an ongoing ceasefire – something it has never done in the past. The PKK's democratic confederalism project provides the possibility of finally achieving a successful peace settlement. Following its launch, the PKK declared new unilateral ceasefires between October 2006 and October 2011. However in February 2011 the PKK moved to a stance of 'active defence', in which its fighters defended themselves if threatened, ending a six-month ceasefire (*al-Ahram*, 24 July 2011).

The PKK asserts that it halted its withdrawal from Turkish Kurdistan in September 2013 due to frustration with the government's pace in introducing democratic reforms meant to address Kurdish grievances. The PKK accuses Ankara of not abiding by the terms of the peace deal agreed between the two sides. A

KCK statement added that the suspension of the withdrawal was 'aimed at pushing the government to take the project seriously and to do what is needed'. The PKK demands amendments to the penal code and electoral laws, as well as the right to education in the Kurdish language and a form of regional autonomy. Prime Minister Erdoğan has already stated that a general amnesty for PKK guerrillas (including for Öcalan) and the right to education in Kurdish were not on the table. No deadline had been set for the withdrawal, but a ceasefire agreement reached in March 2013 said that the peace process could not proceed further until it is completed. The PKK nevertheless promised to respect the ceasefire with Turkish forces (*Ekurd Daily*, 25 September 2013; *Hürriyet Daily News*, 9 September 2013).

In mid-October 2013 Turkey's Ministry of Justice prevented BDP co-chairman Selahattin Demirtaş from visiting Abdullah Öcalan in prison. This was significant, as BDP leaders have acted as mediators in the peace process between the PKK and Ankara. Demirtaş was only temporarily barred, after making critical remarks about the AKP government's democratization package. The PKK deputy commander Mustafa Karasu responded angrily on 18 October 2013, stating that Turkey had 'literally stopped the peace process'. 'We did what we had to do', Karasu stated. 'But now we have stopped withdrawing our guerrillas. We will not give up our struggle on mere words from Turkey.' In August 2013 he had warned: 'If Turkey rejects peace and desires war, then the PKK has the right to defend itself. We are ready for everything' (Rudaw, 2013). In late October 2013, reaffirming his determination to bring the peace process to a successful conclusion, Erdoğan declared that whoever ends the peace process will 'pay the price for its actions' (Munyar, 2013).

In January 2014, however, four Kurdish elected BDP MPs and a pro-Kurdish independent were released from prison and permitted to take their places in the parliament, breathing renewed hope into the precarious peace process. The MPs were among thousands of Kurdish politicians and activists detained in 2009 and 2010 for alleged ties to the PKK. One of the released MPs, the BDP's Selma Irmak, told reporters: 'it's really just a first step.' 'There are dozens of mayors and other elected officials still in jail, so for real progress the anti-terror law must change', she added (Yackley, 2014).

As stated earlier, Cemil Bayık has criticized the focus on withdrawal of PKK forces as the solution to the conflict, highlighting that a ceasefire and the withdrawal of guerrilla forces were components in a democratic political solution to the Kurdish question, which would only have meaning if they were the foundation of an emerging 'democratization in Turkey and the Middle East' (*ANF News*, 2 April 2013).

The ruling AKP continues to give out ambiguous signals regarding its commitment to the peace process. Thus, on 6 November 2011 Erdoğan declared that 'there is no question of giving up arms' against the PKK. He threatened the press with prosecution if it continued to denounce the successive raids on pro-Kurdish media. 'Whether in the media or elsewhere, it should pay attention to what is said about the KCK because it amounts to support of terrorism', he warned (*AFP*, 8 November 2011).

The following day Erdoğan claimed that the continuing crackdown on the KCK had led to the imprisonment of a number of its activists, and commented that the PKK wanted to replace the state apparatus in Turkey, telling reporters that 'no one should expect it to end'. The Turkish prime minister continued: 'There is only one state in Turkey, the Turkish State; there may not be a second.' By this stage around 700 alleged KCK members had already been arrested by the Turkish state, according to government figures – and some 3,000 to 3,500 Kurdish activists (*AFP*, 7 November 2011; 8 November 2011; 26 November 2011).

Then, in January 2013, Erdoğan replaced the controversial minister of the interior İdris Naim Şahin with a moderate from Turkey's Kurdish region. Şahin had adopted a ruthless posture against perceived PKK sympathizers following the 12 June 2011 elections, which the AKP won with 50 per cent of the vote. It was he who instigated the arrests of alleged KCK members (Gursel/*Al-Monitor Turkey Pulse*, 27 January 2013), notoriously prodding police to respond brutally against opposition demonstrations. As one journalist commented: 'Police brutality against demonstrators, primarily their use of pepper gas, had never been so widespread' (Gursel, 2013).

Following his appointment as Şahin's replacement, Minister Muammer Güler told the press: 'We will fly peace doves in the south-east. We will continue to work for happiness, security and welfare of everyone' (Gursel, 2013).

Speaking to Nuçe TV on 2 April 2013, Cemil Bayık, a leading member of both the PKK and the KCK, emphasized that ceasefire and withdrawal of guerrilla forces were both part of a democratic political solution to the Kurdish question. He criticized focusing on the withdrawal of PKK forces. Bayık insisted that the PKK's ceasefire and withdrawal would only be worthwhile if they facilitated the flowering of democratization in Turkey and the region (*ANF News*, 2 April 2013).

In a small but nevertheless symbolic gesture, Turkish security authorities permitted 20,000 of Abdullah Öcalan's supporters to gather in the PKK leader's village of Amara (Ömerli), to celebrate his sixty-fourth birthday on 4 April 2013, following his appeal for a ceasefire. Similar gatherings had been roughly dispersed by the authorities in previous years. PKK supporters sang and danced until late into the night and called for 'freedom for Öcalan' (Çiftçi, 5 April 2013; *AFP*, 4 April 2013).

In a message sent from prison and read before the crowd, Öcalan claimed that the possibility of an honourable peace was more real than ever and referred to the 'rebirth' of the Kurdish community in Turkey. 'Let not a drop of blood be shed during the settlement process', he added (*Today's Zaman*, 4 April 2013).

Prime Minister Erdoğan, for his part, in April 2013 criticized Turkey's parliamentary opposition parties who opposed the peace process, claiming that his Justice and Development Party (AKP) had 'always been alone on the path'. He also conceded that abuses against Kurds in Amed prison after the 1980 coup created conditions in which the PKK was able to thrive, saying that those responsible for such abuse were 'as guilty as those who adopted terrorism' (*Hürriyet Daily News*, 4 April 2013).

In what he believes is a practical way to strive for his new perspective, Öcalan advocates a 'Three-Phases Road Map' to resolve Turkey's Kurdish problem. The first phase of this envisages the PKK initiating 'a permanent ceasefire', to be complemented by a 'Truth and Reconciliation Commission' established by the Turkish government and parliament, together with an amnesty and the release of 'political prisoners'. Finally, the KCK would be legalized, making the PKK obsolete (Öcalan, 2011). Öcalan's book *Prison Writings III: The Road Map to Negotiations* (2012) sets out his plan for peace in Turkey in more detail. The best hope for this bold plan succeeding is the wide support for Kurdish–Turkish peace that exists in Turkey, after decades of bloodshed on both sides. It could succeed, although the obstacles confronting it are daunting, as we have seen.

Abdullah Öcalan took the bold step of declaring a new PKK unilateral ceasefire on 21 March 2013. In a statement issued at the annual Newroz celebration, Öcalan affirmed that it was now not time 'for opposition, conflict or contempt towards each other, it is time for cooperation, unity, embracing and mutual blessing' (Dalay, 2013). Most importantly, he also announced:

> I, myself, am declaring in the witnessing of millions of people that a new era is beginning, arms are silencing, politics are gaining momentum. It is time for our [PKK] armed entities to withdraw from the [Turkish] border. (Dalay, 2013)

The PKK's Hêzên Parastina Gel guerrillas began withdrawing from Turkey in early May 2013. An estimated 2,000 PKK fighters withdrew in stages over several months. The first fighters arrived in Northern Iraq's Qandil Mountains. Turkish security forces manned checkpoints along the mountainous border with Iraq, but did not intervene. Prime Minister Erdoğan publicly undertook to ensure that they would not be targeted during the pull-out (Casey and Parker, 2013; Yackley, 2013). By early June 2013 Atilla Yesilada reported that the PKK had 'largely quit the country, but stands ready to pounce back, if the demands of the Kurdish minority are not met' (Yeşilada, 2013).

PKK-initiated ceasefires have come and gone. As indicated above, some have lasted for years, but none has ever succeeded in convincing Turkey's military also to cease its hostilities. Failure could well be the outcome of this new initiative. On this occasion, though, there is some possibility of success. For the first time the Turkish government is openly engaging in peace negotiations with the PKK leader, and the 'moderate Islamist' Recep Tayyip Erdoğan, now the country's president, has staked his political future on this peace gambit.

Erdoğan is known to be a very ambitious man, who does not take risks lightly – his secular Turkish opponents call him 'the new sultan'. He apparently hopes that peace with the PKK will not only stop the destructive war in Turkey's south-east, but also bring great strategic and economic benefits to Turkey, in the context of the civil wars in neighbouring Iraqi and Syrian Kurdistan. It remains to be seen, of course, whether Erdoğan's ambitions will serve the cause of Kurdish–Turkish peace and justice for the Kurds.

President Erdoğan appears to sincerely desire peace, even though he is capable of deviating from his course at times, on account of electoral and other concerns. In what was hopefully a positive sign, Erdoğan's 2014 New Year Message emphasized the peace process with the PKK. He declared that 'new hope, new excitement, new expectations' lay before all Turkish citizens, as they entered the New Year 'with fresh hope' for an end to war (*Milliyet*, 31 December 2013).

The *Serok* has also stated that his fundamental understanding of the resolution of the Kurdish/Turkish conundrum 'rests on a free and equal rearrangement' of relations between the two peoples (Öcalan, 2011). Such ethnic and political rethinking will require the building of trust between Turks and Kurds in Turkey – and beyond. In 1980 the then security chief of Diyarbakır Prison, Captain Esat Oktay Yıdıran, observed that the PKK had 'three legs': the mountains, the prisons and the pro-PKK groups in Europe. Abdullah Öcalan stated on 23 February 2013 that 'the Kurdish problem' had two parts: one in Iraq's Qandil Mountains and the other in Europe. He even addressed a letter to the Kurdish diaspora in Europe (Kurt, 2013). Journalist Ihsan Kurt points out that Europe's 1.5-million-strong Kurdish diaspora is now 'the most radical, out-of-reach actor on the scene'. Diasporas, it has been said, are either wreckers or promoters of peace processes (Østergaard-Nielsen, 2007: 27; Yossi Shain, cited in Kurt, 2013). Today many in the Kurdish diaspora remain deeply suspicious of Ankara, believing that previous opportunities to end the conflict have always been sabotaged by powerful forces within the Turkish state. Nevertheless, despite their concerns, most remain cautiously optimistic about the process. Given that the diaspora accounts for millions of Kurds and has powerful propaganda tools at its disposal, it can just as easily encourage as spoil the peace effort (Kurt, 2013).

The Kurdish issue will remain of major importance for the Turkish state if it remains committed to accession to the European Union. At the EU's request, Turkey has enacted a number of democratization reforms (albeit sometimes hesitantly and incompletely) that benefit the Kurds. Turkey would prefer to be a part of the EU, but the overly long road to accession has seriously dampened its enthusiasm. In the final analysis, Ankara will agree to full democratization primarily for local reasons, not to please the EU bureaucrats. Thus the EU's pressure regarding Kurdish rights and in support of the peace process will be factors influencing Kurdish/Turkish peace, but not decisive.

However, the recent rise of the Islamic State (IS) group (formerly known as ISIS) to control over one-third of Syria and a very large swathe of Iraq adds further complications to the peace process. In Iraq the IS is based in Mosul, which is part of historic Kurdistan, although outside the Kurdistan Regional Government area. As the IS has pushed northwards into the Kurdish region proper, it has clashed with both the Kurdistan Regional Government's Peshmerga army and the fighters of the PKK's affiliate in Iraqi Kurdistan, the PCDK. In Syrian Kurdistan the local PKK affiliate the PYD has also engaged the IS fighters. Freed from the battlefront in Turkish Kurdistan, the PKK has diverted large numbers of its Hêzên Parastina Gel fighters to support both the PCDK and the PYD against the IS.

Accusations that the Islamic State is entering Syria via Turkey have the potential to adversely affect the Kurdish peace process (Cengiz, 2014). Kurdish politician Ahmet Turk, current leader of the Demokratık Toplum Kongresi – a legal Kurdish party inspired by the PKK – has accused Ankara: 'IS has easy access over the border and the state is looking the other way. This makes the Kurds question the sincerity of the peace process' (*Radikal*, 2014).

For its part, the PKK on 5 August 2014 urged all Kurds to take up the fight against Islamic State: 'All Kurds in the north, east, south and west must rise up against the attack on Kurds in Sinjar [in northern Iraq]' (*Radikal*, 2014).

The belief – widespread among Turkey's Kurds – that Turkey is 'tolerating' IS fighters clearly endangers the peace process in Turkey as IS attacks both Syrian and Iraqi Kurds.

Should the current peace process be successful, it is probable that this will enable the PKK to complete its long transition from terrorists to legitimate rebels. As Evren Balta Paker observes, however, autonomy as a solution 'in countries where regional inequalities are deep' requires 'a deep sense of social justice' (Paker, 2013: 5). This will arise in Turkey only when the ethnic majority not only facilitates the demise of Kurdish under-underdevelopment, but also allows the Kurds to live as full human beings with their own identity intact, free from persecution for merely asserting their Kurdishness. If this can be achieved, then the deadly, bloody pattern of bloodletting/fruitless peacemaking/even worse bloodletting that has haunted the Kurdish/Turkish conflict in Turkey may be banished forever.

References

ABC News (1998), Australian Broadcasting Corporation, 18 November, www.abc.net.au.

Abu Khalil, As'ad (2014) 'The Sufi Gülen on Attacking Kurds', 9 January, http://angryarab.blogspot.com/2014/01/the-sufi-gulen-on-attacking-kurds.html.

AFP (1998) 'More Demonstrations in Front of Italian Missions', 17 November, www.hri.org/news/latest/1998/98-11-off-site.old.html.

AK News (2010) 'PKK Has Repeatedly Asked for a Ceasefire of Peace since Their Establishment in the Past 17 years', 6 December, www.aknews.com/en/aknews/9/193730/?AKmobile=true.

Akkaya, Ahmet Hamdi, and Joost Jongerden (2011) 'The PKK in the 2000s: Continuity through Breaks?', in Marlies Casier and Joost Jongerden (eds), *Nationalisms and Politics in Turkey: Political Islam, Kemalism and the Kurdish Issue*, New York: Routledge, pp. 143–62.

Akşam (2012) '1 Numara Karayılan değil Cemil Bayık', 26 August, www.aksam.com.tr/guncel/1-numara-karayilan-degil-cemil-bayik/haber-135007.

Akyol, Mustafa (2014) 'Turkey: What to Expect in 2014', *Al-Monitor*, 2 January, www.al-monitor.com/pulse/originals/2014/01/turkey-gulen-erdogan-akp-elections-pkk.html.

Al-Ahram (2011) 'Three Turkish Soldiers Killed in PKK Rebel Ambush', 24 July, http://english.ahram.org.eg/NewsContent/2/9/17162/World/International/Three-Turkish-soldiers-killed-in-PKK-rebel-ambush.aspx.

Al Arabiya (2010) 'Turkish Troops and PKK Clash Leaves 13 Dead Tuesday', 6 July, www.alarabiya.net/articles/2010/07/06/113161.html.

Al Arabiya (2011) 'Turkey Bombs PKK Targets in Northern Iraq for Third Day, 19 August, www.alarabiya.net/articles/2011/08/19/163060.html.

Al Arabiya (2012) 'Turkish Warplanes Strike Suspected PKK Targets in Northern Iraq', 12 February, http://english.alarabiya.net/articles/2012/02/12/194167.html.

Al Jazeera (2011) 'Timeline: PKK Attacks in Turkey', www.aljazeera. 19 October, com/news/europe/2011/10/20111019164441520246.html.

Al Jazeera (2012) 'Turkey to Pay Reparations for Slain Kurds', 3 January, www.aljazeera.com/news/europe/2012/01/2012122362249813.html.

Altunişik, Meliha Benli (2005) 'The Turkish Model and Democratization in the Middle East', *Arab Studies Quarterly*, vol. 27, no. 1/2, Winter/Spring: 45–63.

Amarilyo, Eli (2012) 'Is Turkey's Economy on the Brink of Collapse?', *Middle East Economy*, vol. 2, no. 3, March, www.dayan.org/sites/default/files/Iqtisadi_Eng_March2012_Amarilyo.pdf.

Anadolu Ajansi (2012) 'Terör Örgütü Çocukları da Katletti', 20 August, www.aa.com.tr/tr/rss/75114--teror-orgutu-cocuklari-da-katletti.

ANF News (19 April 2011) 'BDP Will Announce on Thursday Its Decision on Elections', http://en.firatnews.com/news/news/bdp-will-announce-on-thursday-its-decision-on-elections.htm.

ANF News (2 April 2013) 'Bayık: Legal Assurance Needed for Withdrawal', http://en.firatnews.com/news/news/bayik-legal-assurance-needed-for-withdrawal.htm.

ANF News (29 June 2013) 'BDP: Attack in Lice is a Massacre Attempt', http://en.firatnews.com/news/news/bdp-attack-in-lice-is-a-massacre-attempt.htm.

ANF News (27 November 2013) 'The PKK Foundation in Sakine Cansız's Words', http://en.firatnews.com/news/news/the-pkk-foundation-in-sakine-cansiz-s-words.htm.

ANF News (14 January 2014) 'New Secret Document on Paris Killings Exposed (full text)', http://en.firatajans.com/news/news/new-secret-document-on-paris-killings-exposed-full-text.htm#.UtVp_QPqitg.twitter.

APS/Central Committee of the Kurdistan Workers Party (1995) 'PKK: Central Committee Statement: 5th Congress of the PKK is a Guarantee of Success and Victory!', February, http://mailman-new.greennet.org.uk/pipermail/old-apc-conference.mideast.kurds/1995–June/000906.html.

Arsu, Sebnem (2009) 'Soldiers Killed in Ambush in Northern Turkey', *New York Times*, 7 December.

Arsu, Sebnem (2013) 'Kurdish Rebel Group to Withdraw From Turkey', *New York Times*, 25 April.

Associated Press (2013) 'Kurdish Rebel Leader Calls for Historic Truce', Ankara, 21 March, http://bigstory.ap.org/article/rebel-leader-expected-declare-cease-fire.

Association for Women's Rights in Development (2013) 'DÖKH's 1st Middle East Women's Conference', 13 March, www.awid.org/Library/Call-for-Participation-DÖKH-s-1st-Middle-East-Women-s-Conference-Amed-Diyarbakir-Turkey-31–May-2–June-2013.

Australian National Security (2014) 'Kurdistan Workers Party (PKK)', www.nationalsecurity.gov.au/Listedterroristorganisations/Pages/KurdistanWorkersPartyPKK.aspx.

Aydin, Zülküf (1986) *Underdevelopment and Rural Structures in Southeastern*

Turkey: The Household Economy in Gisgis and Kalhana, London: Ithaca Press for the Durham Centre for Middle Eastern and Islamic Studies, University of Durham.

Bakan, Şahin (2011) '115 Terörist Etkisiz Hale Getirildi Bakan Şahin, Hakkari'de süren operasyonla ilgili açıklama yaptı', 5 August, www.trthaber.com/haber/gundem/bakandan-teror-bilancosu-50956.html.

Barkey, Henri J., and Graham E. Fuller (1998) *Turkey's Kurdish Question*, with a foreword by Morton Abramowitz, Carnegie Commission on Preventing Deadly Conflict, Lanham MD: Rowman & Littlefield.

Bauer, Otto (2000) *The Question of Nationalities and Social Democracy*, ed. Ephraim J. Nimni, trans. Joseph O'Donnell, Minneapolis and London: University of Minnesota Press.

Bayart, Jean-François (1982) 'La question Alevî dans la Turquie moderne', in Olivier Carré, *L'Islam et l'état dans le monde d'aujourd'hui*, Paris: Presses Universitaires de France, pp. 109–20.

Bayır, Derya (2010) *Negating Diversity: Minorities and Nationalism in Turkish Law*, Ph.D. thesis, Queen Mary University of London.

Baysal, Nurcan (2008) 'An Analysis of Socioeconomic Situation in South-eastern Anatolia', http://nurcanbaysal.blogspot.com/2013/10/an-analysis-of-socioeconomic-situation.html.

BBC News (2015) 'Turkey profile – Timeline', 9 June, www.bbc.com/news/world-europe-17994865.

Bekdil, Burak (2008) 'U.S. Applies Terrorist Designation to Kurdistan Freedom Falcons', *Terrorism Focus*, vol. 5, no. 3, 22 January, www.jamestown.org/single/?tx_ttnews[tt_news]=4672&no_cache=1#.U5J_6S9uEaU.

Bell, Alistair (1995) 'Iran Tentatively Backs Turkey's Anti-Plan', *Reuters*/Nexis, 20 June.

Berkan, İsmet (1996) 'Gladioyo'ya MGK Onayi', *Hürriyet*, 9 December, www.bianet.org/bianet/siyaset/5808-gladyoya-mgk-onayi.

Beşikçi, İsmail (1969) *Doğu Anadolu'nun Düzeni: Sosyo-Ekonomik ve Etnik Temeller*, Istanbul: E Yayınları.

Beyler, Clara (2003) Messengers of Death – Female Suicide Bombers, 12 February, www.ict.org.il/Articles/tabid/66/Articlsid/94/currentpage/20/Default.aspx.

Biehl, Janet (2011) 'Kurdish Communalism', 9 October, http://new-compass.net/article/kurdish-communalism.

Biehl, Janet (2012) 'Bookchin, Öcalan, and the Dialectics of Democracy', presentation to the conference Challenging Capitalist Modernity: Alternative Concepts and the Kurdish Question, Hamburg, February, http://new-compass.net/articles/bookchin-%C3%B6calan-and-dialectics-democracy.

Birand, Mehmet Ali (1992) *Apo ve PKK*, Istanbul: Milliyet Yayınları.

Birand, Mehmet Ali (2012) 'Mega Kurdish State is Being Founded', 27 July, www.hurriyetdailynews.com/mega-kurdish-state-is-being-founded-.aspx?PageID=238&NID=26441&NewsCatID=405.

Bongar, Bruce Michael, Lisa M. Brown, Larry E. Beutler, James N. Breckenridge and Philip G. Zimbardo (eds) (2006) *Psychology of Terrorism*, Oxford and New York: Oxford University Press.

Bookchin, Murray (1990) 'The Meaning of Confederalism', *Green Perspectives* 20.

Bottomore, Tom, and Patrick Goode, (1978) *Austro-Marxism*, Oxford: Clarendon Press.

Bozarslan, Hamit (1992) 'Political Aspects of the Kurdish Problem in Contemporary Turkey', in Philip G. Kreyenbroek and Stefan Sperl (eds), *The Kurds: A Contemporary Overview*, London and New York: Routledge, pp. 95–114.

Bozarslan, Hamit (1997) *La Question Kurde: état et minorités au Moyen-Orient*, Paris: Presses de Sciences Po.

Bozarslan, Hamit (2002) 'Kürd Milliyetçiliği ve Kürd Hareketi (1898–2000)', in Tanıl Bora (ed.) *Modern Türkiye'de Siyasi Düşünce*, vol. 4, Istanbul: İletişim Yayınları, pp. 841–70.

Bozarslan, Hamit (2004) *Violence in the Middle East, the Political Struggle to Self-Sacrifice*, Princeton NJ: Markus Wiener.

Brandon, James (2007) *The PKK and Syria's Kurds*, Jamestown Foundation, *Terrorism Monitor*, vol. 5, no. 3, 15 February.

Cagaptay, Soner (2010) 'What's Really Behind Turkey's Coup Arrests?', *Foreign Policy*, 25 February, www.foreignpolicy.com/articles/2010/02/25/whats_really_behind_turkeys_coup_arrests.

Cagaptay, Soner, and Ali Koknar (2004) 'The PKK's New Offensive: Implications for Turkey, Iraqi Kurds, and the United States', Washington Institute for Near East Policy, *Policy Notes* 877, 25 June, www.washingtoninstitute.org/policy-analysis/view/the-pkks-new-offensive-implications-for-turkey-iraqi-kurds-and-the-united-s.

Cagaptay, Soner, and James F. Jeffrey, (2014) 'Turkey's 2014 Political Transition: From Erdogan to Erdogan?', Washington Institute for Near East Policy, Policy Notes No. 17, January, www.washingtoninstitute.org/policy-analysis/view/turkeys-2014–political-transition.

Cagaptay, Soner, and Zeynep Eroglu (2007) 'The PKK, PJAK, and Iran: Implications for U.S.–Turkish Relations', Washington Institute for Near East Policy, 13 June, www.washingtoninstitute.org/policy-analysis/view/the-pkk-pjak-and-iran-implications-for-u.s.-turkish-relations.

Çağlayan, Handan (2012) 'From Kawa the Blacksmith to Ishtar the Goddess: Gender Constructions in Ideological-Political Discourses of the Kurdish People in Post-1980 Turkey', *European Journal of Turkish Studies* 14, www.ejts.revues.org/4657.

Cakan, Seyhmus (2012) 'Turkish Troops Kill 21 PKK Militants in Clashes', *Reuters* US, 23 August, www.reuters.com/article/2012/08/23/us-turkey-kurds-idUSBRE87M0Z620120823.

Çandar, Cengiz (1997) 'Gul: The Army Has Made Its Worst Mistake', *Hürriyet Daily News*, 8 January, www.hurriyetdailynews.com/default.aspx?pageid=438&n=gul-the-army-has-made-its-worst-mistake-1997–08–01.

Çandar, Cengiz (2009) 'The Kurdish Question: The Reasons and Fortunes of the "Opening"', *Insight Turkey*, vol. 11, no. 4: 13–19, http://arsiv.setav.org/

ups/dosya/7987.pdf.
Çandar, Cengiz (2012) *'Leaving the Mountain': How May the PKK Lay Down Arms? Freeing the Kurdish Question from Violence*, Istanbul: TESEV.
Çandar, Cengiz (2013a) 'The Transformation of Öcalan', *Al Monitor*, 6 January, www.al-monitor.com/pulse/originals/2013/01/turkey-kurds-pkk-peace.html.
Çandar, Cengiz (2013b) 'PKKde değişiklik: Nasıl Okunmalı, ne Anlaşılmalı?', 11 July, www.hurriyet.com.tr/yazarlar/23701266.asp.
Candar, Cengiz (2013c) 'Eğer Gerçekten Kürtlerle Savaş değil barış isteniyorsa…', *Radikal*, 24 October, www.radikal.com.tr/yazarlar/cengiz_candar/eger_gercekten_kurtlerle_savas_degil_baris_isteniyorsa-1157032.
Casey-Baker, Mary, and Jennifer Parker (2013) 'PKK Fighters Begin Withdrawal from Turkey after Nearly 30 Years of Conflict', 8 May, http://foreignpolicy.com/2013/05/08/pkk-fighters-begin-withdrawal-from-turkey-after-nearly-30-years-of-conflict.
Casier, Marlies, and Joost Jongerden (2012) 'Understanding Today's Kurdish Movement: Leftist Heritage, Martyrdom, Democracy and Gender', *European Journal of Turkish Studies* 14: 2–10.
Casier, Marlies, Joost Jongerden and Nic Walker (2011) 'Fruitless Attempts? The Kurdish Initiative and Containment of the Kurdish Movement in Turkey', *New Perspectives on Turkey* 44: 103–27.
Celik, Selahattin (1999) *Türkische Konterguerilla. Die Todesmaschinerie*, Cologne: Mesopotamien Verlag.
Cengiz, Orhan Kemal (2014) 'Turkey Wakes up to Islamic State Threat', *Al-Monitor*, 6 August, www.al-monitor.com/pulse/originals/2014/08/cengiz-isis-mosul-iraq-syria-consul-general.
Cengiz, Seyfi (1990) 'Kürdistan İşçi Sinif ve Disk', *Kürdistanlı Marksist* 2–3, February–March.
Cengiz, Seyfi (n.d.) *Türkiye Kürdistanı İşçi Hareketleri*, London: Yeni Gün Yayınları.
Cetinkaya, H. (1996) *Din Baruunun*, Istanbul: Çağdaş Yayayınları.
Cetinkaya, H. (2004) *Fethullah Gülen'in 40 Yıllık Serüveni*, Istanbul: Gunizi Yayıncılık.
Cetinkaya, H. (2005) *Fethullah Gülen'in 40 Yıllık Serüveni*, vol. 2, Istanbul: Gunizi Yayıncılık.
Cetinkaya, H. (2006) *Din Baron'un Kazlari*, Istanbul: Gunizi Yayıncılık.
Cetinkaya, H. (2007) *Fethullah Gülen ABD ve AKP*, Istanbul: Gunizi Yayıncılık.
Cetinkaya, H. (2008a) *Fethullahçı Gladyo*, Istanbul: Gunizi Yayıncılık.
Cetinkaya, H. (2008b) *Soros'un Çocukları*, Istanbul: Cumhuriyet Kitapları.
Cetinkaya, H. (2009) *Amerikan Mızıkacıları*, Istanbul: Cumhuriyet Kitapları.
Cheviron, Nicolas (2013) 'Thousands Gather for Slain Kurds' Funeral', 17 January, www.dailystar.com.lb/News/Middle-East/2013/Jan-17/202616–thousands-gather-for-slain-kurds-funeral.ashx.
Christian Science Monitor (1998) 'Kurds Flee Persecution for 'Sympathetic Shores' of Greece', 12 January, www.csmonitor.com/1998/0112/011298.intl.intl.2.html/(page)/2.

Christie-Miller, Alexander (2010) 'The PKK and the Closure of Turkey's Kurdish Opening', Middle East Research and Information Project, 4 August, www.merip.org/mero/mero080410.

Christie-Miller, Alexander (2011) 'Turkish Bombing Campaign against PKK Signals Shift in Strategy', *Christian Science Monitor*, 23 August, www.csmonitor.com/World/Middle-East/2011/0823/Turkish-bombing-campaign-against-PKK-signals-shift-in-strategy.

Çiftçi, Ali (2013) 'Öcalan's Birthday Celebrated with Messages of Peace', *SES Türkiye*, 5 April, http://turkey.setimes.com/en_GB/articles/ses/articles/features/departments/national/2013/04/05/feature-02.

Cihan (2012) 'Documents on deaths of 33 soldiers in Bingöl go missing', *Today's Zaman*, 14 November, http://en.dunyatimes.com/article/documents-on-deaths-of-33-soldiers-in-bingol-go-missing-71906.html.

Cindoglu, Dilek (2000) 'Virginity Tests and Artificial Virginity in Modern Turkish Medicine', in Pinar Ilkkaracan (ed.), *Women and Sexuality in Muslim Societies*, Istanbul: Women for Women's Human Rights, pp. 215–28.

Ciwan, Sara (2013) 'Karasu ile 1993'ten Günümüze Ateşkes Süreçleri', 23 April, http://rojaciwan.com/tr/rc/karasu-ile-1993ten-gunumuze-ateskes-surecleri.

CNN (2008) 'Inside the PKK's Hidden Camps', 6 October, www.youtube.com/watch?v=CRP-9ZfzY9A.

CNN (2013) '3 Kurdish Women Political Activists Shot Dead in Paris', 11 January, http://edition.cnn.com/2013/01/10/world/europe/france-kurd-deaths.

CNN Türk (2012) 'Şemdinli'de Çatışma: 2 Şehit, 7 Yaralı', 10 September, www.cnnturk.com/2012/guncel/09/09/semdinlide.catisma.2.sehit.7.yarali/676150.0/index.html.

Cook, Steven A. (2010) 'The Weakening of Turkey's Military', Council on Foreign Relations, 1 March, www.cfr.org/turkey/weakening-turkeys-military/p21548?breadcrumb=%2Fregion%2F358%2Fturkey.

Countryeconomy.com (2014) 'Turkey Unemployment Rate', 13 February, http://countryeconomy.com.

Cutler, David, and Jonathon Burch (2011) 'Timeline – Recent Kurdish Militant Attacks in Turkey', *Reuters*, 19 October, http://uk.reuters.com/article/2011/10/19/uk-turkey-attacks-timeline-idUKTRE79I3VN20111019.

Cyprus Mail (2010) 'Kurds Set Up "Tent City" in Asylum Protest', 22 May, www.cyprusedirectory.com/articleview.aspx?ID=19299.

Dağı, İhsan (2013) 'Kurdish Initiatives Compared: Any Difference?', *Today's Zaman*, 20 January, www.todayszaman.com/columnists/ihsan-dagi-304583-kurdish-initiatives-compared-any-difference.html.

Daily Star (21 December 2013; 8 January 2014; 12 January 2014).

Dalay, Galip (2013) 'Where is Turkey in the Kurdish Peace Process?', 28 September, *Middle East Monitor*, www.middleeastmonitor.com/articles/europe/7570–where-is-turkey-in-the-kurdish-peace-process.

Democratic Turkey Forum (2012) 'Backgrounder on the Union of Communities in Kurdistan, KCK', 22 July, www.tuerkeiforum.net/enw/index.php?title=Backgrounder_on_the_Union_of_Communities_in_Kurdistan,_KCK.

Democratic Turkey Forum (2013) '28–30 June 2013 Daily Human Rights Report', 5 July, www.tuerkeiforum.net/enw/index.php?title=28–30_June_2013_Daily_Human_Rights_Report.

Deutsche Welle (2013) 'Kurds Protest over Murder of Activists in Paris', 12 January, www.dw.de/kurds-protest-over-murder-of-activists-in-paris/a-16517596?maca=en-rss-en-eu-2092–rdf.

Dickey, Christopher (2013) 'Omer Güney Cinayet Mahallinde par Haberdesin', *The Shadowland Journal*, 28 January, http://christopherdickey.blogspot.com/2013/01/video-of-omer-guney-suspect-arrested-in.html.

Diehl, Jörg, Özlem Gezer and Fidelius Schmid (2014) 'Paris Investigation: Tensions Grow over Murder of Kurdish Activists', *Spiegel Online*, 12 February, www.spiegel.de.

Dilorenzo, Sarah (2013) '3 Kurds killed in Paris; Political Motive Claimed Thursday', *Associated Press*, Paris, 10 January, www.wtop.com/?nid=220&sid=3187461&pid=0&page=1.

Dolzer, Martin (2013) 'Aus feudalen Strukturen befreien', *Junge Welt*, 4 October, www.jungewelt.de/2013/10–04/005.php.

Dombey, Daniel (2013a) 'Kurdish Deal Would Fuel Turkey's Goals', *Financial Times*, 19 March, www.ft.com/intl/cms/s/0/d9fc1d48–9090–11e2–a456–00144feabdc0.html#axzz2sJu637t3.

Dombey, Daniel (2013b) 'Historic Address from Kurdish Leader', *Financial Times*, 21 March, http://video.ft.com/v/2242967976001.

Dönmez, Rasim Özgür, and Pınar Enneli (2008) 'The Changing Logic of Political Violence: The Case of the PKK in Turkey after the Invasion of Iraq – Violence for Violence's Sake', in Marika Guggisberg and David Weir (eds) *Understanding Violence: Contexts and Portrayals*, Freeland: Inter-Disciplinary Press, pp. 121–32.

Draper, John William (1875) *A History of the Intellectual Development of Europe*, vol. 2, Melbourne, Sydney and Adelaide: E.W. Cole.

Dublin People (2013) 'A Long Way from Home… But New School Hopes to Bring Kurds Together', 11 February, www.dublinpeople.com/article.php?id=2079&l=101.

Dundar, Can (2006) 'Gizlenen örgütün başındaki adam: Sabri Yirmibeşoğlu 'Özel Harp'çinin tırmanış öyküsü', 8 January, www.milliyet.com.tr/2006/01/08/yazar/dundar.html.

Eccarius-Kelly, Vera (2002) 'Political Movements and Leverage Points: Kurdish Activism in the European Diaspora', *Journal of Muslim Minority Affairs*, vol. 22, no. 1.

Eccarius-Kelly, Vera (2011) *The Militant Kurds: A Dual Strategy for Freedom*, Santa Barbara CA: Praeger.

Economist (2012) 'Istanbuls and Bears', 7 April, www.economist.com/node/21552216?frsc=dg|a.

Economist (2013) 'Turkey Erupts: The New Young Turks. Protests against Recep Tayyip Erdoğan, and His Ham-fisted Response, Have Shaken His Rule and His Country', 8 June, www.economist.com/news/briefing/21579005–

protests-against-recep-tayyip-erdogan-and-his-ham-fisted-response-have-shaken-his-rule-and.

Edmonds, Sibil (2011) 'Turkish Intel Chief Exposes CIA Operations via Islamic Group in Central Asia', 6 January, www.boilingfrogspost.com/2011/01/06/turkish-intel-chief-exposes-cia-operations-via-islamic-group-in-central-asia.

Efendisizler (2013) 'Archiv für Dezember 2013', 12 December, http://efendisizler.blogsport.de/2013/12.

EKurd Daily (2013) 'Turkey–PKK Peace Process in Limbo after Kurd Pull-out Halted', 25 September, www.ekurd.net/mismas/articles/misc2013/9/turkey4778.htm.

EKurd Daily (2014) 'Full Transcript of Alleged Recording of Suspect in Paris Kurd Killings', 13 January, http://ekurd.net/mismas/articles/misc2014/1/turkey4925.htm.

Eliassi, Barzoo (2013) *Contesting Kurdish Identities in Sweden: Quest for Belonging among Middle Eastern Youth*, Basingstoke: Palgrave Macmillan.

Engels, Frederick (1884) *The Origin of the Family, Private Property and the State*, www.marxists.org/archive/marx/works/1884/origin-family/index.htm.

Erdem, Suna (1995) 'Grey Wolf is Power Pivot for Ciller', *Reuters* (Ankara), 6 October.

Ergil, Dogu (2000) 'Suicide Terrorism in Turkey', in Boaz Ganor (ed.), *Countering Suicide Terrorism*, Herzliya, Israel: Institute for Counter-Terrorism, pp. 73–88.

Ergil, Dogu (2001) 'Suicide Terrorism in Turkey: The Workers' Party of Kurdistan', in *Herzlia: Countering Suicide Terrorism, An International Conference*, Herzliya, Israel: International Policy Institute for Counter-Terrorism, pp. 105–14, 118–28.

Ersever, Ahmet Cem (1993) *Kürtler, PKK ve A. Öcalan*, Ankara: Milenyum Yayınları Politika Dizisi, http://kitabxana.net/files/books/file/1278322274.pdf.

Esayan, Markar (2013) 'Ergenekon: An Illegitimate Form of Government', *Insight Turkey*, vol. 15, no. 4, Fall: 7–18.

Ethnologue (2015a) 'Sweden', www.ethnologue.com/country/SE.

Ethnologue (2015b) 'Switzerland', www.ethnologue.com/country/CH.

Ethnologue (2015c) 'Austria', www.ethnologue.com/country/AT.

Ethnologue (2015d) 'Norway', www.ethnologue.com/country/NO/languages.

Ethnologue (2015e) 'Italy', www.ethnologue.com/country/IT.

European Parliament (2009) 'Leyla Zana: European Parliament's Sakharov Prize Winner of 1995: Background Note', www.europarl.europa.eu/meetdocs/2004_2009/documents/fd/nt_zana_/nt_zana_en.pdf.

Expatica (2004) 'Dutch police raid "PKK paramilitary camp"', 12 November, www.expatica.com/nl/news/local_news/dutch-police-raid-pkk-paramilitary-camp-13898.html.

Fanon, Frantz (1965) *The Wretched of the Earth*, New York: Grove Press.

Farrar, Max (2012) 'Fethullah Gülen and the Kurdish Question in Turkey Today', 7 November, http://maxfarrar.org.uk/max-blog/blog/

fethullah-gulen-and-the-kurdish-question-in-turkey-today.

Fattah, K., and K.M. Fierke (2009) 'A Clash of Emotions: The Politics of Humiliation and Political Violence in the Middle East', *European Journal of International Relations*, vol. 15, no. 1: 67–93.

Fdesouche (2011) 'Île-de-France: Violences après l'interpellation de trois Kurdes', 5 June, www.fdesouche.com/216599–ile-de-france-violences-apres-linterpellation-de-trois-kurdes.

Fine, Jonathan (2008) 'Contrasting Secular and Religious Terrorism', *Middle East Quarterly*, Winter: 59–69, www.meforum.org/1826/contrasting-secular-and-religious-terrorism#_ftnref39.

Fırtına, Çiler (2011) 'Herr Gülen löst die Kurdenfrage', *Agendakurd*, www.agendakurd.com/index.php?option=com_content&view=article&id=650:herr-guelen-loest-die-kurdenfrage&catid=57:ciler-frtna.

FM News Weekly (2011) 'Turkey's Erdogan Demands Hollande Explain Meeting with Militants', www.fmnewsweekly.com/turkeys-erdogan-demands-hollande-explain-meeting-with-militants.

Franz, Erhard (1989) 'Das "Güneydoğu Anadolu Projesi/GAP" in Stichworten', *Dokumentation der Internationale Konferanz 'Menschenrechte in Kurdistan'*, Bremen: Initiative 'Menschenrechte in Kurdistan', pp. 187–98.

Freely, Maureen (2007), 'Why They Killed Hrant Dink', *Index on Censorship*, vol. 36, no. 2, May: 15–29.

Ganser, Daniele (2005a) *NATO's Secret Armies: Operation Gladio and Terrorism in Western Europe*, London and New York: Frank Cass.

Ganser, Daniele (2005b) 'Terrorism in Western Europe: An Approach to NATO's Secret Stay-Behind Armies', *Whitehead Journal of Diplomacy and International Relations*, Winter/Spring: 69–95.

GAP: Southeast Anatolia Project Regional Development Administration (2006) 'History of Southeastern Anatolia Project', http://web.archive.org/web/20080422165950/www.gap.gov.tr/gap_eng.php?sayfa=English/Ggbilgi/gtarihce.html.

Gediman, M. Fatih (2013) 'PKK Bildirisinde Gözden Kaçan Alevi Ayrıntısı', 13 July, www.hurhaber.com/pkk-bildirisinde-gozden-kacan-alevi-ayrintisi/haber-562411.

Ghareeb, Edmund (1981) *The Kurdish Question in Iraq*, New York: Syracuse University Press.

Gill, Paul (2013) 'Tipping Point – The Adoption of Suicide Bombings', *Psicología Política* 46, May: 77–94.

Gökalp, Deniz (2010) 'A Gendered Analysis of Violence, Justice and Citizenship: Kurdish Women Facing War and Displacement in Turkey', *Womens Studies International Forum*, vol. 33, no. 6: 561–9.

Goktas, Hidir (2007) 'Kurd Rebel Group Deny Carrying out Ankara Attack', *Reuters*, 23 May, www.reuters.com/article/2007/05/23/us-turkey-explosion-id USL2326260920070523?pageNumber=2&virtualBrandChannel=0.

Guardian (2012) 'Turkish Troops Die in Clash with Kurds', 3 September, www.guardian.co.uk/world/2012/sep/03/turkish-troops-die-clashes-kurds.

Gülen, M. Fethullah (2011) 'Terör ve Izdırap – Fethullah Gülen Hocaefendi Bamteli Sohbet Arşivi', 24 October, http://vimeo.com/31138232.

Gülen, M. Fethullah (2012) 'Fethullah Gülen Kürtlere beddua etti mi, Fethullah Gülen Ölüm Emri Verir mi?', 3 January, http://tr.fgulen.com/content/view/20100/172/#mfg9.

Gündem (2014) 'Paralel Yapının Biat Mektupları', 30 January, www.aktuel.com.tr/gundem/2014/01/30/iste-o-mektuplar.

Gündeş, Osman Nuri (2010) *İhtilallerin ve Anarşinin Yakın Tanığı, Kadıkoy*, Istanbul: VPA Grup Basım Yayım.

Gunes, Cengiz (2012) *The Kurdish National Movement in Turkey: From Protest to Resistance*, Abingdon and New York: Routledge.

Gunter, Michael (1990) *The Kurds in Turkey: A Political Dilemma*, Boulder CO, Westview Press.

Gunter, Michael (1997) *The Kurds and the Future of Turkey*, New York: St. Martin's Press.

Gunter, Michael (2011) *Historical Dictionary of the Kurds*, Lanham MD: Scarecrow Press.

Gunter, Michael (2012) 'The Closing of Turkey's Kurdish Opening', 20 September, http://jia.sipa.columbia.edu/online-articles/closing-turkeys-kurdish-opening/#_ednref7.

Gürbuz, Mustafa (2014) 'Drowning the Turkish Watergate, Playing the Kurdish Card', 21 January, www.todayszaman.com/blog/mustafa-gurbuz/drowning-the-turkish-watergate-playing-the-kurdish-card_337159.html.

Gursel, Kadri (2013) 'Kurds Welcome Change of Turkish Interior Minister', *Al-Monitor*, 27 January, www.al-monitor.com/pulse/originals/2013/01/idris-naim-sahin-turkey-interior-minister-replaced.html.

Güzeldere, Ekrem Eddy (2010) 'Kurdish Opening – How Far, How Sincere?', www.academia.edu/1712797/Kurdish_opening_-_how_far_how_sincere.

Haber Türk (2011) 'İşte KCK'nın şeması', 5 November, www.haberturk.com/gundem/haber/685703–iste-kcknin-semasi.

Haynes, Deborah (2007) 'The Kurdish Women Rebels Who are Ready to Fight and Die for the Kurdish Cause', *Kurd Net*, 24 October, www.ekurd.net/mismas/articles/misc2007/10/turkeykurdistan1455.htm.

Heinrich, Lothar A. (1989) *Die Kurdische Nationalbewegung in der Türkei*, Hamburg: Deutsches Orient-Institut.

Hevidar, Lorin (2004) 'Kongra Gel Engulfed by Troubles – Again', 12 June www.kurdmedia.com/article.aspx?id=9659.

Human Rights Watch (2012) 'Turkey: Clampdown on Journalists, Kurdish Activists, Government Critics', 22 January, www.righttoremain.org.uk/coi/turkey-clampdown-on-journalists-kurdish-activists-government-critics.

Hürriyet (13 August 1997; 3 March 1999; 14 March 1999; 25 October 2007; 24 October 2007a; 24 October 2007b).

Hürriyet (2008) 'Bir dönemin acı bilançosu', 16 September, www.hurriyet.com.tr/gundem/9914612.asp?gid=0&srid=0& oid=0&l=1

Hürriyet Daily News (2013) 'PKK Halts Withdrawal but Vows to Continue Cease-

Fire', 9 September, www.goodmorningturkey.com/pkk-halts-withdrawal-vows-continue-cease-fire.

Ideas and Action, 2 March 2011, http://ideasandaction.info/2011/03/interview-with-turkish-anarchists.

İkibine Doğru (1989), 22 October.

Immigration and Refugee Board of Canada (November 1996–April 1998) 'Turkey: Reports of Human Rights Violations Committed by the Turkish Military against Civilians Living in the Bingol Province, Particularly in the Kigi district', www.refworld.org/docid/42df61b11.html.

Imset, Ismet G. (1992) *The PKK: A Report on Separatist Violence in Turkey, 1973–1992*, Ankara: Turkish Daily News Publications.

Independent (2007) 'Turkey "faces choice between democracy and dictatorship"', 9 July, www.flash-bulletin.de/2007/eJuly10.htm#1.

İnsan Hakları Ortak Platformu/Human Rights Joint Platform (2011), 'The Diyarbakır Trial against the KCK', 14 April, www.ihop.org.tr/dosya/diger/20110414_KCK_ENG.pdf.

Institut de Criminologie, Paris (1995) 'Le Party des Travailleurs du Kurdistan, PKK, Chronologie, 1974–1995, Notes and Etudes', October, Embassy of the Republic of Turkey, Washington DC, http://turkey.org/turkey.

Institut Kurde de Paris (2015) 'Diaspora Kurde', www.institutkurde.org/kurdorama.

International Crisis Group (2013) *CrisisWatch* 114, 1 February, www.crisisgroup.org/en/publication-type/media-releases/2013/crisiswatch/crisiswatch-114.aspx.

Isku (1997) 'Zur Geschichte und Politik der Arbeiterpartei Kurdistans (PKK)', *Informationstelle Kurdistan*, www.nadir.org/nadir/initiativ/isku/hintergrund/geschichte/hausarbeitpkk.htm.

İstegün, Aziz (2011) 'Is the KCK a Party, an Organization or an Alternative State Structure?', *Today's Zaman*, 6 November, www.todayszaman.com/news-262009–is-the-kck-a-party-an-organization-or-an-alternative-state-structure.html.

Jafar, Majeed R. (1976) *Under-Underdevelopment: A Regional Case Study of the Kurdish Area in Turkey*, Helsinki: Social Policy Association.

Jamestown Foundation (2008) 'Leading PKK Commander Cemil Bayik Crosses into Iran', 20 May, www.jamestown.org/single/?tx_ttnews%5Btt_news%5D=4938#.VaW4bSqqpBc.

Jamestown Foundation (2009) 'The PKK Extends its Unilateral Ceasefire', 3 June, www.jamestown.org/single/?tx_ttnews%5Btt_news%5D=35077&no_cache=1#.VYDwIFWqpBc

Jenkins, Gareth H. (2007) 'Turkey Weighs Military Options against PKK Camps in Iraq', *Global Terrorism Analysis*, vol. 4, no. 33, 16 October.

Jenkins, Gareth H. (2009) *Between Fact And Fantasy: Turkey's Ergenekon Investigation*, Washington DC: Central Asia–Caucasus Institute and Silk Road Studies Program.

Jenkins, Gareth (2010) 'Target Practice – PKK Militants Attack Turkish Infrastructure', *Jane's Intelligence Review*, 7 September.

Jenkins, Gareth H. (2013) 'The AKP's New Dialogue with Öcalan: A Process but Which Process?', *Turkey Analyst Archive*, vol. 6, no. 1, 16 January, www.turkeyanalyst.org/publications/turkey-analyst-archive/item/21–the-akps-new-dialogue-with-öcalan-a-process-but-which-process?.html.

Jongerden, Joost (2008) 'PKK', *CEU Political Science Journal*, vol. 3, no. 1: 127–32.

Jongerden, Joost (2012) 'Rethinking Politics and Democracy in the Middle East', 5–6 December, http://peaceinkurdistancampaign.files.wordpress.com/2012/12/joost-jongerden.pdf.

Jongerden, Joost, and Ahmet Hamdi Akkaya, (2011) 'Born from the Left: The Making of the PKK', in Marlies Casier and Joost Jongerden (eds), *Nationalisms and Politics in Turkey: Political Islam, Kemalism and the Kurdish Issue*, London: Routledge, pp. 123–42.

Jongerden, Joost, and Ahmet Hamdi Akkaya (2013) 'Democratic Confederalism as a Kurdish Spring: The PKK and the Quest for Radical Democracy', www.academia.edu/3983109/Democratic_Confederalism_as_a_Kurdish_Spring_the_PKK_and_the_quest_for_radical_democracy.

Jongerden, Joost, and Ahmet Hamdi Akkaya (2014) 'The Kurdistan Workers Party and a New Left in Turkey: Analysis of the Revolutionary Movement in Turkey through the PKK's Memorial Text on Haki Karer', *European Journal of Turkish Studies* 14, http://ejts.revues.org/4613.

Jyllands Posten (2006) 'Fakta: Kurdere i Danmark', 8 May, http://jyllands-posten.dk/indland/ECE5105449/fakta-kurdere-i-danmark.

Kafaoğlu, Arslan Başer (1991) 'Proje Mi, Balon Mu?', *Demokrat*, April: 44–5.

Kahraman, Berna (2011) 'Youth Unemployment and Unemployment in Developing Countries: Macro Challenges with Micro Perspectives', http://scholarworks.umb.edu/cgi/viewcontent.cgi?article=1035&context=doctoral_dissertations.

Kanaltürk (2006) 'Interview with Nurettin Veren', 26 June.

Karaca, Banu (2013) 'Suspending the Limits of the Sayable', 31 October, www.culanth.org/fieldsights/402–suspending-the-limits-of-the-sayable.

Karasu, Mustafa (2000) 'Zilan Yoldaş: Ulusal Demokratik Devrimimizin: Zafer Tacıdır', *Serxwebûn*, June, www.serxwebun.org/arsiv/222/files/assets/downloads/page0027.pdf.

Karaveli, Halil M. (2011) 'Erdoğan's War: Will Turkey's Most Powerful Leader since Atatürk Succeed in Securing the Country's Unity?', *Turkey Analyst*, vol. 4, no. 16, 29 August.

Karpat, Kemal H. (1973) 'Structural Change, Historical Stages of Modernization, and the Role of Social Groups in Turkish Politics', in Kemal Karpat (ed.), *Social Change and Politics in Turkey: A Structural-Historical Analysis*, Leiden: Brill, pp. 11–92.

Kavakci, Merve (2009) 'Turkey's Test with Its Deep State', *Mediterranean Quarterly*, vol. 20, no. 4, Fall: pp. 83–97.

Kaya, Serdar (2009) 'The Rise and Decline of the Turkish "Deep State": The Ergenekon Case', *Insight Turkey*, vol. 11, no. 4: 99–113.

Kaya, Zeynep N. (2012) *Maps into Nations: Kurdistan, Kurdish Nationalism and International Society*, Ph.D. thesis, London School of Economics.

Kendal [Nezan, Kendal] (1982) 'Kurdistan in Turkey', in Gerard Chaliand (ed.), *People Without a Country*, with a preface by Maxime Rodinson, trans. Michael Pallis: London: Zed Books, pp. 47–106.

Koma Jinên Bilind (2011) 'The Kurdistan Women's Liberation Movement for a Universal Women's Struggle', www.kjb-online.org/hakkimizda/?lang=en.

Korn, David A. (1995) 'Turkey's Kurdish Rebellion', *Freedom Review*, vol. 26, no. 3, May–June.

Kurd Net (2010) 'Nine Kurdish PKK Rebels, Turkish Soldier Killed in Clashes', 7 September, www.ekurd.net/mismas/articles/misc2010/9/turkey2921.htm.

Kurd Net (2011a) 'Turkey: Armed with Stones, Petrol Bombs: Kurdish Youth Claim Mission', 19 May, www.ekurd.net/mismas/articles/misc2011/5/turkey3221.htm.

Kurd Net (2011b) 'Turkey Requests US Help against Kurd PKK Separatists', 21 September, www.ekurd.net/mismas/articles/misc2011/9/turkey3396.htm.

Kurdeng (1995) 'Women's Army: PKK 5th Congress Reso', 7 August, http://mailman.greennet.org.uk/pipermail/old-apc-conference.mideast.kurds/1995-August/000972.html.

Kurdish Globe (2010) 'Two Kurdish PKK Rebels Killed in Southeast Turkey', 17 April, www.kurdishglobe.net/displayArticle.jsp?id=502D1DB7AC2E102 F881A7BAECAA2421C.

Kurdish Info (2014) 'Flautre: Useful dialogue with PM Erdoğan but Not Convincing', 23 January, www.kurdishinfo.com/flautre-useful-dialogue-pm-erdogan-convincing.

Kurdistan Democratic Communities' Union (2013) 'To Our Peoples and the Public Opinion', Info/Koma Ciwakên Kürdistan, 19 January, http://peaceinkurdistan campaign.com/2014/01/21/kck-these-murders-couldnt-have-taken-place-intelligence-services.

Kurdistan Report (1991) '15 August 1984–15 August 1991. Seven Years of Valiant Struggle!', October: 1.

Kurdistan Report (1998) 'Interview with Members of the Central Committee of the PKK', September–November, https://groups.google.com/forum/#!topic/misc.activism.progressive/svald4wUuU8.

Kurdistan Tribune (2014) 'BDP MPs Hold Press Conference on Öcalan and the Peace Process', 14 February, http://kurdistantribune.com/2014/bdp-mps-hold-press-conference-on-ocalan-peace-process.

Kurdpress News Agency (2013) 'PKK Makes Changes in the Organization', 6 November, http://kurdpress.com/En/NSite/FullStory/News/?Id=5846#Title=PKK%20makes%20changes%20in%20the%20organization.

Kurdpress News Agency (2014) 'Five Released BDP Lawmakers Take Oath in Parliament', 8 January, http://kurdpress.com/En.

Kürkçü, Ertugrul (1996) 'The Crisis of the Turkish State', *Middle East Report* 199, Spring: 2–7.

Kurt, Ihsan (2013) 'Kürt Diasporası Unutulmasın', 10 March, www.radikal.com.tr/radikal.aspx?atype=haberyazdir&articleid=1124651.

Kurt, Umit (2010) 'The Doctrine of "Turkish–Islamic Synthesis" as Official Ideology of the September 12 and the "Intellectuals' Hearth – Aydınlar Ocağı" as the Ideological Apparatus of the State', *European Journal of Economic and Political Studies*, vol. 3, no. 2: 111–25.

Kutschera, Chris (1979) *Le Mouvement National Kurde*, Paris: Flammarion.

Kutschera, Chris (1994) 'Mad Dreams of Independence: The Kurds of Turkey and the PKK', *Middle East Report*, vol. 24, no. 4, July–August.

Landau, Jacob M. (1974) *Radical Politics in Modern Turkey*, Leiden: Brill.

Landauro, Inti, and Joe Parkinson (2013) 'Kurdish Killings in Paris Cloud Peace Effort: Three Women Are Shot Dead in Office With Ties to Militant Leader Involved in Talks with the Turkish Government', 10 January, http://online.wsj.com/news/articles/SB10001424127887324081704578233074109454456.

Lenin, V. I. (1963a) *Collected Works*, vol. 18, Moscow: Progress Publishers.

Lenin, V.I. (1963b) '"Cultural–National" Autonomy', *Collected Works*, vol. 19, Moscow: Progress Publishers; first published in *Za Pravda* 46, 28 November 1913.

Lenin, V. I. (1964) *Collected Works*, vol. 24, Moscow: Progress Publishers.

Levitt, Wendy Kirstianasen (1991) 'Letter from Mardin', *Middle East International* 405, 26 July: 24.

Libcom.org (2010) 'Wildcat Strike in Diyarbakır Ends with Victory', 22 April, http://libcom.org/news/wildcat-strike-diyarbak%C4%B1r-ended-victory-22042010.

Libération (2011) '"Trois cadres importants du PKK en France: ont été interpellés', 5 June, www.liberation.fr/societe/2011/06/05/trois-cadres-importants-du-pkk-en-france-ont-ete-interpelles_740669.

Löwy, Michael (1976) 'Marxists and the National Question', *New Left Review* 96, March–April: 81–100.

Lyon, Alynna J., and Emek M. Uçarer, (1998) 'The Transnational Mobilization of Ethnic Conflict: Kurdish Separatism in Germany', paper prepared for presentation on the panel on 'Stateless Ethnic Nations', International Studies Association annual meeting, Minneapolis, Minnesota, March, www2.hawaii.edu/~fredr/kurds.htm.

Mango, Andrew (2005) *Turkey and the War on Terror: 'For Forty Years We Fought Alone'*, London: Routledge.

MAR Project (2010) 'Chronology for Kurds in Turkey', 10 August, www.cidcm.umd.edu/mar/chronology.asp?groupId=64005.

Marcus, Aliza (2007) *Blood and Belief: The PKK and the Kurdish Fight for Independence*, New York and London: New York University Press.

Marcus, Aliza (2010) 'Troubles in Turkey's Backyard', *Foreign Policy*, 12 July, www.foreignpolicy.com/articles/2010/07/09/troubles_in_turkey_s_backyard.

Margulies, Ronnie, and Ergin Yıldızoğlu (1987) 'Agrarian Change: 1923–70', in Irvin C. Schick and Ertuğrul Ahmet Tonak, (eds), *Turkey in Transition: New Perspectives*, New York and Oxford: Oxford University Press, pp. 269–92.

Mavioglu, Ertugrul (2008) '2003 Was a Year of Coup Plans, Shows Report',

Turkish Daily News, 15 November, http://arama.hurriyet.com.tr/arsivnews.aspx?id=-635136.

McDonald, Susan (2001) 'Kurdish Women and Self-Determination: A Feminist Approach to International Law', in Shahrzad Mojab (ed.), *Women of a Non-State Nation*, Costa Mesa CA: Mazda, pp. 135–60.

McDowall, David (1996) *A Modern History of the Kurds*, London and New York: I.B. Tauris.

MED TV press release (1999), 18 February, www.kurdistan.org/AKIN/press20.html.

Middle East Newsline (25 May 2008) 'New PKK Leadership Takes over Insurgency', www.menewsline.com/article-809-New-PKK-Leadership-Takes-Over-Ins.aspx.

Middle East Times (1995) 'Notes From the Region: Turkey Says PKK Regrouping in Iran', 25 June–1 July.

Milliyet (17 December 1998; 3 March 1999; 28 May 2009; 27 June 2011; 31 December 2013).

Ministry of Foreign Affairs Turkey (2014) 'A Report on the PKK and Terrorism', www.fas.org/irp/world/para/docs/mfa-t-pkk.htm.

Minorsky, Vladimir (1986) 'Kurds, Kurdistan', in *The Encyclopaedia of Islam*, vol. V, pp. 438–86.

More, Christiane (1984) *Les Kurdes Aujourd'hui. Mouvement National et Partis Politiques*, Paris: Éditions L'Harmattan.

Morgan, Lewis H. (1877) *Ancient Society, or Researches in the Lines of Human Progress from Savagery, through Barbarism to Civilization*, Chicago: Charles H. Kerr.

MSNBC (2011) 'Turkey PM Promises Great Revenge after Deadly PKK Attacks', 19 October, www.sott.net/article/236494–Turkey-PM-promises-great-revenge-after-deadly-PKK-attacks.

Munyar, Vahap (2013) 'Whoever Ends Kurdish Bid Will Pay the Price: Turkish PM Erdoğan', *Hürriyet*, 26 October, www.hurriyetdailynews.com/whoever-ends-kurdish-bid-to-pay-price-says-turkish-pm-erdogan.aspx?pageID=238&nID=56817&NewsCatID=338.

National Consortium for the Study of Terrorism (2013) 'Terrorist Organization Profile: Kurdistan Freedom Hawks', www.start.umd.edu/tops/terrorist_organization_profile.asp?id=4381.

National Turk (2012) 'Turkey: Former Chief of Staff Arrested by Court over Coup Attempt', 6 January, www.nationalturk.com/en/turkey-former-chief-of-staff-arrested-by-court-over-coup-attempt-15743.

NIS News Bulletin (2004) 'PKK Training Camp Dismantled near Eindhoven, 38 Arrests', 3 November, www.nisnews.nl/public/131104_1.htm.

Noi, Aylin Ünver (2012) 'The Arab Spring, Its Effects on the Kurds, and the Approaches of Turkey, Iran, Syria, and Iraq on the Kurdish Issue', *Middle East Review of International Affairs*, vol. 16, no. 2, June, www.rubincenter.org/2012/07/the-arab-spring-its-effects-on-the-kurds-and-the-approaches-of-turkey-iran-syria-and-iraq-on-the-kurdish-issue.

Northern Ireland Neighbourhood Information Service (2011) 'Ethnic Group – Full Detail_QS201NI', www.ninis2.nisra.gov.uk/Download/Census%20 2011_Excel/2011/QS201NI.xls.

NTV–MSNBC (2005) 'Süleyman Demirel: İki devlet var', 16 November, http://arsiv.NTV–MSNBC.com/news/349780.asp.

NTV–MSNBC (2012) 'Gaziantep'te Bombalı Saldırı: 9 Ölü', 20 August, www.NTV–MSNBC.com/id/25375804.

Nurhak, Delal Afsin (2013) 'The Kurdistan Woman's Liberation Movement', www.pkkonline.com/en/index.php?sys=article&artID=180.

Oakland Tribune (2007) 'Stories Differ on Turkish "Hot Pursuit" into Iraq', 7 June, www.insidebayarea.com/oakland-tribune.

Öcalan, Abdullah (1999) *Kürt Aşkı*, Istanbul: Aram Yayınları.

Öcalan, Abdullah (2000) *Nasıl Yaşamalı*, vol. 1, Istanbul: Mem Yayınları.

Öcalan, Abdullah (2002) *Özgür Yaşamla Dialoglar*, ed. Nesrin Esen, Istanbul: Çetin Yayınları.

Öcalan, Abdullah (2009) *War and Peace in Kurdistan: Perspectives for a Political Solution of the Kurdish Question*, trans. International Initiative, 2nd edn, Cologne: International Initiative.

Öcalan, Abdullah (2010a) 'A Conspiracy Against Peace', trans. David Macdonald, *il Manifesto*, 13 February, www.freedom-for-ocalan.com/english/hintergrund/schriften/ilmanifesto.htm.

Öcalan, Abdullah (2010b) 'Öcalan: I am withdrawing because I could not find an interlocutor', 29 May, www.kurdishaspect.com/doc052910KI.html.

Öcalan, Abdullah (2011) 'Declaration on the Democratic Solution of the Kurdish Question: Translation of Abdullah Öcalan Defence Argument in 1999', trans. Zagro Palani Jaff, Council of Kurdish Resurrection and Kurn Net, 17 February, www.ekurd.net/mismas/articles/misc2011/2/turkey3139.htm.

Öcalan, Abdullah (2012) *Prison Writings III: The Road Map to Negotiations*, trans. Havin Guneser with a preface by Immanuel Wallerstein, Cologne: International Initiative.

Öcalan, Abdullah (2013) 'The Kurds Must Evaluate Their Own Position in Face of the Latest Developments', 27 April 2011, www.pkkonline.com/en/index.php?sys=article&artID=130.

Öcalan, Abdullah (2014) 'Öcalan: My Real Role in Kurds' Struggle for Freedom', 20 January, http://peaceinkurdistancampaign.wordpress.com/2014/01/21/ocalan-my-real-role-in-kurds-struggle-for-freedom.

Oda TV (2010) 'CIA Neden Fethullah Gülen'i Destekliyor', 3 May, www.odatv.com/n.php?n=cia-neden-fethullah-guleni-destekliyor-0305101200.

Østergaard-Nielsen, Eva (2007) 'The Kurdish Diaspora from Turkey', in Bahar Baser and Mirella Pejčić (eds), *Diasporas and Their Involvement in Peace Processes*, Department of Peace and Conflict Research, Uppsala University, pp. 26–30, www.academia.edu/349477/_Diasporas_and_Their_Involvement_in_Peace_Processes.

Özel, Soli (2011) 'Silahla söz arasında', 19 August, www.haberturk.com/yazarlar/soli-ozel/660628–silahla-soz-arasinda.

Özgür Gündem (1993), 19 July.
Özmaya, Cahit (2012) 'Politik Ekoloji', *Özgür Gündem*, 20 November, www.ozgur-gundem.com/haber/55982/politik-ekoloji.
Paker, Evren Balta (2013) 'Autonomy and Conflict: Looking into the Kurdish Question in the Light of Different Experiences', www.hyd.org.tr/staticfiles/files/article_-_autonomy_and_conflict_-_evren_balta_paker.pdf.
Panico, Christopher (1995) 'Turkey's Kurdish Conflict', *Jane's Intelligence Review*, vol. 7, no. 4, 1 April.
Pariscinayeti (2014) 'Paris assassiner de trois timon – Omer Ziya guney vérité', 12 January, http://pariscinayeti.blogspot.de/2014/01/paris-assassiner-de-trois-timon-omer.html.
Park, Bill (2010) 'Turkey and Ergenekon: from Farce to Tragedy', 10 March, www.opendemocracy.net/bill-park/turkey-and-ergenekon-from-farce-to-tragedy.
Parkinson, Joe, and Ayla Albayrak (2014) 'Gulen Blasts Turkey Leader', *Acturka/Wall Street Journal Europe*, 21 January, http://acturca.wordpress.com/2014/01/21/gulen-blasts-turkey-leader.
Peker, Emre (2013) 'Turkish Court Upholds Jailing of Military', 9 October, http://online.wsj.com/news/articles/SB40001424052702304520704579125071654564740.
Peker, Emre (2014) 'Turkey's Military Moves against Coup Cases as Judiciary Fights Government', *Wall Street Journal*, 3 January, http://blogs.wsj.com/emergingeurope/2014/01/03/turkeys-military-moves-against-coup-cases-as-judiciary-fights-government.
People's Daily Online (2007), 'Suicide Bomber Carries Out Blast in Turkish Capital', 23 May, http://en.people.cn/200705/23/eng20070523_377245.html.
PKK (Partiya Karkerên Kurdistan) (1991) '15 Ağustos Atılımı'nın 7. Zafer Yılı Ulusal Kurtuluş Mücadelemizin Altın Yılı Olmuştur', *Serxwebûn*, October: 4–13.
PKK (1995a) *Programm und Statut*, Cologne: Weşanên Serxwebûn.
PKK (1995b) 'PKK Party Program – Chapter Three', trans. Arm the Spirit, 24 January, http://212.150.54.123/documents/documentdet.cfm?docid=27.
PKK (1996) 'Zeynep Kınacı (Zilan)', www.pkkonline.com/en/index.php?sys=article&artID=153.
PKK (2005) *Partiya Karkerên Kurdistan PKK Yeniden Inşa Kongre Belgeleri*, Istanbul: Çetin Yayınları.
PKK Central Committee (1984 [1978]) *PKK Kuruluş Bildirisi*, n.p., *Weşanen Serxwebûn* 25, http://rojbası.files.wordpress.com/2012/01/pkk-kurulus-bildirgesi2.pdf.
PKK Central Committee (1999) 'PKK Central Committee Statement – Newroz 1999', 15 March, www.humanrights.de/doc_en/archiv/t/turkey/apo/archiv/pkknewroz_d.htm.
Pollock, David, and Soner Cagaptay (2013) 'The PKK Announcement: Can Turkey Build a Kurdish Cordon?', 25 March, www.washingtoninstitute.org/policy-analysis/view/the-pkk-announcement-can-turkey-build-a-kurdish-cordon.

PKK Central Committee (1999) 'PKK Central Committee Statement – Newroz 1999', 15 March, www.humanrights.de/doc_en/archiv/t/turkey/apo/archiv/pkknewroz_d.htm.

Pope, Hugh (2013) 'Turkey and Its Rebel Kurds May Want Peace This Time', 16 January, www.crisisgroup.org/en/regions/europe/turkey-cyprus/turkey/op-ed/pope-turkey-and-its-rebel-kurds-may-want-peace-this-time.aspx.

Popp, Maximilian (2014) 'A Brother's Vengeance: The Preacher Who Could Topple Erdoğan', *Spiegel Online*, 1 September, www.spiegel.de/international/world/turkey-erdogan-sees-power-threatened-by-muslim-cleric-guelen-a-942296.html.

Pravda (2011) 'Turkey's Conflict with Kurds Turns into Critical Military Confrontation', 4 October, http://english.pravda.ru/hotspots/conflicts/04–10–2011/119223–turkey_kurdish-0.

Press TV, various dates.

Prohayat (2014) 'KCK Yapılanması', 8 August, www.prohayat.com/2011/11/17/kck-semasi-ve-sozlesmesi.

The Province (2013) 'Three Kurdish Women, Including PKK Founder, Shot Execution-style in Paris', 10 January, www.theprovince.com/news/Three+Kurdish+women+including+founder+shot+execution+style+Paris/7801122/story.html.

Radikal (2012) '14 Hedef Vuruldu, 25 PKK'lı Öldürüldü', 11 September, www.radikal.com.tr/turkiye/14_hedef_vuruldu_25_pkkli_olduruldu-1099856.

Radikal (2014) 'Ahmet Türk: IŞİD'e destek barış sürecini sorgulatıyor', 16 July, www.radikal.com.tr/politika/ahmet_turk_iside_destek_baris_surecini_sorgulatiyor-1202252.

Rathmell, Andrew, and Michael M. Gunter, (2014) 'Turkey: Kurdish Struggle, 1984–2000s', *Sharpe Online Reference*: 'World Terrorism', www.sharpe-online.com/SOLR/a/show-content/fullarticle/23/Book022–PART1–article196.

Renner, Karl (1918 [1899]) *Das Selbstbestimmungsrecht der Nationen in besonderer Anwendung auf Österreich, Deuticke, Leipzig and Vienna*, Leipzig and Vienna: F. Deuticke.

Republic of Turkey, Ministry of Foreign Affairs (2011) 'PKK/KONGRA-GEL', www.mfa.gov.tr/pkk_kongra-gel.en.mfa.

Reuters (2010) 'Twenty-two Dead as Turkish Troops Clash with PKK', 19 June, www.reuters.com/article/2010/06/19/us-turkey-kurds-idUSTRE65I0JL20100619.

Reuters AlertNet, 14 March 2010.

Rodrik, Dani (20 January 2014) 'Turquie: la démocratie perdante', *Acturka/La Tribune*, http://acturca.wordpress.com/2014/01/20/turquie-la-democratie-perdante.

Romano, David (2006) *The Kurdish Nationalist Movement: Opportunity, Mobilization, and Identity*, Cambridge: Cambridge University Press.

Rote Zora (1995) 'You Have the Power, but the Night Belongs to Us', communiqué, July, http://apa.online.free.fr/article.php3?id_article=725.

RT/Reuters (2011) 'Kurdish Threat Makes Turkey Flip Flop on Iran', 21 October, http://rt.com/news/turkey-iran-kurds-war-401.

Rudaw (2011) 'Spaniard Pushes Cultural Ties with Kurdistan', 28 November, http://web.archive.org/web/20120221034238/http://www.rudaw.net/english/kurds/4182.html.

Rygiel, Kim (1998) 'Stabilizing Borders: The Geopolitics of National Identity Construction in Turkey', in Simon Dalby and Gearóid Ó Tuathail (eds), *Rethinking Geopolitics*, New York: Routledge, pp. 106–30.

Sabah (4 August 1996; 30 January 2014).

Sadiki, Larbi (2013) 'From Taksim to Tahrir: A Turkish "Arab Spring"', 18 June, http://studies.aljazeera.net/en/reports/2013/06/201361811185042329 4.htm.

Şahin, Bakan (2011) '115 Terörist Etkisiz Hale Getirildi Bakan Şahin, Hakkari'de süren operasyonla ilgili açıklama yaptı', *TRT Haber*, 5 August, www.trthaber.com/haber/gundem/bakandan-teror-bilancosu-50956.html.

Sakallioğlu, Ümit Cizre (1996) 'Parameters and Strategies of Islam–State Interaction in Republican Turkey', *International Journal of Middle East Studies* 28: 231–51.

Saktanber, Ayse (2002) *Living Islam: Women, Religion and the Politicization of Culture in Turkey*, London and New York: I.B. Tauris.

Samim, Ahmet (1981) 'The Tragedy of the Turkish Left', *New Left Review* 126, April/May: 60–85.

Sayın, Mahir (1998) *Erkeği Öldürmek*, Istanbul: Zelal Yayınları.

Schmid, Estella (2012) 'PYD Leader Puts the Kurdish Case for Achieving Peace in Syria', 8 December, www.kurdmedia.com/article.aspx?id=16915.

Scotland Census (2013) 'Scotland's Census 2011 – National Records of Scotland: Ethnic group (detailed): All people', www.scotlandscensus.gov.uk/documents/censusresults/release2a/rel2A_Ethnicity_detailed_Scotland.pdf.

Şehirli, Atila (2000) *Türkiye'de Bölücü Terör Hareketleri ve Devletin Aldığı Tedbirler*, Istanbul: Burak Yayınları.

Seibert, Thomas (2009) 'Return of Kurds Puts Turkey in a Bind', *The National*, 30 October, www.thenational.ae/news/world/europe/return-of-kurds-puts-turkey-in-a-bind#ixzz303H2FYbI.

Sénat de Belgique (1991) 'Enquête parlementaire sur l'existence en Belgique d'un réseau de renseignements clandestine international', 1 October, Documents du Sénat de Belgique 1117 (1990–1991), *Annales du Sénat*, www.senate.be/lexdocs/S0523/S05231297.pdf.

Serxwebûn (October 1991; February 1999; September 2012), www.serxwebun.org.

Sharon-Krespin, Rachel (2009) 'Fethullah Gülen's Grand Ambition: Turkey's Islamist Danger', *Middle East Forum*, Winter, www.meforum.org/2045/fethullah-gulens-grand-ambition.

Shekhani, Sherzad (2013) 'PKK Elects New Leadership as Iran Steps up Border Presence', *Asharq Al-Awsat*, 11 July, www.aawsat.net/2013/07/article55309299.

Şık, Ahmet (2013) *Dokunan Yanar*, www.antenna-tr.org/media/files/pdf/160148216.pdf.

Silverman, Reuben (2013) 'The Long Road: Mehmed Uzun and the Kurdish Struggle for Rights', 26 December, http://reubensilverman.wordpress.com/2013/12/26/the-long-road-mehmed-uzun-and-the-kurdish-struggle-for-rights.

Smith, Helena (1999) 'Athens in Crisis over CIA Links to Ocalan Capture', 19 February, *Guardian*, www.theguardian.com/world/1999/feb/19/kurds.helenasmith.

Soleimani, Kamal (2011) 'Gülen's Latest Speech On Kurds – "It is really shameful, embarrassing, that the state has not killed them all"', *Kurdish Media*, 21 December, www.kurdmedia.com/article.aspx?id=16835.

Stalin, J.V. (1913) 'Marxism and the National Question', *Prosveshcheniye* 3–5, March–May, http//www.marxists.org.

Statistics Finland (2015) 'Language According to Age and Sex by Region 1990–2014', http://pxweb2.stat.fi/Dialog/varval.asp?ma=030_vaerak_tau_102_en&path=../database/StatFin/vrm/vaerak/&lang=1&multilang=en.

Sunday's Zaman (2008) 'Senior General Knew about Lieutenants' Ergenekon Contacts', 24 September, www.todayszaman.com/newsDetail_getNewsById.action;jsessionid=A78393A7F2814F246DD8FAC709D21AE0?newsId=154149.

Taka (2013) 'Kandil'den Alevi Açilimi', 11 July, www.takaonline.com/etiket/alevi-kokenli-bese-hozat.

Taraf (2010) '*Darbenin adı Balyoz*', 20 January, www.taraf.com.tr/haber/darbenin-adi-balyoz.htm.

Taraf (2012) 'Bu Mektup Aysel Tuğluk u Zora Sokacak', 20 September, www.internethaber.com/bu-mektup-aysel-tugluku-zora-sokacak-377954h.htm.

Taşpınar, Ömer (2012) 'Turkey's Kurdish Predicament', Brookings Institution, 22 April, www.brookings.edu/research/opinions/2012/04/22–turkey-kurds-taspinar.

Tatort Kurdistan (2013) *Democratic Autonomy in North Kurdistan: The Council Movement, Gender Liberation, and Ecology – in Practice. A Reconnisance into Southeastern Turkey*, Porsgrunn, Norway: New Compass Press.

Taylor-Lind, Anastasia (2010) 'No Friends but the Mountains: Women of the PKK', www.anthropographia.org/2.0/?p=126.

T.C. İstanbul Cumhuriyet Başsavcılığı (2011–12) 'Tutuklu İş', www.ankarastrateji.org/_videos/kckkk.pdf.

Tempo (18 October 2007).

Tezcur, Gunes Murat (2010) 'Turkey's Referendum: A Democratic Dynamic', *Open Democracy*, 15 September, www.opendemocracy.net/gunes-murat-tezcur/turkey's-referendum-power-democracy-nexus.

Tezcur, Gunes Murat (2011) 'The AKP Years in Turkey: The Third Stage', *Open Democracy*, 20 September, www.opendemocracy.net/gunes-murat-tezcur/akp-years-in-turkey-third-stage.

Tezcür, Güneş Murat (2013) 'Prospects for Resolution of the Kurdish Question: A Realist Perspective', *Insight Turkey*, vol. 15, no. 2: 69–84.

Times of Malta (2014) 'Kurds Protest in Valletta', 25 October, www.timesofmalta.com/articles/view/20141025/local/kurds-protest-in-valletta.541187.

Today's Zaman (2012) 'Camps Built in Germany, Austria to Win New Members for PKK, Reports Reveal', 9 August, www.todayszaman.com/news-289089-camps-built-in-germany-austria-to-win-new-members-for-pkk-reports-reveal.html.

Torchia, Christopher (2007) 'Iraqi Kurds: Turkey Shells Across Border', *Washington Post/Associated Press*, 8 June, www.washingtonpost.com/wp-dyn/content/article/2007/06/08/AR2007060800462.html.

Trading Economics (2014a) 'Turkey Inflation Rate', 13 February, www.tradingeconomics.com/turkey/inflation-cpi.

Trading Economics (2014b) 'Turkey External Debt', 13 February, www.tradingeconomics.com/turkey/external-debt.

Trading Economics (2014c) 'Turkey Unemployment Rate', 5 June, www.tradingeconomics.com/turkey/unemployment-rate.

Tran, Mark (2007) 'Turkey Kills 34 Kurdish Fighters in Northern Iraq', *Guardian*, 24 October, www.guardian.co.uk/world/2007/oct/24/turkey.iraq.

Traynor, Ian, and Constanze Letsch, (2013) 'Locked in a fateful embrace: Turkey's PM and his Kurdish prisoner', *Guardian*, 1 March, www.theguardian.com/world/2013/mar/01/turkey-pm-kurdish-prisoner-peace.

Truthhugger (2008) Female Fighters: We Won't Stand for Male Dominance, http://truthhugger.com/2008/10/07/female-pkk-warriors-wont-stand-for-male-dominance.

Tuğluk, Aysel (2007) 'Sevr Travması ve Kürtlerin Empatisi', *Radikal*, 27 May, www.radikal.com.tr/ek_haber.php?ek=r2&haberno=7097.

Turkish Daily News (21 July 1993; 13 August 1998; 22 December 1998; 17 September 2004).

Turkish Statistical Institute (2013) 'Gross Domestic Product, III. Quarter 2013', 10 December, www.turkstat.gov.tr/HbGetirHTML.do?id=13645.

Türkiye (2008) '16 Mart Katliamı Davası Düştü', 15 December.

Uluslararası İşçi Dayanışması Derneği (2013) 'Van'da Taşeron İşçileri Sendika Hakkı için Greve çıktı', 7 July, http://uidder.org/van_da_taseron_iscileri_sendika_hakki_icin_greve_cikti.htm.

Ünal, Ali (2014) 'Peace Process Remains on Track Without Problems', 29 May, www.dailysabah.com/politics/2014/05/23/peace-process-remains-on-track-without-problems.

United Nations OHCHR (2004) 'Report Of The Committee Against Torture', www.refworld.org/cgi-bin/texis/vtx/rwmain?page=search&docid=43214e144&skip=0&query=Report%20Of%20The%20Committee%20Against%20Torture%202004.

US Department of State (1994) *Turkey Human Rights Practices, 1994*, www.hri.org/docs/USSD-Rights/94/Turkey94.html.

US Department of State (1995) *Patterns of Global Terrorism: 1994*, www.hri.org/docs/USSD-Terror/94.

Uslu, Emrullah (2009) 'The PKK Extends its Unilateral Ceasefire', *Eurasia Daily Monitor*, vol. 6, no. 106, 3 June, www.jamestown.org/single/?no_cache=1&tx_ttnews[tt_news]=35077.

Uslu, Emrullah (2013) 'Leadership Change in the PKK', *Today's Zaman*, 10 July, www.todayszaman.com/columnist/newsDetail_openPrintPage.action?newsId=320526.

Uygur, Ercan (2010) *The Global Crisis and the Turkish Economy*, Penang: Third World Network.

Uzun, Adem (2014) *'Living Freedom' – The Evolution of the Kurdish Conflict in Turkey and the Efforts to Resolve It*, Berghof Transitions Series No. 11, www.berghof-foundation.org/fileadmin/redaktion/Publications/Papers/Transitions_Series/transitions11_turkey.pdf.

van Bruinessen, Martin (1991) 'Religion in Kurdistan', *Kurdish Times*, vol. 4, nos 1/2, Summer–Fall: 5–27.

van Bruinessen, Martin (1995) 'Forced Evacuations and Destruction of Villages in Dêrsim (Tunceli), and Western Bingöl, Turkish Kurdistan September–November 1994', www.academia.edu/6250323/Forced_evacuations_and_destruction_of_villages_in_Dersim_Tunceli_and_Western_Bingol_Turkish_Kurdistan_September-November_1994.

van Bruinessen, Martin (1996), 'Kurds, Turks and the Alevi Revival in Turkey', *Middle East Report* 200, Summer: 7–10.

van Bruinessen, Martin (1997) 'Ismail Beşikçi: Turkish Sociologist, Critic of Kemalism, and Kurdologist', www.hum.uu.nl/medewerkers/m.vanbruinessen/publications/ismail_besikci.htm.

van Bruinessen, Martin (1998) 'Shifting National and Ethnic Identities: The Kurds in Turkey and the European Diaspora', *Journal of Muslim Minority Affairs*, vol. 18, no. 1: 39–52.

van Bruinessen, Martin (2000) *Transnational Aspects of the Kurdish Question*, Working Paper No. 22, Robert Schuman Centre for Advanced Studies, European University Institute, www.academia.edu/707649/Transnational_aspects_of_the_Kurdish_question.

Vanly, Ismet Cherif (n.d.) *Survey of the National Question of Turkish Kurdistan with Historical Background*, Zurich: Hevra.

Voice of America (1999) Kurdish language service, 17 February.

Voice of America News (2009) Turkish Revenge Brigade Claims Responsibility for Bomb Blast in Kurdish Area', 31 October, www.voanews.com/content/a-13-2006-09-13-voa48/316089.html.

Wahby, Taufiq (1982) *The Origins of the Kurds and Their Language*, Stockholm: KKSE.

Wall Street Journal (European edition) (9 August 1996).

Washington Times (2007) 'Turkish Troops Said in Hot Pursuit in Iraq', 7 June, www.washingtontimes.com/news/2007/jun/7/turkish-troops-said-in-hot-pursuit-in-iraq/?page=all.

Watson, Ivan, and Yesim Comert (2012) 'Report Says Turkey's Kurdish Conflict Has Turned More Violent', CNN, 18 September, http://edition.cnn.com/2012/09/18/world/europe/turkey-war-within/index.html.

Wereldjournalisten.nl (2007) 'Kurds in Netherlands', 23 May, www.wereldjournalisten.nl/factsheet/2007/05/23/factsheet_koerden_in_nederland.

White, Paul J. (1997) 'Turkey: From Total War to Civil War?', in Paul J. White and William S. Logan (eds), *Remaking the Middle East*, Oxford and New York: Berg, pp. 225–57.

White, Paul J. (2000) *Primitive Rebels or Revolutionary Modernizers? The Kurdish National Movement in Turkey*, London: Zed Books.

White, Paul J. (2004) 'Die Entstehung kurdischer nationaler Identität unter kurdischen Frauen aus der Türkei in Nordwest-Melbourne, Australien', in Siamend Hajo, Carsten Borck, Eva Savelsberg and Şukriye Doğan (eds), *Gender in Kurdistan und der Diaspora*, Münster: Unrast, pp. 327–45.

Wilgenburg, Wladimir van (2010) 'Kurdish PKK Using PJAK to Isolate Turkey', *Terrorism Monitor*, vol. 8, no. 33, 19 August.

Wood, Graeme (2007) 'Among the Kurds', 26 October, http://gcaw.net/2007/10/26/among-the-kurds.

World Bulletin (2010a) 'Turkish Troop Killed in PKK clash', 16 April, www.worldbulletin.net/?aType=haber&ArticleID=57125.

World Bulletin (2010b) 'PKK Attack Kills 8 Turkish Soldiers', 19 June, www.worldbulletin.net/?aType=haber&ArticleID=60178.

World Bulletin (2010c) 'Turkish Army Kills 46 PKK Militants in Last Month', 14 July, www.worldbulletin.net/?aType=haber&ArticleID=61333.

Yackley, Ayla Jean (2013a) 'Kurdish Rebel Group Sees Nationalist Hand in Paris killings', *Reuters*, 11 January, www.reuters.com/article/2013/01/11/us-france-kurds-idUSBRE90907B20130111.

Yackley, Ayla Jean (2013b) 'Kurdish Rebels Begin Withdrawal from Turkey', *Daily* Star, 8 May, www.dailystar.com.lb/News/Middle-East/2013/May-08/216307-kurdish-rebels-begin-to-withdraw-from-turkey-pro-kurdish-party.ashx.

Yackley, Ayla Jean (2014) 'Turkey's Pro-Kurdish MPs Sworn in after Freed from Prison', *Reuters*, 7 January, www.reuters.com/article/2014/01/07/us-turkey-kurds-idUSBREA060RW20140107.

Yanardağ, Merdan (2006) *Türkiye Nasıl Kuşatıldı? Fethullah Gülen Hareketinin Perde Arkası* (35 Yıllık Yol Arkadaşı Nurettin Veren Anlatıyor), Istanbul: Siyah Beyaz.

Yesilada, Atilla (2013) 'Turkey Unrest Threatens Financial Flows and Economic Stability', 4 June, http://blogs.ft.com/beyond-brics/2013/06/04/guest-post-turkish-unrest-threatens-financial-flows-and-economic-stability.

Yetkin, Murat (2013) 'Who killed 3 PKK Members in Paris?', *Hürriyet Daily News*, 11 January, www.hurriyetdailynews.com/who-killed-3–pkk-members-in-paris.aspx?pageID=449&nID=38816&NewsCatID=409.

Yildiz, Yesim Yaprak (2013) 'Turkey and the PKK: The Kurdish Women who Take up Arms', *BBC News*, 15 January, www.bbc.co.uk/news/world-europe-21026273.

Yılmaz, İhsan (2013) 'The İmralı Peace Process and Defaming Hizmet', *Today's Zaman*, 18 March, http://en.fgulen.com/press-room/columns/4543-ihsan-yilmaz-todays-zaman-the-imrali-peace-process-and-defaming-hizmet.

Young Civilians and Human Rights Agenda Association (2010) 'Ergenekon Is Our Reality', July, http://ergenekonisourreality.files.wordpress.com/2010/07/ergenekonisourreality-final.pdf.

YouTube (2014) 'ParisteUc Fidan Cinayeti', 12 January, www.youtube.com/

watch?v=9hqODiGQ_us.

Yuksel, Aslan Alper (2008) 'Turkish Attacks in Iraq "exclusively target PKK"', *Daily Star*/Turkish Embassy Beirut (press release), 28 February, www.dailystar.com.lb/News/Middle-East/Feb/28/Turkish-attacks-in-Iraq-exclusively-target-PKK.ashx#axzz2aaOvJZ6H.

Zagros Newroz Aryan Kurdistan (2012) 'March 8, International Women's Day of Kurdish Womens Amazons', 7 March, www.youtube.com/watch?v=lbgfg_87sx4.

Zaman (2007) 'Turkish Vengeance Brigade Founder Detained, Alleged Connections with Generals', 2 April, http://dlib.eastview.com/browse/doc/11848726.

Zaman, Amberin (1998) *Voice of America*, 16 November.

Zanotti, Jim (2012) 'Turkey: Background and U.S. Relations', Congressional Research Service, 2 February, http://fpc.state.gov/documents/organization/185939.pdf.

Zedalis, Debra D. (2004) 'Female Suicide Bombers', Strategic Studies Institute, www.strategicstudiesinstitute.army.mil/pdffiles/pub408.pdf.

Zibak, Fatma Dişli (2013) 'New EMASYA-like Protocol Involves Military in Domestic Security', 28 June, www.todayszaman.com/news-319464–new-emasya-like-protocol-involves-military-in-domestic-security.html.

Zürcher, Erik J. (1995) *Turkey: A Modern History*, London and New York: I.B. Tauris.

Index